ALL ABOUT DIVIDEND INVESTING

OTHER TITLES IN THE "ALL ABOUT . . ." SERIES

All About Asset Allocation

All About Bonds, Bond Mutual Funds, and Bond ETFs

All About Commodities

All About Derivatives

All About Exchange-Traded Funds

All About Futures

All About Hedge Funds

All About High-Frequency Trading

All About Index Funds

All About Investing

All About Market Indicators

All About Market Timing

All About Options

All About Short Selling

All About Six Sigma

All About Stock Market Strategies

All About Stocks

All About Technical Analysis

ALL ABOUT DIVIDEND INVESTING

The Easy Way to Get Started

SECOND EDITION

DON SCHREIBER, JR.
GARY E. STROIK

New York   Chicago   San Francisco   Lisbon   London
Madrid   Mexico City   Milan   New Delhi   San Juan
Seoul   Singapore   Sydney   Toronto

1 2 3 4 5 6 7 8 9 0   DOC/DOC   1 5 4 3 2 1 0

ISBN: 978-0-07-163713-8
MHID: 0-07-163713-3

This publication is designed to provide accurate and authoritative information in regard to the subject matter covered. It is sold with the understanding that the publisher is not engaged in rendering legal, accounting, or other professional service. If legal advice or other expert assistance is required, the services of a competent professional person should be sought.

—From a declaration of principles jointly adopted by a committee of the American Bar Association and a committee of publishers

McGraw-Hill books are available at special quantity discounts to use as premiums and sales promotions or for use in corporate training programs. To contact a representative, please e-mail us at bulksales@mcgraw-hill.com.

This book is printed on acid-free paper.

DISCLAIMER

Please remember that different types of investments involve varying degrees of risk. Therefore, there can be no assurance that the future performance of any type of investment, investment strategy, style, system, or product made reference to directly or indirectly in this book will be profitable or equal historical or anticipated performance level(s), or be appropriate for your personal situation. Moreover, you should not assume that any discussion or information contained in this book serves as the receipt of, or as a substitute for, personalized investment advice from its authors or from any other investment professional. To the extent that a reader has any questions regarding the applicability/suitability of any specific issue and/or investment discussed in this book for his/her individual situation, he/she is encouraged to consult with the professional advisor(s) of his/her choosing.

Although based on circumstances drawn from a variety of case histories, all characters and events described in the examples used in this book are fictional, and are not intended to portray any particular person or event.

CONTENTS

Acknowledgments   ix

Introduction   xi

Part 1

Laying the Foundation: The Basis for Dividend Investing   1

Chapter 1

The Compelling Evidence for Dividend Investing   3

Chapter 2

Dividends 101: A Basic Primer   15

Chapter 3

New Advantages of Dividend Investing   25

Chapter 4

Head Start for Income Investors   39

Chapter 5

Advantages for Growth Investors   57

Chapter 6

Why Conventional Approaches Fail Investors   69

Part 2

Using the Toolbox: How to Get It Done   81

Chapter 7

Doing Your Homework   83

Chapter 8

Filling Your Toolbox   111

Chapter 9

Laying the Foundation   123

Chapter 10

Building Your Portfolio   141

Chapter 11

Safeguard Your Capital   167

Chapter 12

DRIPs, Folios, Mutual Funds, and ETFs   183

Chapter 13

Staying on Course   203

Appendix   209
Glossary   217
Index   233

ACKNOWLEDGMENTS

Over the years, we have been helped in countless ways by wonderful people too numerous to mention. To a large extent, we owe the benefits of where we are today to all those who have contributed to our success. We would be remiss, however, if we didn't pay special thanks to those who have most recently helped us with the preparation and completion of this book.

Thanks to Larry Chambers for providing his experience and expertise as an editor. We are constantly amazed by his ability to spin straw into gold. Thanks as well to Sydney LeBlanc for her editorial help in preparing the second edition.

Our team at WBI Investments pitched in to pick up the slack on those many occasions when we were sequestered away, hammering out reluctant text for days on end. Whether by helping with research or by keeping the business humming along without us, *their* efforts made *our* efforts possible. Special thanks go out to Bob Confessore. Not only has he been instrumental in making WBI Investments the company it is today, but his generous advice helped turn our initial manuscript drafts into something more closely resembling a book.

Neither of us is a particular joy to live with when we're *not* obsessed with a project as time-consuming as writing a book, and it takes a special brand of patience to support us when we are. For putting up with our frequent absence—and worse, our preoccupied presence—we owe a special debt of gratitude to our families. They listened as we tried out ideas, they poured over thousands of words, and they served as our first line of defense against financial jargon. To the extent that the concepts in this book are easy to understand, they deserve much of the credit.

Finally, we offer thanks to our clients. Our business continues to thrive and grow because of their confidence and support. We recognize how fortunate we are to be able to do what we love for a living. By allowing us to help them achieve their personal hopes and dreams, they are helping us to achieve ours.

INTRODUCTION

The only constant in investing is dividends.

It is dividends that give you superior performance in both good and bad markets. It was dividend stocks that investors moved into after the 1929 crash—during the 1940s, 1950s, and 1960s—because of the return that dividends provided. In the last few years, investors have again rediscovered the benefits of dividend stocks. Yes, the only constant in investing is dividends.

The world of investing has changed dramatically, as conventional passive growth stock approaches have failed investors. If they followed the buy-and-hold mantra and stayed the course from 2000 through 2009, investors booked losses of as much as 44 percent instead of gains. The once high-flying NASDAQ growth stock index devastated investors with losses of 44.50 percent over that 10-year period. According to conventional theory, market returns will always bail you out, so investors should not worry about short-term losses. But in reality, this loss of capital makes it difficult for investors to fund their retirement sufficiently and might cause them to outlive their stream of income. Now is the time for investors to back away from conventional approaches they have been taught. Why? Simply because they do not work!

In 2008, investors found that traditional approaches failed them. Portfolio management strategies that were considered sound faltered. The markets defied the tenets of modern portfolio theory, seeing asset classes fall—and fall hard—across the board. Conventional portfolio construction theory has traditionally put forth the notion that asset diversification reduces risk sufficiently to allow investors to buy and hold. Unfortunately, this theory and actual investor experience seem diametrically opposed, suggesting the assumption is fundamentally flawed. To meet the "acid test," investment approaches must work in both good and bad market cycles. Today more than ever, investors need to pay attention to the evidence indicating that dividend-paying stocks, not growth stocks, should be the foundation on which portfolios are built.

Times and tax laws may change, but fundamentals never change. The fundamentals of investing are

- Dividends can lower risk.
- Dividends can help investors enhance returns when markets are favorable.
- Dividends give investors the ability to achieve positive results even when markets are unfavorable.

During the 1990s, investors who owned dividend-paying stocks did extremely well. They were rewarded with high returns as prices appreciated, and their dividends further enhanced those high returns. These same investors were rewarded again during the bear market of 2000–2002 and the financial crisis of 2008 by not losing almost everything, as so many growth stock investors did. The consistent cash flow return from dividends sustained them and helped them stay on track to achieve their goals.

The Jobs and Growth Tax Relief Reconciliation Act of 2003 (JGTRRA) drastically reduced the tax that investors have to pay on dividends. Investors currently pay a tax of just 5 or 15 percent, depending on their income. But proposals are coming out of Washington for broad-based tax increases. Odds are the top dividend tax will likely increase by 5 percent or more as the government grapples with budget deficits. The good news is that the tax rates on dividends should remain on a par with the rates on capital gains, maintaining preferential rates that are significantly lower than those for ordinary income.

Your authors are Don Schreiber, CEO and president of WBI Investments, Inc., and Gary E. Stroik, vice president and portfolio manager of WBI Investments, Inc. (a money management firm located in Little Silver, New Jersey). Together we bring you 50 years of experience in researching, designing, and managing portfolios. Over that time we have learned three important truths regarding investing and making money:

1. Most investors are concerned with the safety of their capital and have a low tolerance for volatility. This can cause them to panic and bail out at all the wrong times.
2. In order for investors to be protected from panicking and bailing out, they need to have an investment process in place that allows them to manage the risk of owning stocks while providing them with the return they need.

3. By combining the cash flow and inflation protection strengths of dividend-paying stocks, investors can position themselves to reliably capture the return they need to achieve their goals.

Over the years, we have found that dividend stocks have been the solution to a host of investment problems. They have been the glue that holds our clients' portfolios together. In Part 1 of this book, we'll explore why dividends work for just about everyone, whether they are just beginning to save or are already in retirement. We'll demonstrate how dividends lower risk, provide growth, and steadily increase income over time.

Our observation became the driving force behind a powerful investment methodology. We have spent the last 17 years focused on building portfolios with high-yielding dividend stocks. In Part 2, we detail the fundamentals of our selection process and explain how investments in dividend-paying stocks can be diversified by growth, value, yield, financial stability, and overall quality. We'll show how to develop a very logical process for building and maintaining a portfolio that can help reduce or even eliminate the kinds of emotion-based investment decisions that almost always set investors up for failure.

We believe investors should "get paid" while they wait for stock prices to appreciate and that they should guard their investment capital. That capital is the engine that produces growth or income. It should never be compromised. The risk-managed investment approach outlined here will help you respond appropriately to bull and bear investment cycles. Our goal is to help you develop an approach that will provide consistent, reliable returns with substantially less risk of capital loss than the traditional approaches you may have used in the past. Now is the time to learn how to build an investment program that focuses on a stock's dividend and on a company's ability to grow dividends. Dividend investing is the foundation for building your wealth steadily year after year, in good markets and bad. All it requires is that you invest some time in reading this book.

ALL ABOUT
DIVIDEND
INVESTING

Laying the Foundation: The Basis for Dividend Investing

CHAPTER 1

The Compelling Evidence for Dividend Investing

For every action there is an equal and opposite reaction.

—Sir Isaac Newton

Newton's third law of motion has a practical ability to help us understand not just physics but the effects and consequences that market cycles have on investor behavior. The idea that you will "buy and hold" through any market decline, secure in the knowledge that markets always recover as your portfolio value vanishes before your eyes, is pure nonsense! This is evidenced by the rampant but faulty "buy high, sell low" investor behavior that Wall Street thrives on.

But what if investors held stocks that provided return from two sources: price appreciation and dividends? Stock prices fluctuate; they always have and they always will. While you may not be able to count on the return from stock price appreciation, you can *bank* on the return you will get from dividend payments. Dividends arrive every quarter, pretty much without fail. In addition, you do not have to sell the stock to get the dividend. Once received, the tangible dividend can be reinvested, used to diversify your investment position and risk, or used to support your lifestyle.

To clearly understand the dramatic benefits that dividends might have for us in the future, let's look at what an investor might have garnered in the past.

A CLASSIC DIVIDEND STORY

Example: The owner of a grocery store in New York City who saved most of what he made during his life, Joe was one of the fortunate people who came through the Depression with some cash. In 1944, he gave $10,000 to each of his 25-year-old twin sons, Robert and Michael. Though $10,000 was a princely sum in those days—almost enough to buy a modest home—his only proviso regarding the gift was that Robert and Michael not spend the money but instead invest it against a rainy day.

It had been only a few years since the collapse of the stock market, and many investors had lost everything. And if that wasn't bad enough, we were fighting World War II.

Like everyone else, Robert and Michael didn't know where to invest the money. Their father suggested they buy big-name companies in the Dow Jones Industrial Average (DJIA) Index, those stocks that had survived the economic collapse. He also told his sons to let the dividends work for them by reinvesting them. In 1944, the DJIA offered a pretty generous dividend yield of 4.47 percent. (To calculate the dividend yield of the DJIA Index, add up all the dividends paid by the 30 stocks in the index and then divide by the total combined prices of all the stocks in the index.)

Although Michael didn't spend the gift, he could not resist spending the dividend income his stocks provided in the first year. He had good intentions to reinvest his dividends in the future but always seemed to find a reason to spend them. Like a lot of people, Michael found that spending his dividends was easier than saving them. As the years went by, Michael enjoyed his lifestyle and the extra cash his dividends provided. His initial $10,000 investment continued to grow, and by the end of 2009 it had reached $767,000, more than 76 times his initial investment. His dividends also continued to increase, providing him with more income to spend each year. The $483 in dividends that Michael received in his first year grew to more than $21,000 by 2009, providing him with 45 times more purchasing power. Amazingly, his stocks provided him with more than $370,000 in dividend income from 1944 through 2009!

Robert also took his dad's suggestion and bought the companies that made up the DJIA, but unlike his brother Michael, he chose to follow his dad's advice about reinvesting his dividends. He allowed his dividends to reinvest until he retired in 1984, when he needed his dividend income to help support his lifestyle. By 2009, Robert's initial investment increased in value, just as Michael's had, to $767, 000, but the additional shares he bought by reinvesting his dividends grew in value to more than $4.7 million. That's right, almost $5 million! By letting his dividends work for him, Robert's initial gift increased in value from $10,000 to a total of $6.5 million, more than 650 times his initial investment. His annual dividend income also soared from $492 to more than $132,000! Since 1984, he has collected more than $1.7 million in dividends from his stocks. *Now that's inflation protection.* (See Exhibits 1.1 and 1.2.)

EXHIBIT 1.1

Robert versus Michael—Portfolio Value

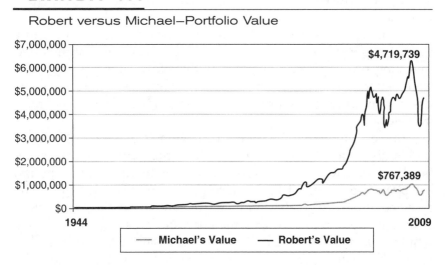

EXHIBIT 1.2

Robert versus Michael—Dividend Income

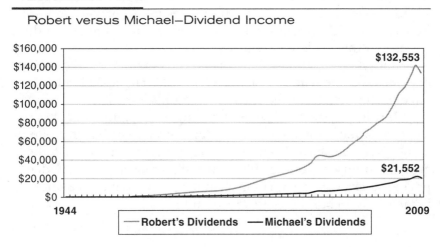

Over 65 years, his dad's initial gift and the classic advantages of dividends made Robert rich. By reinvesting his dividends, Robert unleashed two powerful investment forces—compounding and dollar cost averaging—to build his wealth. *Compounding* builds your shares as dividends are reinvested to buy more shares each quarter. As the number of shares increases, so does the dividend, driving your share balance higher. *Dollar cost averaging* is the practice of systematically investing money (reinvested dividends), usually monthly or quarterly, over a long period of time. Systematic investing leads to lowering the average purchase price of shares as stock prices fluctuate. When share prices are lower, you purchase more shares.

If you find these results almost unbelievable, join the club. Many people are unaware of the tremendous benefits that dividend investing provides. And as good as this story is, it's about to get even better. These results ignore the effect of taxes, but the 65 years covered by this story sported some of the highest income tax rates in history.

If we assume that Robert paid an average tax rate of 35 percent on his dividends, he would have paid almost $395,000 in taxes on his dividends. Robert had to pay tax on his dividends even though he reinvested them. Michael had to pay tax on his dividends as he received them. As their dividends increased, so did their taxes. Although both came to love their dividend-paying stocks, they would always grumble at holiday parties about having to work just to pay the tax man. With the lower tax rates on dividends under the Jobs and Growth Tax Relief Reconciliation Act of 2003 (JGTRRA), the highest tax rate is just 15 percent. This lower tax rate would have saved Robert more than $225,000 in taxes in our 65-year example. Robert and Michael are ecstatic about the reduction in tax on dividends that this tax law provides!

Robert has begun to share his holdings with the children, but his gifts do come with one string attached. You guessed it: his kids have to continue to let the dividends work for them.

Turning $10,000 in dividend-paying stocks into millions is not a get-rich-quick story, but it is a history lesson. The benefits of dividend investing have been all but forgotten by many of today's growth-hungry investors. It's ironic that they equate dividend-paying stocks with the rocking chair set and miss out on a safe and reliable way to build wealth. (See Exhibit 1.3.)

EXHIBIT 1.3

Classic Dividend Story Summary

	Robert's Story	Michael's Story	Difference
The Dividend Income Advantage			
Total Dividends Paid 1944–2009	$2,072,306	$373,037	$1,699,269
Total Cash Dividends Taken in Retirement 1984–2009*	$1,789,843	$291,013	$1,498,830
Total Dividends Taken in Cash Before Retirement	$0	$82,024	−$82,024
Average Annual Dividend Income During Retirement	$31,399	$5,652	$25,746
Dividend Income in 1944	$481	$473	$8
Dividend Income in 2009	$132,553	$21,552	$111,001
Average Dividend Yield 1944–2009	3.99%	3.99%	0.00%
The Dividend Growth Advantage			
Initial Investment in 1944	$10,000	$10,000	$0
Value of Initial Shares in 2009	$767,389	$767,389	$0
Value of Dividend Shares in 2009	$3,952,350	$0	$3,952,350
Total Value of Shares 2009	$4,719,739	$767,389	$3,952,350
Total Value of Shares Plus Dividend Income	**$6,509,582**	**$1,140,426**	**$5,369,156**

*Robert starts to take dividends in cash at retirement in 1984; Michael takes dividends in cash from the beginning.

THE DIVIDEND ADVANTAGE

Following are five reasons that explain why dividend investing works so well for investors.

Reason 1: Dividends Provide a Steady Stream of Income

This income stream delivers a return you can count on regardless of the price movements of the stocks you own or the moves in the markets in general. You can spend your stream of dividend payments as another source of ordinary income. Michael's initial investment paid just $483 in dividends in 1944, but by 2009, his yearly dividends had increased to more than $21,000, a 4,362 percent increase.

Over 65 years, he collected $373,000 in dividends on his initial investment of $10,000.

Reason 2: Dividend Stock Prices Increase Over Time

As more investors are attracted to stocks that pay dividends, the value of those shares is likely to grow over time. The underlying stock prices of companies that pay dividends tend to rise as their dividends increase, which helps keep pace with inflation. The underlying value of Michael's initial $10,000 worth of shares acquired in 1944 increased in value over time to $767,000.

Reason 3: Dividend Reinvestment Allows Your Investment to Grow at a Compounded Rate of Growth

Each time Robert's stocks paid a quarterly dividend, the dividend money bought more shares. At the end of each quarter, he received dividends on those additional shares and bought even more shares. And so on. By the time he retired in 1984, he had not only a much greater number of shares spinning off dividend income, but he had the appreciated value of the additional shares as well.

Reason 4: Dividend Reinvestment Promotes Dollar Cost Averaging

This process of systematically reinvesting dividends leads to lowering the average purchase price of shares as a stock's price fluctuates. When stock prices fall, you buy more shares with each dividend payment.

Reason 5: Dividend-Paying Stocks Generally Have Lower Price Volatility

One of the benefits of providing investors with a reliable return through dividend payments is the *lower risk* that these stocks can offer. In declining markets, the dividend income stream becomes even more important to investors who can no longer count on share price appreciation to provide them with a return.

HOW DIVIDENDS WIN BIG IN BOTH BULL AND BEAR MARKETS

Typically, dividend stocks fall much less than the overall equity market as investors flock to the safety net that dividends provide. *During the 2000–2002 bear market, the DJIA, which is made up of large mature dividend-paying stocks, fell 37.85 percent, while the more growth-oriented indexes like the NASDAQ and the S&P 500 fell 77.93 percent and 49.15 percent, respectively (from their highest closing values in 2000 to their lowest closing values in 2002).*

Both Robert and Michael were happy that their portfolios mirrored the DJIA instead of the more volatile indexes; an almost 38 percent decline in value was more than enough for them. Even with the declines, they felt lucky because their dividends provided them with additional return. Over the three-year bear market period, Michael collected almost $40,000 in dividend income, while Robert collected more than $250,000. Of course, Robert spent years reinvesting his dividends before the bear market started and Michael didn't. And even amid the financial crisis in 2008, they were both pleasantly surprised as the dividend-focused DJIA proved to be a less volatile bet, falling 33.84 percent, less than the more growth-oriented S&P 500 (−38.75 percent) and NASDAQ (−40.55 percent).[1]

Without dividends, market performance would be truly disappointing. The return on the DJIA from price appreciation over the past century has averaged only 4.89 percent—certainly nothing to write home about.[2] Not many investors would be excited about investing in stocks if they were to disregard the additional return from dividends. Yet in a bull market with inflated price appreciation, investors typically forget about the consistent return benefits from dividends.

Through years of extensive research, we have noticed that bull and bear market cycles tend to last longer than most people tend to remember—about 17 years on average. These major trends in market price momentum are extremely important to understand because they affect the way you should invest. In major bull trends, investing looks easy as the rising tide of prices seems to lift most stock prices. During a major bull overperformance cycle, the market's rate of return is much higher than the average 10 percent return that equity investing has provided investors during the past 100 years, just as major bear trends provide investors with lower returns than the historical average. *These bear market cycles remind investors that investing is never easy.*

The exact turning points of cycles are difficult to spot, but by looking at the history of past market trends, certain themes should become clear:

- The DJIA Index's historical 10 percent average rate of return over the past 100 years has been generated almost *equally* from *price appreciation* and *dividends*.
- Dividend-paying stocks work in both bull and bear market cycles.
- During an underperformance cycle, dividends provide a positive return on your investment while the return from price appreciation alone may be nonexistent or negative.
- During an overperformance cycle, dividends enhance returns generated by price appreciation.

From Exhibits 1.4 and 1.5, you can see that these major performance cycles follow one another. Bull cycles are always followed by bear cycles, and these cycles last a long time. The tip-off to determining the beginning of a bear market underperformance cycle is a bear market decline. Bear markets are generally characterized by

EXHIBIT 1.4

Market Performance Cycles, DJIA Index

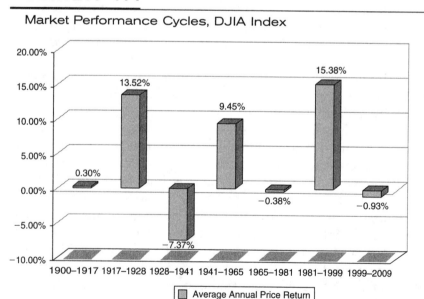

| 1900–1917 | 1917–1928 | 1928–1941 | 1941–1965 | 1965–1981 | 1981–1999 | 1999–2009 |

0.30%   13.52%   −7.37%   9.45%   −0.38%   15.38%   −0.93%

☐ Average Annual Price Return

EXHIBIT 1.5

History of Market Performance Cycles, DJIA Index, 1900–2009

Type of Cycle	Period	Years	Average Price Return
Underperformance	1900–1917	17	0.30%
Overperformance	1917–1928	11	13.52%
Underperformance	1928–1941	13	−7.37%
Overperformance	1941–1965	24	9.45%
Underperformance	1965–1981	16	−0.38%
Overperformance	1981–1999	18	15.38%
Underperformance	1999–2009*	10	−0.93%

*Market cycle in progress.

a drop of at least 20 percent from the previous high reached, and the negative trend typically lasts for six months or more, such as we experienced from March 2000 until April 2003.

In 1966, the markets moved into an *underperformance cycle*. At the time, the dividend yield on the DJIA was 3 percent—well below the historical average of 4.21 percent. The lower yield was a reflection of the inverse relationship that yield has with stock price movements. As stock prices soared from 1941 through 1965, the yield on the DJIA fell. From 1966 through 1981, the economy and markets faltered as they were battered by a combination of rising interest rates and commodity prices. You may recall that the United States was in the grip of *stagflation*—an economic recession combined with soaring interest rates.

If history repeats itself yet again, the current bear market trend is a signal to investors that they may be in for a fairly long stretch of disappointing returns, especially from price appreciation. The good news is that if you know where you are in the cycle, you can make your investment decisions accordingly.

The inverse relationship between price and dividend yield may not be widely understood, but it isn't really a mystery. For a stock, the dividend yield is calculated by dividing the dividend per share by the stock's price. For an index, you find the dividend yield by adding up all the dividends paid on the stocks in the index and dividing by the sum of all of the stock prices included in the index. If we assume a constant dividend, when a stock's price falls, its dividend yield rises. The reverse is also true: as the price rises, the dividend yield falls. (Stock prices and dividends per share information are listed daily in most major newspapers and online.)

The underperformance period that began in 1966 included the shocks of the 1970s. Investors had to cope with oil embargoes, gas lines, and falling stock prices. As if the grinding declines in the market and poor economic conditions weren't enough, at the same time the very fabric of our society was being tested by the political turmoil caused by the war in Vietnam. But even during these very troubled times, companies did their best to keep their commitments to shareholders. Surprisingly, the companies in the DJIA were actually able to increase dividend payouts by an average of 4.46 percent per year. Exhibit 1.5 also shows that returns from price appreciation were negative over the 16-year period. But the increasing dividend stream paid to investors provided them with positive returns.

This negative performance period turned out to be the second worst underperformance cycle of the twentieth century. If you were invested in growth stocks that did not pay a dividend, you almost certainly lost money. However, if you bought stocks that paid dividends, you probably garnered a positive return.

If you had invested $100,000 in the DJIA Index in 1966, the value of your initial shares would have declined over 16 years to $90,275 by 1981. During this underperformance cycle, stock prices declined, and return from price appreciation was nonexistent.

By reinvesting dividends, you would have acquired more shares at a time when prices were falling. Your reinvested dividends would have helped you accumulate additional shares worth $96,386, and your total account value would have increased to $186,661. If you had taken your dividends in cash instead of reinvesting, you would have received $64,978 in cash dividends over the period, and instead of losing almost $10,000 in value, you would have netted almost $50,000. (See Exhibit 1.6.)

In contrast, let's look at how dividend-paying stocks perform during bull market overperformance cycles. One could argue that the period from 1982 through 1999 was an unusually good period for the economy and the markets. This nearly 20-year period provided the longest economic expansion and the greatest bull market in history.

Stock market prices advanced from 875, the value of the DJIA at the start of 1982, to 11,497, its closing value in 1999. These

EXHIBIT 1.6

DJIA Dividends Reinvested Summary, 1966–1981

Initial Investment 1/1/1966	$100,000
Value of Initial Shares (with Price Appreciation)	*$90,275*
Value of Additional Shares from Dividends	$96,386
Total Value*	$186,661
Total Value of Dividends Reinvested*	$64,978

*Assumes dividends reinvested

tremendous returns from price appreciation caused many otherwise conservative dividend investors to abandon their tried-and-true strategy of investing in dividend stocks for the more glamorous growth stock sectors like technology and communications. This decision looked good for a while because these non-dividend growth stocks soared in value, outpacing the price appreciation of their dividend-paying counterparts. In 1999, the technologies-heavy NASDAQ Index advanced a whopping 85 percent, dwarfing the 25 percent advance in the DJIA.

Many growth investors who forgot to factor risk into their investing equation were caught by surprise as the bull cycle faded in 2000. But investors did not need to take more risk to get great returns; dividend-paying stock prices also increased, and their dividends enhanced the stunning returns from appreciation that the great bull market trend provided.

If you had invested $100,000 in the DJIA during the great bull market from 1982 through 1999, the value of your original shares would have grown to $1,302,760 as a result of price appreciation, but with dividends reinvested, the value would have been increased by an *additional* $753,348 to $2,056,109. (See Exhibit 1.7.)

EXHIBIT 1.7

DJIA Dividends Reinvested Summary, 1982–1999

Initial Investment 1/1/1982	$100,000
Value of Initial Shares (Price Appreciation Only)	$1,302,760
Value of Additional Shares from Dividends	$753,348
Total Value of Shares with Dividend Reinvested*	$2,056,109
Total Value of Dividends Reinvested*	$199,686

*Assumes dividends reinvested

EXHIBIT 1.8

DJIA Dividends Reinvested Summary, 2000–2009

Initial Investment 1/1/2000	$100,000
Value of Initial Shares (Price Appreciation Only)	$90,701
Value of Additional Shares from Dividends	$23,267
Total Value of Shares with Dividend Reinvested*	$113,968
Total Value of Dividends Reinvested*	$23,008

*Assumes dividends reinvested

Investors experienced the powerful benefits of dividends once again from 2000–2009 when the markets reverted to a negative price appreciation cycle. Even though the DJIA Index performed dramatically better than the S&P 500 and NASDAQ, an investor who held through this period's two bear market declines would have suffered a loss without dividends. Returns from price appreciation would have turned a $100,000 investment into $90,701. But here again, dividends bailed investors out. With dividends reinvested, an investor would have ended the period with $113,968. (See Exhibit 1.8.) By comparison, the growth-oriented S&P 500 and NASDAQ would have turned $100,000 into $75,900 or $55,760.

Under just about any market conditions, history provides compelling evidence of the benefits of dividend-paying stocks, both for investors who are just starting out and for those already in retirement. And as good as these classic advantages are, there are new advantages based on demographics and tax law changes that will make dividend-focused investing even better. But before we explore these new advantages, it may be helpful to review some of the basic information you need to know about dividends.

ENDNOTES

1. Thomson Baseline, a product of Thomson Reuters.
2. Global Financial Data.

Dividends 101: A Basic Primer

What is a cynic? A man who knows the price of everything, and the value of nothing.

—*Oscar Wilde*

WHAT ARE DIVIDENDS?

A dividend is a distribution of profit earned from company operations or investment activity that is paid to shareholders. A company's board of directors declares cash dividends periodically (quarterly, semiannually, or annually), and dividends can be paid to shareholders as cash or as additional shares of stock. Whereas cash dividends are very common, stock dividends are less common and are usually declared when the directors of a company want to reinvest the cash generated from company operations to grow the company.

When investors buy shares in a company, they receive stock certificates indicating the number of shares they have acquired. If that company pays a dividend, each share they own entitles them to a proportionate share of the total dividend relative to the total number of shares outstanding.

Many established public companies pay cash dividends and have a dividend policy that is well known to their investors. Some of these companies have been paying cash dividends for a very long time. Banking was one of the first industries to develop in the United States. The Bank of New York started paying dividends

EXHIBIT 2.1

S&P 500 Century Dividend Payers

Company	Cash Dividends Paid Each Year Since
Stanley Works	1877
Consolidated Edison	1885
Lilly (Eli)	1885
Johnson Controls	1887
Procter & Gamble	1891
Coca-Cola Co.	1893
General Electric	1899
PPG Industries	1899
TECO Energy	1900
Pfizer, Inc.	1901
Chubb Corp.	1902
Bank of America	1903

Source: Standard & Poor's Quantitative Services.

more than two centuries ago, in 1785. Citicorp, one of the largest banks in the world, started paying dividends in 1813.

The popular S&P 500 Index is made up of 500 of the largest U.S. companies across every major industry group in America. This index information is tallied and published on a continuous basis by Standard & Poor's Quantitative Services. While there are literally thousands of U.S. companies whose stocks are traded on major exchanges, only a few stocks from each industry are included in the S&P 500. Twelve of the companies in the S&P 500 today started paying dividends more than a century ago. (See Exhibit 2.1.)

WHAT DICTATES DIVIDEND POLICY?

Management determines whether it is going to distribute earnings in the form of a dividend or reinvest all earnings to further the business plan of the company. The ratio of dividends paid out to investors versus the amount of earnings retained is called the *payout ratio*. Changes in tax law and investor preference can influence decisions in the corporate boardroom regarding how much profit to retain or to pay out to investors in the form of dividends. However, dividend increases often lag behind an increase in earnings because management will want to be certain that a new higher dividend payment will be sustainable going forward.

EXHIBIT 2.2

Dow Jones Industrial Average Dividend Yield, 1920–2009

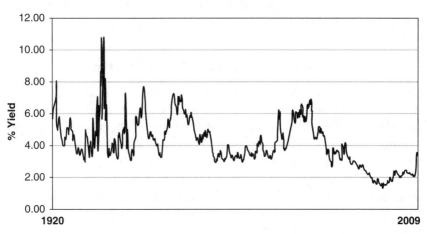

Looking back over market history, we can see that dividend policy and payouts have remained relatively steady and that any change in dividend yield has had a lot more to do with the change in stock prices than with changes to dividend policy made by corporate directors. The relationship between dividend yield and stock prices can be seen in Exhibit 2.2.

Management is usually very reluctant to reduce dividends because a cut is often perceived as a sign of financial weakness. Even during the Great Depression, companies were loath to cut dividends. From 1929 to 1932, dividend yields soared because most companies maintained their dividends as stock prices collapsed in the crash. But as stock prices rose from 1933 to 1936, dividend yields fell—even though companies were actually increasing the dividends they paid.

This inverse relationship between dividend yield and price was particularly evident during the huge bull market run from 1982 to 1999. Companies increased dividends steadily over the period, actually increasing dividends paid by almost 400 percent. Yet the dividend yield collapsed to historic lows because stock prices increased by 1,500 percent.

Occasionally, some companies do run into trouble and cut or omit their dividend payments, but this is the exception rather than the rule. The typical dividend-paying company not only maintains the dividend payout it establishes but follows a policy of steadily increasing its dividend as earnings increase, as we will shortly see.

Some companies increase their dividend payments every quarter, some once a year, and others only as profits allow. Some companies will even pay extra or special dividends if earnings have been quite good for a number of years.

The Two Dates You Need to Know

Once a company's directors declare or change the dividend payment, two important dates are established: the record date and the distribution date. The *record date* is the date the books of the corporation are closed. Everyone who is a shareholder on the books of the corporation at the end of that day will receive a dividend.

After the record date, the stock is said to trade *ex-dividend*—meaning without the dividend. The price of the stock is reduced by the amount of the dividend that has been declared because the purchaser will not get the current dividend.

The second date to remember is the *distribution date*. This is when the dividend will actually be paid to shareholders. It may be a few days or several weeks after the record date.

EVALUATING DIVIDEND-PAYING COMPANIES

A company should be evaluated on three dividend attributes:

1. Reliable dividend payment history
2. A record of increasing dividends
3. A relatively high dividend yield

A company's dividend history is factored into the company's stock price. One with a superior history of paying and increasing dividends will usually command a higher price than a company that has a poor record. A high dividend yield will often attract more investors to a stock, and this can translate into higher prices as investors buy up shares to lock in a generous stream of dividends. A track record of dividend growth is an important indication of the company's ability to grow earnings. The concept of growing dividends is so important that Standard & Poor's maintains a number of indexes that specialize in tracking companies that have a long record of increasing dividends every year. The S&P 500 Dividend Aristocrats Index is designed to measure the performance of S&P 500 companies that have increased dividends every year for at least 25 years. (See Exhibit 2.3.)

EXHIBIT 2.3

S&P 500 Dividend Aristocrats Index

	Ticker	Name	Sector
1	MMM	3M Co	Industrials
2	ABT	Abbott Laboratories	Health Care
3	AFL	AFLAC Inc	Financials
4	APD	Air Products & Chemicals Inc	Materials
5	ADM	Archer-Daniels-Midland Co	Consumer Staples
6	ADP	Automatic Data Processing	Information Technology
7	BCR	Bard, C.R. Inc	Health Care
8	BDX	Becton, Dickinson & Co	Health Care
9	BMS	Bemis Co Inc	Materials
10	BF.B	Brown-Forman Corp B	Consumer Staples
11	CTL	Centurytel Inc	Telecommunication Services
12	CB	Chubb Corp	Financials
13	CINF	Cincinnati Financial Corp	Financials
14	CTAS	Cintas Corp	Industrials
15	CLX	Clorox Co	Consumer Staples
16	KO	Coca-Cola Co	Consumer Staples
17	ED	Consolidated Edison Inc	Utilities
18	DOV	Dover Corp	Industrials
19	EMR	Emerson Electric Co	Industrials
20	XOM	Exxon Mobil Corp	Energy
21	FDO	Family Dollar Stores Inc	Consumer Discretionary
22	GWW	Grainger, W.W. Inc	Industrials
23	TEG	Integrys Energy Group Inc	Utilities
24	JNJ	Johnson & Johnson	Health Care
25	KMB	Kimberly-Clark	Consumer Staples
26	LEG	Leggett & Platt	Consumer Discretionary
27	LLY	Lilly, Eli & Co	Health Care
28	LOW	Lowe's Cos Inc	Consumer Discretionary
29	MCD	McDonald's Corp	Consumer Discretionary
30	MHP	McGraw-Hill Cos Inc	Consumer Discretionary
31	PEP	PepsiCo Inc	Consumer Staples
32	PBI	Pitney Bowes Inc	Industrials
33	PPG	PPG Industries Inc	Materials
34	PG	Procter & Gamble	Consumer Staples
35	STR	Questar Corp	Utilities
36	SHW	Sherwin-Williams Co	Consumer Discretionary
37	SIAL	Sigma-Aldrich Corp	Materials
38	SWK	Stanley Works	Industrials
39	SVU	Supervalu Inc	Consumer Staples
40	TGT	Target Corp	Consumer Discretionary
41	VFC	VF Corp	Consumer Discretionary
42	WAG	Walgreen Co	Consumer Staples
43	WMT	Wal-Mart Stores	Consumer Staples

Source: Standard & Poor's Quantitative Services, December 2009.

Investors tend to view these higher-yielding, consistent dividend payers as a safe haven during falling markets. Not only does the dividend yield tend to be higher—2.90 percent for the Dividend Aristocrats Index versus 2.00 percent for the S&P 500 Index—but the stocks also tend to perform better. For the three years ending January 31, 2010, the S&P 500 Dividend Aristocrats Index lost 2.04 percent per year, while the S&P 500 index lost 9.28 percent per year.[1]

But beware of a company with a high dividend yield that has an eroding earnings outlook. Just because it has a generous dividend yield does not mean the company can support the payments if it gets in trouble. General Motors, the largest car company in the world, had to eliminate its dividend in 2008 to avoid bankruptcy. Prior years' profit losses should have been a clear sign to investors to be wary. Remember, a company can pay dividends only from current or accumulated earnings. Without good earnings, there is a good chance that the high dividend you covet may be cut. Chapters 7, 8, and 9 provide more detail on the process you should follow to evaluate dividend-paying stocks before you buy.

BUSINESS AND DIVIDEND LIFE CYCLES

Business life cycles are most influenced by access to resources and capital. A company's success and development are also affected by a host of outside factors—competition from companies in the same industry, economic conditions, and even changing consumer preferences. (See Exhibit 2.4.)

There are six phases in a company's development that influence its dividend policy:

1. In the *start-up phase*, someone invests cash for stock in the business to develop products, hire employees, pay for equipment, and rent space. It is not unusual for a company to raise seed money from professional investors and enter the start-up phase with a hundred or more employees. A small company needs to plow all profits back into growing and perfecting its business model to survive.

2. If the company launch is successful, it will enter the *early growth phase*. As the demand for its products or services increases, sales and profits increase. The company still needs to reinvest all cash flow and profit to achieve competitive scale.

E X H I B I T   2 . 4

Business and Dividend Life cycles

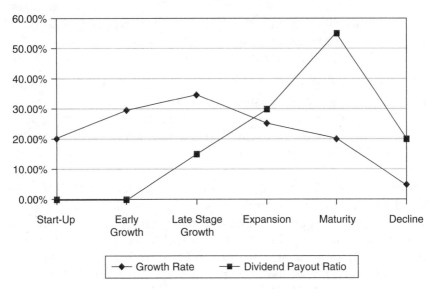

Legend: Growth Rate · Dividend Payout Ratio

(X-axis categories: Start-Up, Early Growth, Late Stage Growth, Expansion, Maturity, Decline)

3. In the *late-stage growth phase*, the company continues to grow and may begin to pay a small dividend, usually 10–15 percent of earnings. This is a clear signal to investors that the company has reached a level of stability in profits and cash flow necessary to support a dividend.

4. If the company is well run, it will enter the *expansion phase*. Its rate of growth might slow as competitors take some of the company's market share. Companies at this stage generally increase their dividend payout ratio to approximately 30–40 percent of earnings.

5. Companies can continue to expand even as they reach their *maturity phase*, but their growth rate usually slows measurably. Well-run mature companies can continue to be competitive forces in their respective industries for decades or even several generations. Many of the companies shown in Exhibit 2.3 are mature companies, a few over a century old. It is during this stage that companies tend to increase their dividend payout ratios to 50–60 percent of earnings, which provides investors with generous dividend income.

6. In the latter stages, many companies fail to innovate—to keep their competitive advantage. These companies will enter the *decline phase*, and unless they reinvent themselves, they will eventually cease to exist. In this phase, as sales and profits decline, they will eventually reduce or eliminate their dividend payouts.

Beware of attempting to buy or hold the stock of a company in the final stages of its business life cycle.

AT&T is a great example of a company currently in decline, possibly on its way to extinction. At one time, AT&T was the most widely held stock in America. The company paid its first dividend in 1893 and became known as the "widows and orphans" stock because it was such a consistent source of dividend payments for investors. AT&T's history dates back to 1875. The company's founder, Alexander Graham Bell, invented the telephone and together with several investors started the American Telephone and Telegraph Corporation. As a telephone company, AT&T was so successful it achieved regulated monopoly status. In 1984, the U.S. Department of Justice broke the AT&T monopoly into eight companies: seven regional operating "Baby Bells" and AT&T.

For most of its history, AT&T had been largely insulated from market pressures and competitive forces. After the breakup, smaller and leaner communication companies stole AT&T's market share, first through price competition and later by becoming product innovators. For the new AT&T to successfully compete in an unregulated environment would require a drastic change in corporate culture. Over the years, operations and profits continued to decline, and AT&T was struggling to survive up until BellSouth Corporation acquired AT&T on March 6, 2006, at fire sale prices. Although the AT&T brand was adopted by the merged company, investors may never achieve the value they once had when AT&T was a strong competitor.

AT&T's story of dominance and decline highlights the constant need to follow up your initial purchase analysis with a routine review to see if the companies you hold are performing as expected. Each time you decide to continue to hold a stock, you are in fact making a new buying decision. Understanding the business life cycle outlined here will enable you to identify companies that are about to emerge as great dividend payers, as well as help you to spot the mature companies headed down the road to extinction.

NOT ALL DIVIDENDS ARE CREATED EQUAL

The rights and benefits of a stockholder depend on the *type* of stock he or she owns. The two main categories of stock are *common* and *preferred*.

Common stock is the most popular and widely held form of stock. The vast majority of the stocks listed in the Unites States are common. Investors who hold common stock have the last claim on the earnings and assets of a company. Common stockholders are entitled to a share in the profits of the company in the form of dividend payments and appreciation through an increase in the stock price, which reflects growth in the value of the company's assets. After initial issue, common stock has no fixed dollar value; the stock price rises and falls with the company's fortunes. Common stockholders can benefit more from a company's prosperity or lose more from a company's adversity.

Whereas the dividend payout on common stocks is variable, *preferred stocks* pay a fixed dividend, and owners are entitled to receive dividends before any dividends are distributed to other shareholders. Preferred stock ownership may also entitle shareholders to preferred assets of the company in the event of dissolution. Most firms have only one issue of common stock, but they may have several issues of preferred stock.

Stocks with first preference in the distribution of dividends or assets are called *first preferred* or *preferred A*; the next in the series is called *second preferred* or *preferred B*; and so on. The fixed dividend on a preferred stock is paid from profits (current or accumulated), and a company may not declare or pay a dividend if it does not have profits. If the dividend is omitted, then it is said to be "in arrears." Most preferred issues are considered cumulative because dividends that are not paid accumulate to be paid later. There are noncumulative preferred issues whose dividends do not have to be made up if missed. In addition, some issues have a conversion feature that allows the preferred stock to be converted to common.

STOCK VERSUS CASH DIVIDENDS

Some firms pay stock dividends in addition to or in lieu of cash dividends. Stock dividends are a form of recapitalization and do not affect the assets and liabilities of the firm. There is a misconception that stock dividends increase the ability of the firm to grow. Many investors believe that stock dividends preserve cash and actually allow the firm to reinvest more for growth. Because of this belief, many stocks trade higher after paying a stock dividend. However, stock dividends do not increase the earning power of the company.

If an investor receives additional shares from a stock dividend (and the investor does not have the option to take the dividend in cash), there is no tax consequence until the investor sells the stock. For example:

Example: Assume you purchase 100 shares of XYZ Company at $10 per share for a total investment of $1,000, and the company elects to pay a stock dividend of 10 percent a year later. After the stock dividend, you would own 110 shares. For tax purposes, your new "adjusted cost basis" on the shares you now own is calculated by taking your original investment of $1,000 and dividing by the new number of shares, or 110, to arrive at an adjusted cost basis per share of $9.09. If you decide to sell a few months later for $12 per share, you would use this adjusted cost basis to calculate your taxable gain. In this example, you would have a gain per share of $2.91 and a total gain of $320.

All this being said, the concept of paying dividends is now being presented as a *new* benefit—all due to JGTRRA. We'll look at why JGTRRA is having this effect in the next chapter.

ENDNOTE

1. Standard & Poor's Quantitative Services, January 31, 2010.

New Advantages of Dividend Investing

We must all hang together, or assuredly we shall all hang separately.

—Benjamin Franklin

THE DEMOGRAPHIC EFFECT

As 80 million or more American baby boomers leave the workforce over the next two decades and the nearly 25 million people in the gap generation retire, the ranks of retired people will swell from 35 million to more than 140 million. By 2020, nearly one in two Americans will be retired. The problems caused by this ratio are further compounded by the fact that today's seniors and baby boomers are the wealthiest generations the world has ever seen. (See Exhibits 3.1 and 3.2.)

As their long-term investments for capital growth give way to retirees' need for income to support their lifestyles, this enormous group of people will need to reposition their assets. The much smaller group of people in the generations still working will not have the investment dollars required to purchase the stocks being sold. This potential supply and demand imbalance could create a vortex of falling stock prices.

EXHIBIT 3.1

U.S. Population Census by Age Group

Age Group Designation	Years to Retirement	Age	Number of People	% of Population
Generation Y	46–65	0–19	80,473,265	28.60%
Generation X	31–45	20–34	58,855,725	20.91%
Baby Boomers	11–30	35–54	82,826,479	29.43%
Gap Generation	1–10	55–64	24,274,684	8.63%
Seniors		Over 65	34,991,753	12.43%
Totals			**281,421,906**	**100.00%**

Source: U.S. Census Bureau, Census 2000.

EXHIBIT 3.2

U.S. Demographics by Age

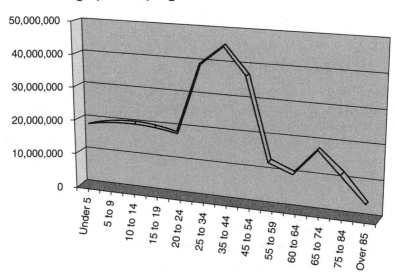

THE TAX EFFECT

The good news is that, by reducing the tax on dividends, the Jobs and Growth Tax Relief Reconciliation Act of 2003 (JGTRRA) may have set the stage for the rescue of U.S. equity markets and the protection of the U.S. economy. Taxes are a fundamental part of every investment decision. Investor behavior indicates that investors are very motivated to reduce taxes whenever possible and by whatever means they can employ. Investors know that the more they pay to the tax man, the less they get to spend or to keep reinvesting to fund their goals.

JGTRRA cut the tax on dividend income significantly, creating a competitive environment in which market forces compel companies to pay dividends. This could provide the solution to the retirement income dilemma if market holdings are repositioned from traditional growth stocks to dividend stocks that don't have to be liquidated to generate income.

The government did not hand investors this windfall out of the kindness of its heart. After all, dividends had been taxed *twice*—once at the corporate level as profits, and then again when paid to investors as investment income. The government had a strong incentive to cut the tax to stimulate the economy and to draw investors back into the stock market after the second worst bear market in history.

A similar situation occurred more than 20 years ago, in 1981, when the government cut the tax on capital gains. The tax on investment asset appreciation (capital gains) was reduced from ordinary income rates as high as 50 percent to a new preferential rate for long-term capital gains of 20 percent. Before the tax cut, you paid $500 in federal tax on a $1,000 long-term gain; after the tax cut, you paid only $200. That represents a whopping 60 percent reduction in tax!

Prior to 1981, the United States economic engine and stock markets had faltered. The economy was in recession while, at the same time, inflation was running rampant—a painful combination known as *stagflation*. The Dow Jones Industrial Average (DJIA), which soared to 1,000 in 1966, sat at just 875 by the close of 1981: 16 years of depressing performance. Investors were dismayed, to say the least, because it seemed that they could not make money investing in stocks. But even with poor stock performance and terrible economic conditions, investors took the tax bait and rushed to buy stocks.

As we reflect on what has happened since then, it's clear that this fiscal stimulus was a key factor in the longest economic expansion on record and set the stage for the greatest bull market move in history! From the Dow's low of 777 in 1982 to its high mark of 11,497 in 1999, we saw a stunning 15-fold increase in value.

If the capital gains tax break could bring investors back to the market after one of the worst long-term performance cycles on record, then what is the dividend tax cut likely to do today? History tells us that investors could once again rush to take advantage of the tax benefits being offered. This time, our government has even raised the stakes.

Depending on your tax bracket, the reduction in tax on dividends is as high as 85 percent. That's right. Before the JGTRRA, every dollar in dividend income was taxed at your highest ordinary income tax rate (which could have been as high as 38.6 percent in 2002). Now the highest federal tax rate on qualifying dividends is 15 percent and, depending on your tax bracket, you can pay as little as 5 percent on your dividend income!

SWIMMING WITH THE TIDE

In 1980, 94 percent of the corporations that made up the S&P 500 routinely paid out 50 percent of their earnings (payout ratio) in dividends to investors. With the advent of preferential tax rates on long-term capital gains, investors shifted their focus from stocks that paid dividends to stocks that reinvested their profits to drive growth. Corporate policy followed this trend, and, by 2002, only 74 percent of S&P 500 companies paid dividends, and the payout ratio plummeted to just over 30 percent, leaving plenty of room for a widespread increase in payout ratios.

In March 2000, the annualized dividend yield on the DJIA fell to a century low of 1.49 percent. But low yields have been steadily increasing as companies compete for investor capital under these new market forces that favor dividend stocks over traditional growth stocks. From 2003 to 2008, S&P 500 Index companies increased dividend payouts at one of the fastest paces on record. By the end of 2009, the DJIA yield had more than doubled, to 3.30 percent. And while the 2008 financial crisis caused many companies, especially in the financial sector, to eliminate or reduce dividends, the worst may be over. It's likely to take a couple of years, but as the economy and corporate earnings improve, companies will begin to restore and increase dividends back to record levels.

To illustrate the dramatic effect that increases in payout ratios can have, let's look at the following example.

Example: A company has a dividend payout ratio of 30 percent and is paying $1 in dividends per share to shareholders. Further, we will assume that business is good for the company, and earnings increase by 50 cents to $3.83 per share. If the company follows its existing payout policy, it would increase dividends by 15 cents per share to $1.15. But let's assume that the company's board of directors decides to increase the payout ratio from 30 to 50 percent to attract a new breed of dividend-hungry investors. The new dividend would increase to $1.92 per share, a 67 percent increase over the dividend rate of $1.15 per share under the old payout ratio.

This renewed emphasis on dividends fits well into the post–Enron, WorldCom, Global Crossing, and tech stock world, because companies can't jury-rig dividend payouts as they did their earnings to boost stock prices. After watching skyrocketing appreciation vanish, badly burned growth stock investors are looking for tangible value—checks in their mailboxes. Companies need real earnings to pay dividends.

THE TECH STOCK FACTOR

Y2K was widely anticipated to become a disaster of monstrous proportions, with predictions of massive computer hardware and software malfunctions that would cause a total meltdown of global computer networks and financial systems. The concern over the looming computer disaster gained worldwide attention and led businesses to upgrade hardware and to rewrite or replace all existing software.

The late 1990s buying binge unleashed a cycle of increased revenue and earnings in the technology sector at a pace never seen before. Earnings did not just exceed expectations—they exploded! As stock prices soared, investors cashed in their gains and went on their own buying binge that lifted activity across all sectors of the economy. This rising tide of earnings announcements became a self-fulfilling prophecy, attracting more of the U.S. population into buying stocks than ever before. The major stock indexes rose to new highs, most sporting staggering advances. Watching financial news programs seemed to replace baseball as America's favorite pastime.

Even the experts were caught up in the speculative frenzy, condoning ridiculous stock prices and unprecedented valuations and predicting ever higher prices to follow—all the while concocting a number of "this time, it's different" theories to justify bubble pricing. Fundamental value criteria were completely discounted; it did not matter if companies had profits or even revenue. If you can believe it, professionals were basing prices and valuations on how many eyeballs a Web site recorded. The greater fool theory was in full swing; if you bought an overpriced stock, so what, someone would likely pay you an even higher price for it tomorrow!

Unfortunately, times are never different, and investors paid a huge price for abandoning well-reasoned investment disciplines for the emotional decisions that abound during market mania. In this case, the experts had figured Y2K wrong. The looming disaster wasn't about computers at all. *The year 2000 will always be remembered as the beginning of the second worst bear market period in history.* The once high-flying NASDAQ lost almost 70 percent in value from its peak, but many investors who had concentrated their assets in the technology sector faired even worse, losing 85 percent or more of their account values.

As the speculative bubble burst in 2000, the economy faltered, and economists, politicians, and even the Federal Reserve Board chairman feared a possible slide into deflation. To its credit, the government took appropriate steps to avoid a dire economic scenario. Once again it took out its magic tax wand to entice investors back into the market and to jump-start the economy. This time it not only reduced the tax on ordinary income and capital gains but on dividends, too.

JGTRRA IN PLAIN ENGLISH

Public Law 108–27, the Jobs and Growth Tax Relief Reconciliation Act of 2003 (JGTRRA), signed by President Bush on May 28, 2003, includes five basic changes to the tax law that are important to investors:

1. The maximum tax rate on net capital gain (i.e., net long-term capital gain reduced by any net short-term capital loss) was reduced from 20 percent to 15 percent (and from 10 percent to 5 percent for taxpayers in the 10 to 15 percent tax rate brackets) for property sold after May 5, 2003. The reduced rate applies to both regular tax and the alternative minimum tax. Because of the expansion of tax brackets, some people who were paying 20 percent tax on capital gains found their new tax rate reduced by 75 percent, to only 5 percent.

EXHIBIT 3.3

Changes in Taxation for Dividend Investors

Old Law Tax Rate on Dividends	New Tax Rate on Dividends	% Reduction in Tax Rate	Tax Under New Law	Tax Under Old Law	Increase in Retained Income
Dividend Income Assumption:			$1,000		
10%	5%	50.00%	$ 50	$ 100	5.56%
15%	5%	66.67%	$ 50	$ 150	11.76%
27%	15%	44.44%	$ 150	$ 270	16.44%
30%	15%	50.00%	$ 150	$ 300	21.43%
35%	15%	57.14%	$ 150	$ 350	30.77%
38.60%	15%	61.14%	$ 150	$ 386	38.44%

2. The same 15 percent (or 5 percent) maximum tax rate that applies to net capital gains also applies to dividends paid by most domestic and foreign corporations after December 31, 2002. According to Section 302 of the new tax law, qualifying dividends will now be taxed on "Schedule D" of the income tax return, just like capital gains, instead of being taxed at ordinary income rates as high as 38.6 percent for high-income investors. This means a 61 percent reduction in tax on dividends that qualify. (See Exhibit 3.3.)

3. Federal income tax rates were reduced on ordinary income. The tax rate brackets of 27, 30, 35, and 38.6 percent have been reduced to 25, 28, 33, and 35 percent, respectively. These reductions in tax brackets will reduce the amount of tax investors will have to pay on interest from savings accounts, money market funds, certificates of deposits, and bonds.

4. Federal income tax brackets were expanded, increasing the amount of income an individual could have and still qualify for a lower bracket. For example, in 2002 a married couple filing a joint return moved to a higher than 15 percent tax bracket when their taxable income exceeded $46,700. Under the new law, the same couple was able to book taxable income up to $56,800 and still pay the 15 percent tax rate. This expanded bracket allowed more investors to take maximum advantage of

E X H I B I T   3 . 4

Old Tax Law Rates versus New Tax Law Rates

New Tax Law				
Federal Tax Rate Tables Married Filing Jointly				
Taxable Income Over	Taxable Income Not Over	Amount	Plus%	Of Amt Over
$0	$14,000	$0.00	10%	$0
$14,000	$56,800	$1,400.00	15%	$14,000
$56,800	$114,650	$7,820.00	25%	$56,800
$114,650	$174,700	$22,282.50	28%	$114,650
$174,700	$311,950	$39,096.50	33%	$174,700
$311,950	–	$84,389.00	35%	$311,950

Old Tax Law				
Federal Tax Rate Tables Married Filing Jointly				
Taxable Income Over	Taxable Income Not Over	Amount	Plus%	Of Amt Over
$0	$12,000	$0.00	10%	$0
$12,000	$46,700	$1,200.00	15%	$12,000
$46,700	$112,850	$6,405.00	27%	$46,700
$112,850	$171,950	$24,265.50	30%	$112,850
$171,950	$307,050	$41,995.50	35%	$171,950
$307,050	–	$89,280.50	38.6%	$307,050

the lowered capital gains and dividend rates. Many more low- and middle-income investors fell into or below the 15 percent tax bracket and pay 75 percent less tax on some, if not all, of their dividend income. (See Exhibit 3.4.)

5. Section 303, Sunset of the Act, specifies that these beneficial provisions shall not apply to taxable years beginning after 2008 and that the Code shall be applied and administered to such years as if those provisions had never been enacted. But the dividend preference granted under the JGTRRA tax law has an excellent chance of staying on the books for a very long time, just like the preference on capital gains that has been the law of the land for almost 30 years.

With these sunset provisions, it is true there is the risk that the investor-friendly provisions enacted will expire in 2011. But don't fret—these new dividend tax benefits have become so popular with investors that they will revolt rather than give them up. Early drafts of the new tax proposals keep the dividend and capital gain preference in place, but the tax rates are slightly higher. Seniors have one of the strongest political lobbies in the country, and as their ranks swell as the gap generation and aging baby boomers retire, it could be akin to political suicide to try to take the dividend tax benefits away. It would be similar to reducing Social Security benefits!

DIVIDENDS THAT QUALIFY

Not all stocks qualify for the new dividend tax. The obvious winners will be those stocks that qualify for the new dividend tax preference. Generally, dividend income paid by U.S. corporations, as well as by qualified foreign corporations, is eligible for the new lower tax treatment under the JGTRRA. A qualified foreign corporation is one whose stock or American Depositary Receipts (ADRs) are traded on an established securities market in the United States, or a foreign corporation that is eligible for the benefits of an income tax treaty with the United States.

Some stocks already have some tax preferences built in, like real estate investment trusts (REITs) and master limited partnerships (MLPs), and, thus, do not qualify for lower tax rates on their dividends.

Other dividends that *do not* qualify under the law are

- Dividends on preferred stocks that are treated as a debt instrument
- Dividends from mutual funds attributable to interest or short-term gains
- Dividends from tax-exempt organizations, including certain savings institutions
- Dividends paid on money market funds
- Dividends paid on insurance policies
- Dividends paid into IRAs or tax-deferred retirement accounts
- Dividends from S-corporations (with limited exceptions)
- Dividends you receive as a nominee

Dividends that do not qualify under the law are treated as ordinary dividends and are included as ordinary income on your tax return.

HOLDING PERIOD REQUIREMENT

The law also requires that you meet holding period rules for dividends that do qualify. For a dividend to satisfy these rules, you are required to hold the stock for more than 60 days during the 120-day period beginning 60 days before the ex-dividend date. For preferred stock dividends, you must hold the stock for 90 days during the 180-day period beginning 90 days before the preferred stock's ex-dividend date. Holding periods include the day you sell but not the day of purchase. (As we write this book, the IRS has extended the holding period from 120 to 121 days for common stock and 180 to 181 days for preferred stock to make the holding period easier to satisfy.)

Let's try that one again! If you want a stock dividend to qualify for the lower tax rate, you must buy the stock at least one day before the ex-dividend date and hold it for 60 more days. To shed additional light on the complex holding period requirement rules, let's review a couple of paraphrased examples from the IRS 2003 Form 1040 instructions:

Example 1.   You bought 5,000 shares of XYZ Corp common stock on July 1, 2003. XYZ Corp paid a cash dividend of 10 cents per share. The ex-dividend date was July 9, 2003. Your form 1099-DIV from XYZ Corp shows $500 in box 1a (ordinary dividends) and in box 1b (qualified dividends). However, you sold the 5,000 shares on August 4, 2003. You held your shares of XYZ Corp for only 34 days of the 120-day holding period that began on May 10 and ended on September 6, 2003. Even though the dividends from the XYZ Corp technically qualify, your holding period does not.

Example 2.   Assume the same facts as in Example 1, except that you bought the stock on July 8, 2003 (the day before the ex-dividend date), and you sold the stock on September 9, 2003. You held the stock for 63 days (from July 9, 2003, through September 9, 2003). Now comes the tricky part: you have no qualified dividends from XYZ Corp because you held the stock for only 60 days of the 120-day period (from July 9, 2003, through September 6, 2003).

Remember, the day you bought the stock does not qualify as a holding day under the rule. The 121-day qualifying period allowed your holding period to qualify in this example.[1]

Mutual fund dividends that qualify are subject to the same holding period requirement as stock dividends. Your mutual fund company will let you know the portion of dividends eligible to be treated as qualified dividends, but you still must satisfy the holding period for the mutual fund shares you purchase.

The new holding period requirement is designed to *prevent* investors from using dividend capture strategies that rely on buying stocks just before the ex-dividend date to capture the dividend and then immediately selling the stock while obtaining the tax breaks being offered. Most investors calculate their holding periods as a matter of course prior to selling to ensure they pay the lower tax on dividends.

In summary, since most stocks pay dividends quarterly, the revised 121-day holding period covers the entire period from ex-date to ex-date. So the ex-date is the important date to remember. You can purchase a stock up to 60 days (but at least 1 day) before the ex-date, and your dividends will qualify so long as you hold the stock 61 days before selling.

WHAT *IS* PREDICTABLE

Every investor needs to rethink his or her investment plan right now; there is no time to lose. The powerful investment benefits of dividend stock investing are not widely known and appreciated by most investors. As investors shun the conventional growth stock "buy and hope" approaches, there will be a rush into dividend payers that will dramatically drive prices up and yields down. Unfortunately, many investors are sitting on the sidelines because they were burned by losses incurred in the 2008 bear market.

What most investors don't know is that market cycles are fairly predictable. This is good news! In March 2009, the markets reversed the bear trend created by the financial crisis. Most investors, retail and institutional alike, were caught by surprise sitting in cash. Once again, a good working knowledge of market history would have allowed them to anticipate a significant move to the upside. After every major market decline, markets have snapped back with a

EXHIBIT 3.5

Don't Miss the Relief Rallies: DJIA Index Correction and Rally
Cycles 1900–2009

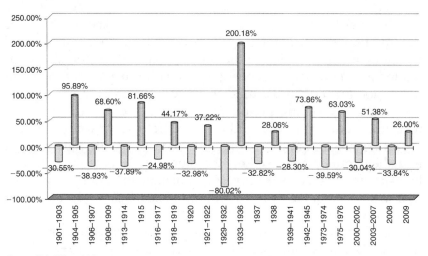

Source: Global Financial Data

short-term (cyclical) bull market rally. These up-trends tend to be
very powerful, lifting investors' account balances and spirits at the
same time.

Exhibit 3.5 shows the powerful relief rallies that have followed each market decline as measured by the year-over-year
change in the DJIA Index. It's as if the markets understand
Newton's law of physics: that for every action there is an equal
and opposite reaction. After each correction, a rally has helped to
salvage investors' fortunes.

YOU CAN'T AFFORD TO MISS THE POWERFUL RELIEF RALLIES

Oh, what a relief! The market rally of 2009 lifted the S&P 500 Index
to a positive return of 26 percent. The market bounced off bottom
on March 9 and never stopped rising for the balance of the year.
That's great for investors if they were fully invested when the rally
started. Unfortunately, most investors sold to protect capital as the
markets fell, and many never reinvested because they were afraid
the rally was nothing but a head fake.

They missed an historic buying opportunity to pick up equities at low prices in the spring of 2009. The single most important premise of investing is to "buy low and sell high," yet investors battered by losses are often reluctant to invest when markets bottom because risk is still high and they don't want to lose more money. The severity of losses seems to dictate the amount of time an investor sits on the sidelines in cash. One of the benefits of hindsight is to correct investment decisions that seem to be irrational. But many of the same investors who failed to believe that the 2009 relief rally was a normal consequence of markets adjusting to an oversold and severely undervalued condition missed the same opportunity in 2003 as the markets recovered from the 2002 market lows.

The question of the day seems to be, how high will the markets go? Or, has this "relief rally" already run its course? While nobody has a crystal ball, a careful review of market history may give us some clues. Since 1900, the DJIA has posted 11 cyclical year-over-year corrections of 20 percent or more, followed by a relief rally that helped investors recover lost capital. The average correction posted a 38 percent loss, while the average rally posted a 74 percent gain. The average relief rally was strong enough to lift account values to 103 percent of their precorrection value. But it helped investors only if they stayed the course.

The 2008 correction shaved 33.84 percent off the DJIA, so the rally that started in March 2009 would have to lift the DJIA back to 13,700 to follow the historical trends. This would impute a gain of 51 percent on the starting value of the DJIA of 8,776.39 in 2009. While we believe we are a long way from a new sustainable secular (long-term) bull market, these short-term rallies can be more powerful and last longer than the skeptics believe. Rallies off market bottoms happen quickly, and to capture the return, investors must be invested, not sitting on the sidelines in cash. The duration of relief rallies tends to be about as long as the previous declines, but they don't last forever, so investors need to be cautious.[2]

The best way to win in cyclical markets is to incorporate cash flow from dividends as the foundation of portfolio strategy. With dividends you get paid to patiently wait until the appreciation happens. To stay comfortably invested, investors also need to manage risk to capital. This involves developing a process to buy low and sell high systematically, in an attempt to capture the elusive gains offered during these short rallies. Twenty years from now, we may look back and realize that the dynamic changes in demographics and tax incentives paved the way to a new golden age of dividend investing.

ENDNOTES

1. Paraphrased from the Department of the Treasury, Internal Revenue Service, 2003 Form 1040 instructions, page 23, for Line 9b, Qualified Dividends.
2. Global Financial Data.

CHAPTER 4

Head Start for Income Investors

Perfection as an ideal is beyond human perception.

—*Plato*

After years of saving and growing their asset bases, investors approaching retirement change their objective from growing capital to generating income from their investments to support their lifestyle needs.

GENERATING INCOME FROM STOCKS

Eureka—there's gold in them there dividend stocks! A perfect income portfolio needs to include a healthy dose of these stocks. Bonds may have higher yields and generate more cash for each dollar invested, but their income streams are fixed and do not keep pace with inflation. Since dividend-paying stocks do keep pace with inflation, we have found that a balanced approach of investing about half of an income portfolio in bonds and the other half in high-yielding dividend-paying stocks works best. (See Exhibit 4.1.)

If dividend-paying stocks should be part of the perfect income portfolio, then why aren't more retired investors using them?

There are basically two reasons:

1. Most stocks have low dividend yields.
2. Stocks are volatile and are viewed as too risky.

EXHIBIT 4.1

EXHIBIT 4.1

Characteristics of Bonds and Stocks

Attribute	Bonds	Stocks
High Current Income	+	−
Increasing Income	−	+
Asset Appreciation	−	+
Tax Efficiency	−	+
Volatility & Risk	+	−
Positive (+) Negative (−)		

There are many books and online resources where you can find information about how to invest in bonds.

Stocks that pay dividends tend to increase dividends over time. And the prices of stocks generally appreciate over long periods of time, allowing the income investor to reposition a portion of the stock portfolio to increase income. Dividend stocks are also generally less volatile than typical growth stocks. During the three-year Y2K bear market, dividend stocks actually held their value better than their growth counterparts. Because dividend-paying stocks from big companies in mature industries don't fall as much in a market decline, they are considered defensive stocks. They tend to hold their value because investors buy these types of companies as they bail out of more risky growth plays. The ensuing influx of cash into these issues helps them maintain their value even in declining markets.

Income investors should focus their search on dividend stocks that have yields high enough to generate the income they require. If you need an income stream equal to 4 percent of invested capital, then you should look for stocks with yields in the 4 percent range. There are thousands of stocks, so to make your job of finding the right dividend stocks easier, we suggest you mentally group them into three distinct yield categories.

Category 1. Low-Yielding Stocks

These are issues that have a dividend yield of less than the yield on the S&P 500 Index. As we write this book, the yield on the S&P 500 Index is about 1.52 percent. Although they do pay a dividend, they tend to reinvest most of their earnings to foster growth in value through price appreciation. These stocks are very appropriate for growth investors, but they may fail to meet your income requirement. (Look for more information on the advantages of these stocks for growth investors in Chapter 5.)

Category 2. Medium-Yielding Stocks

These are issues with dividend yields that are equivalent to the index's yield or higher and tend to be companies focusing on providing a balanced return from both dividends and price appreciation. When screening for stocks, we target stocks with yields that are at least 150 percent of the index's yield. They are committed to their dividend program and pay out from 30 to 50 percent of earnings in dividends. You can shop in this group for income, but remember that the object of your search is to find stocks that meet your income requirement, so you should concentrate on stocks with higher yields.

Category 3. High-Yielding Stocks

These are issues with yields today in the 4 to 5 percent range or higher and are companies that are generally in mature industries that focus on providing investors with returns through dividends. They pay out 50 percent or more of their earnings to attract investors with a high dividend yield. Mature industries that fit this category are utilities, banks, pharmaceuticals, energy, and real estate investment trusts (REITs). As mentioned earlier, the dividends from REIT stocks and energy (MLPs) do not qualify for the new lower tax rate. Don't fail to include them for consideration, though, because their high yields are compelling, and their after-tax yield may more than offset the difference in the tax on these issues versus dividend stocks that do qualify for the new lower tax.

As portfolio managers, we have been able to find a fair supply of high-yielding stocks with dividend yields equivalent to most bonds' yields. It just depends on where you look. You can find stocks with yields in excess of 4 percent from mature companies in certain industries like utilities that focus on attracting investors with their high dividend yields.

You can also find undervalued stocks with juicy yields that have fallen out of favor with investors. In many cases, their prices have declined while their dividends have remained stable, increasing the stocks' yields in the process. Analyze these situations carefully to determine why the stock has declined in price and if its dividend is secure. There is often a fundamental business reason why the stock price is declining: failing to meet earnings expectations, declining revenue, increasing debt levels, etc. Your job is to determine if the price decline is a temporary setback or part of a larger negative trend. If you're confident that the pricing adjustment is based on temporary conditions that you see improving, then you may have found a nugget of gold!

Since you get to spend only the income you retain after you pay your taxes, it is imperative to analyze your investment options carefully to try to keep your tax burden to a minimum. Although we believe every citizen should pay his or her fair share of taxes, paying more than your fair share is a direct loss of wealth. Savings vehicles and government and corporate bond interest will be taxed at your highest ordinary income tax rate, and the interest you earn will be added with all your other income to determine your tax bracket. On the other hand, qualifying dividends will be taxed at a lower preference rate of 5 or 15 percent, depending on your income level and tax bracket. (See Exhibit 4.2.)

Determine your tax bracket and then calculate the net yield or after-tax income you will receive by investing in the income generator of your choice.

We have spent years searching for the one investment that could provide income investors with what they require. Unfortunately, there does not seem to be one perfect income investment that meets all these criteria.

Traditional investments like bonds, munis, certificates of deposits, and money market accounts are good income generators, but they do not increase their income over time to help you keep pace with rising costs due to inflation.

Stocks provide inflation protection through a growing stream of dividend payments (dividend stocks) and growth in value through price appreciation, but they fail the safety of principal test due to their wide swings in price. Exhibit 4.3 shows how traditional income investments either pass or fail the requirements test.

What's an investor to do? The answer lies in combining a collection of investments into a coherent portfolio. Based on years of

EXHIBIT 4.2

Comparing After-Tax Yields on Income Investments

Income Investment Type	Yield	Taxable As	Highest Federal Tax Rate	After-Tax Net Yield
Fixed Income				
CDs (5 Year Maturity)	2.65%	Interest Income	35.00%	1.72%
Money Markets	0.50%	Interest Income	35.00%	0.33%
30-Year Government Bonds	3.70%	Interest Income	35.00%	2.41%
Coporate Bonds	5.50%	Interest Income	35.00%	3.58%
Junk Bonds	6.50%	Interest Income	35.00%	4.23%
Munis	4.05%	Tax-Free	0.00%	4.05%
Stocks				
Low Yielding Dividend Stocks	1.50%	*Qualified Dividends*	15.00%	1.25%
Medium Yielding Dividend Stocks	3.00%	*Qualified Dividends*	15.00%	2.55%
High Yielding Dividend Stocks	5.00%	*Qualified Dividends*	15.00%	4.25%
REITs	6.00%	Taxable Dividends	35.00%	3.90%
MLPs	6.00%	Taxable Dividends	35.00%	3.90%

EXHIBIT 4.3

Assessing Traditional Income Alternatives

What Income Investors Want	CDs	Money Markets	Gov't Bonds	Corp. Bonds	Junk Bonds	Munis	Dividend Stocks
High Current Income	Yes	No	Yes	Yes	Yes	Yes	Yes
Reliable Income Stream	Yes	Yes	Yes	Yes	Yes	Yes	Yes
Safety of Principal	Yes	Yes	Yes	Yes	No	Yes	No
Tax Efficiency	No	No	No	No	No	Yes	Yes
Inflation Protection	No	No	No	No	No	No	Yes

experience from working with clients to understand their needs, we have found that the perfect income portfolio for most people shares these basic characteristics:

- The investments in the portfolio are safe.
- The income generated by the portfolio is predictable.
- The income is sufficient to support your lifestyle needs.
- The income rises over time to keep pace with rising costs due to inflation.

Most people who are taking income from their portfolios are at a stage in their lives when they are no longer willing or able to build their fortunes all over again. Often, this income stream is the difference between (A) a comfortable lifestyle and the peace of mind they dreamed of as they looked forward to their "golden years" and (B) subsistence living characterized by just trying to get by on a fixed pension and Social Security.

The more we rely on the income from our portfolios, the more predictable it has to be. Bills have a way of showing up every month, whether we've got income coming in or not. No matter what's going on with interest rates, stock prices, or the economy, the income check has to show up in the mailbox each month because the bills have to be paid. So the income from your investments must be secure, and your income portfolio principal needs to be maintained so your income continues to flow uninterrupted. If you can't count on the income to arrive as needed, you can't plan and can't really count on maintaining any particular standard of living.

Retired investors understand that as long as their principal is safe, it will continue to generate income to support their lifestyles. Maintaining their capital is directly related to maintaining their income. As much as they need income, they're not prepared to take on much risk to get it.

Think of your investment capital as the engine that generates income. If you assume an income rate of 5 percent, then $1,000,000 of capital could generate $50,000 in annual income. If you lost $200,000 of your capital base, then your smaller engine would generate only $40,000 in annual income. As you lose capital, your ability to generate income is impaired.

How many people do you know who retired on a fixed income and then struggled to keep up with the ever-rising cost of living as the years went by? If you live long enough, what once seemed like a princely sum can easily turn into a pauper's pittance as inflation causes prices to march relentlessly higher. Today you would need to spend almost $5.71 to buy the same goods and services that could be purchased for $1.00 in 1970. This is the functional equivalent of having an account that was worth $100,000 in 1970 shrink in value to $17,508! Exhibit 4.4 illustrates the crushing inflation that took place from 1970 to 2009.

Not many people are in a position that permits them to lose over 80 percent of their real purchasing power and still maintain their standard of living. A dollar may still be a dollar years from

EXHIBIT 4.4

The Effect of Inflation on $1.00 of Purchasing Power

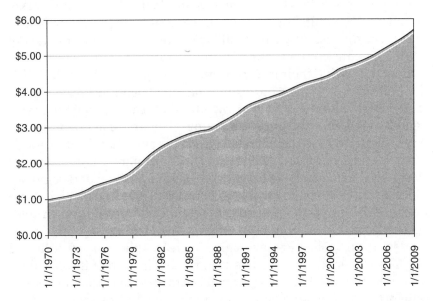

now, but you only have to look back over your own lifetime to see how the purchasing power of each dollar can fade away. How much did you pay for your first new car or first house? How much would a similar car or house cost you today? Inflation affects the price of everything we use in our everyday lives. A bottomless cup of coffee cost a quarter 25 years ago; today, a cup of coffee at Starbucks costs $1.95, and there is no such thing as a free refill. Remember, our ideal income portfolio is supposed to be safe, not just project the illusion of safety. To do that, the income it produces must rise to keep pace with inflation.

TRADITIONAL SOURCES OF RETIREMENT INCOME

Now that we have a clearer picture of what an income portfolio should be, let's take a look at some of the methods investors have traditionally used to generate income from investments.

Systematic Withdrawal Plans

One common method of generating income from investments was to buy a stock or fund that you thought would grow over time and then sell all or part of your position, hopefully at a higher price, to generate the income you need. This once popular strategy is known as a *systematic liquidation plan* and looks great as the market advances, but capital liquidation accelerates as the markets fall.

Over the last 30 years, Wall Street sold retirees on the idea of getting income from investing in growth stocks and then systematically withdrawing their income from appreciation. During the 1990s the bull market soared, but as the markets began to fall, plans for systematic withdrawal from growth funds became dollar cost averaging's evil twin, "dollar lost averaging." Dollar lost averaging is the term we use to describe the negative effects systematic withdrawals can have on a portfolio's value in volatile or falling markets. As the stocks go down, you have to sell more of your position and begin liquidating more of your capital base in order to meet the given income need. And it turns the potential for compound growth when reinvesting into compound liquidation when taking income. In its mildest form, dollar lost averaging increases the risk of outliving capital. Grim investor experience shows that in each of the last long-term negative market cycles from 1929 to 1941 and 1965 to 1981, a retired investor using a systematic withdrawal from growth stocks approach would have run out of money before the next bull market cycle started.[1] And the most recent negative cycle, while not yet over as of this writing, is likely to yield the same devastating result.

Fixed-Income Investing

A second method for generating income is to invest in bonds, CDs, and/or money market accounts. Unfortunately, these investments don't keep pace with inflation, and this is a must with longer life spans. Today, with interest rates at 45-year lows, the income these investments generate is not going to be enough to get the job done. And worse yet, you will pay tax at the highest rates on the income you do receive.

Dividend Investing

The third method is to buy stocks or funds that generate a dividend to help take care of income needs without forcing the investor to sell the investment. In working with hundreds of retired clients, we have found that they typically need about six percent in income from their assets to support their lifestyles.

Mature industries such as utilities, financial services, real estate, pharmaceutical, and energy generally provide dividend yields in excess of the general market and approach the income required by retirees.

More on Dollar Lost Averaging

It seems that during every bear market cycle, we witness the carnage inflicted upon scores of investors who are blinded by the illusion of easy gains during a bull market's spectacular run. They don't fully appreciate the risk factors involved in chasing the high returns offered by growth stocks. Many of these investors are retired people who need income to support their lifestyles, yet they abandon more conservative income-generating portfolios to get more growth. They often adopt systematic withdrawal plans to support their income needs.

Example: One of these unfortunate couples was Tom and Judy Miller (not their real names) who were referred to us by a longtime client. Tom told us that he and his wife were retired and in their mid-seventies and were taking systematic withdrawals from their portfolio to the tune of $10,000 per month. Before the markets corrected, their portfolio, heavily weighted with growth stocks, was worth $2.5 million. As the bear markets depressed stock prices, their portfolio had lost more than $1 million in value. Tom was pretty concerned about his ability to continue to support his income need of $10,000 per month and realized that he and his wife were steadily liquidating their principal—even as it continued to decline in value.

We told Tom that systematic withdrawal plans were a precarious way to meet their income needs and, even worse, his portfolio was concentrated in growth stocks, which we felt was wholly inappropriate for a retired couple needing income. Because yields had also collapsed, we thought it was unlikely that the remaining $1.5 million could be invested in bonds and generate the $120,000 per year in income that Tom and Judy required. We suggested that they study their expenses to see where they could cut and then reposition their investment portfolio in a more conservative income-oriented program without relying on liquidating principal.

Unfortunately, Tom was too attached to the companies he had invested in and felt he was justified in holding his positions.

He called us several times over the next few months to discuss his eroding situation, until their portfolio value had slid to under $800,000. Yet even in the face of his desperation, Tom still wanted to hold on to his stocks.

The following year the equity markets bottomed, and growth stocks recovered some of the ground they had lost, and so did Tom and Judy's portfolio. But by then, it was too late. Too much of the portfolio had been liquidated for the income they needed. Although the relief rally looked spectacular, it only increased their portfolio value to $1,025,000, still not nearly enough capital to generate the necessary $10,000 per month.

The sad thing is that Tom and Judy had built a capital base large enough to easily support their income needs throughout retirement. Now they need nothing short of a market performance miracle. Without it, they will continue to liquidate their capital until they run out.

Investing is a serious business, and most of us do not have enough assets to take a risk on systematic withdrawal plans for the promise of higher returns. In fact, most people are lucky if they accumulate enough capital to provide a comfortable retirement income. But you can learn from Tom and Judy's mistakes:

- Don't use systematic withdrawal plans to generate income.
- Don't ignore risk to shoot for high returns.
- Don't fall in love with any of the securities you own. They are only tools to help you achieve your investment goals. If they're not working, find some others that will.

More on CDs, Savings, and Money Market Accounts

The big attraction of the choices in this group is their safety of principal. In fact, they are considered so safe that they are generally lumped together as an asset class called "cash/cash equivalents." For the purpose of this discussion, let's call them all "cash."

The main attraction of cash is simple—the value of the principal does not fluctuate and may even be guaranteed, depending on the amount of the investment. Put a dollar in, and you'll get a dollar back, plus interest. In addition, the assets in the cash group can generally be "cashed in" at full value on short notice (although CDs may have meaningful early surrender penalties). No matter what gyrations the stock market or interest rates are going through, the value of these assets stays the same. Most financial planners will recommend that you have enough money salted away in cash/cash equivalents to cover three to six months' living expenses, plus an amount to cover any known major outlays you'll have to make in the next year or two. This group of assets can also add stability to your portfolio—because their value is stable. All in all, cash plays a key role in building a portfolio as a sound foundation for funding emergencies or contingent expenses—but not for income!

Many investors confuse safety of principal with a "sure thing investment." Cash accounts provide investors with peace of mind because their principal does not fluctuate in value and because interest is added to the account on a periodic basis. The institution providing the savings vehicle invests the money deposited by the investor in loans and bonds. They take the dual risks of volatility and loss of capital—not the investor. Unfortunately, investor peace of mind is an illusion, because the real enemy is not fluctuation of principal, it is inflation! And "cash" investments do not keep pace with inflation! As inflation robs investors of their purchasing power, they must invade principal to buy the goods and services they need to live. As the years go by, the poor investors' peace of mind is replaced by fear as they continually dip into their principal to pay for lifestyle expenses that rise with inflation.

In fact, cash flunks one of the most important tests we set for our perfect income investment. In exchange for safety of principal and liquidity, the returns on cash are generally very low. In fact, at current rates, the return on most cash alternatives isn't even as high as the rate of inflation, as measured by the Consumer Price Index (CPI). In other words, the interest on your money would not be sufficient to replace the purchasing power you're losing to inflation.

The story for cash type assets—money markets, CDs, and other cash equivalents—is much the same. And if you're holding these investments in a taxable account, the news is even worse. The after-tax return on Treasury bills recently has been just about 0.30 percent, or three tenths of 1 percent assuming a 30 percent tax rate! Even though you think cash passes the safety of principal test because your principal does not fluctuate in value, it fails three other important safety tests. First, the safety of cash begins to look suspect if you're losing the true value of your money—the ability to buy the things you need—because of inflation. Second, since the yield is so low, the income generated by cash is not sufficient to buy the goods and services you need, which will force you to liquidate your principal. Finally, the false illusion of safety is compounded because the low yield on cash is further reduced by taxes. Worse yet, you will pay tax at your highest marginal rate. Unfortunately the combination of a high tax rate and a low yield only increases your need to liquidate assets. Well, so much for safety!

The more you study the inflation problem, the more you realize how important it is to a successful retirement plan. Inflation has been pretty tame over the past 10 years, averaging only 2.43 percent per year. Don't be lulled into a false sense of security and allow yourself to think inflation is not going to be a big problem for you in the future.

In the 1970s, inflation averaged just over 7.4 percent. By the 1990s, inflation had moderated to an average of just over 2.9 percent. Still, as you can see in Exhibit 4.5, we moved from a very high inflationary period in the 1970s to a more moderate inflation period of just 2.43 percent over the past 10 years. The average inflation rate for the entire 100-year period from 1909 through 2009 was 3.33 percent. Typically, rising inflation will also drive interest rates on saving vehicles higher for a short period of time. Generous yields can cause investors to mistakenly believe they can count on a high level of interest income indefinitely. Unfortunately, higher yields can fade quickly! Over the past 25 years, 3-month CD rates (annualized) have ranged from a high of 10.37 percent in 1984 to a low of 0.56 percent in 2009.

Just a small increase in inflation can be crushing to retirees. You would need to invest a lot more money initially in a cash investment to provide enough interest to be reinvested against the day when you need to take more income to keep up with rising costs.

EXHIBIT 4.5

Inflation Is the Retired Person's Greatest Enemy

Time Period	Number of Years	Average Inflation Rate
1909–2009	100	3.33%
1959–2009	50	4.05%
1969–2009	40	4.53%
1979–2009	30	3.25%
1989–2009	20	2.79%
1999–2009	10	2.43%

Since CDs have a higher yield than money markets, we'll use them for this example:

Example: Let's say you had an income need of $3,000 per month, and you noticed you could buy a 5-year CD with a current yield of 4 percent (a generous assumption based on current yields). To generate an income of $3,000 per month or $36,000 per year, you would need to deposit $900,000 in the bank.

The first year everything seems to work well, but in the second year you notice two problems:

1. You had to pay taxes on your interest income, and you had not factored that into the equation. Where do you get the tax money?

2. Your living costs are rising, and you forgot to factor in inflation. (If inflation averages just 3 percent for the first year, your annual expenses would increase by an additional $1,080, compounding your income need. So after only the first year, you would have to start liquidating principal to buy the same goods and services you enjoyed the year before.)

Safe but Sorry

Over the years, we have seen many people make the same big mistake—they opt for the safety of principal that cash investments offer and ignore inflation risk. In 1984, a recently retired advertising manager came to us with a retirement plan rollover that needed to be invested. At age 62, Dave's objectives were to conserve his capital and to generate $1,000 per month in income to help support his expenses during retirement. He had about $150,000 to invest after he rolled his retirement plan over into an IRA. Dave told us that he was seriously considering putting the money into a CD yielding 10 percent for five years because he knew his principal would be safe. The CD really sounded good to him because he had been burned by investing in equities during the 1973–1974 bear market. Like so many investors, Dave had sold at or near the bottom of that market and promised himself that he would never again invest in stocks. The only reason he was talking with us was because his good friend Jim had been working with us for a number of years and was very happy with our investment results.

We let Dave know right away that inflation was his greatest enemy and that while his principal would not fluctuate in a CD, it would not provide him with a growing income stream or grow in value enough to keep pace with inflation. At the time, inflation was at the forefront of everyone's thinking because of the rampant inflation caused by the oil embargo during the late 1970s. We also told him that CD rates, which had been as high as 16 percent a few years earlier, were rapidly declining, and he ran the risk that he would renew his CD at a much lower interest rate when it matured in five years.

Our advice was to build in the inflation protection he needed by investing 30 percent of his IRA in stocks that paid dividends. The dividend yield on the DJIA at the time was in excess of 6 percent.

Unfortunately, Dave's fear of losing his capital pushed him to discount the inflation risk and invest his entire IRA in the 10 percent CD. He figured he could reinvest the extra $3,000 per year he would earn on the CD that exceeded the $12,000 in income he needed to spend to supplement his expenses and not have to worry about losing his principal. Dave failed to appreciate the magnitude of the inflation problem and the ultimate impact it would have on his ability to meet his retirement expenses.

As inflation robbed him of his purchasing power, Dave came to realize that his illusion of safety would cost him dearly! Interest rates continued to decline, and when Dave's CD matured in 1989, he was able to renew at only 8 percent interest. He locked in for another five years, but when the next renewal came up, in 1994, the interest rate on CDs was another 2 percent lower. Dave was in real trouble because 6 percent would not generate nearly enough income for the $17,346 he now needed per year to buy the same goods and services that $12,000 had bought him in 1984.

Up to this point, Dave had been able to pay his expenses without dipping into his original capital. He was on a slippery slope—the more principal he took out, the less income he produced. For a short time, his adult children helped him with some of the expenses, but Dave did not want to become a burden. He knew they had families of their own to support; besides, he had hoped that he would be able to help *them*.

Exhibit 4.6 illustrates Dave's CD investment and his losing fight against inflation. Dave finally came to terms with the fact that inflation was the enemy—not the risk of losing his capital.

EXHIBIT 4.6

Dave's Account Using Only CD Investments

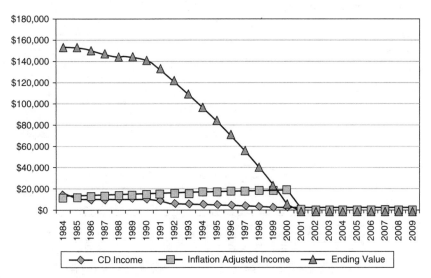

The combination of rising expenses due to inflation along with falling interest rates on CDs caused Dave to run out of income and capital in 2002. Dave's aversion to stocks caused him to miss out on the greatest bull market run of all time. The DJIA closed at 1,213 in 1984 and soared to over 11,497 in 1999, an 850 percent increase in value.

As it turned out, if Dave had taken our advice and invested as little as 30 percent of his IRA in dividend-paying equities, he would have been able to meet his income needs without depleting his capital base.

Exhibit 4.7 shows the difference that dividend-paying stocks can make.

The CD does not fare any better in the combined portfolio and still needs to be liquidated. But after 25 years of taking income and keeping pace with inflation, the $45,000 invested in the DJIA's dividend-paying stocks would be worth more than the total $150,000 original investment.

The classic problems of low yield, high taxes, and no inflation protection are pretty common to all types of fixed-income investments. Bonds start out with a little more income for each dollar invested but suffer the same defects that cash investments do.

EXHIBIT 4.7

Dave's Account Using 70 Percent CDs and 30 Percent
Stock Investments

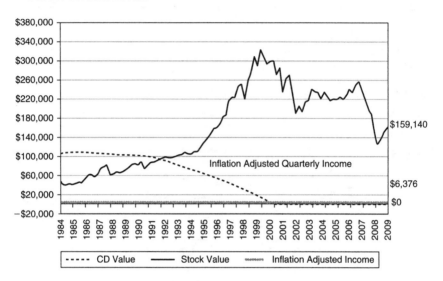

And though it may not be widely understood by most investors, bonds can also suffer from high volatility and risk under the right circumstances.

Bonds Will Be the Big Loser

This group of investments comprises bonds of all types, including government bonds, corporate bonds, high-yield (junk) bonds, and municipal bonds. It has historically been the most popular choice for investors seeking income. While there's tremendous variation among the kinds of bonds available—credit quality, duration, issuer, and so on—bonds share some important similarities that define how well they fit the bill for income investors.

Bonds are IOUs, loans that you as an investor make to an issuer in exchange for a promise to get your money back on a certain day, with regular installments of interest paid to you every month or quarter along the way. The interest that the issuer agrees to pay each year is known as the coupon. The coupon rate, multiplied by the principal of the bond, provides the dollar amount of interest paid. For example, a bond with a 5 percent coupon rate and a principal of $1,000 will pay annual interest of $50.

Example: Let's say Company A is issuing a new 30-year bond with a 6 percent coupon and you decide to buy $10,000 worth. You have just loaned Company A your $10,000 for the next 30 years. Assuming it can afford to do so, the company will pay you $300 every six months for the next 30 years and then return your $10,000 when the bond matures. If you need to get your money back for some reason before then, you'll have to find someone else to buy your bond from you. How much you'll get for your bond will depend on a lot of things, including the current financial condition of Company A and how much the new bonds being issued are paying. If interest rates have gone higher and new bonds are yielding 10 percent per year, you obviously won't be able to sell your bond for full price. Why would anyone pay you $10,000 to get $600 per year when they could buy a new bond for that price and make $1,000 per year? You'd probably have to settle for something closer to $6,000 for your bond, because at that price, your bond's $600 is also a 10 percent yield. And if rates fall so that new bonds are paying only $300 per year, or a 3 percent yield, then your bond would be worth to other investors about twice what you paid for it.

Of course, this is an oversimplified example. In real life, there are lots of things that affect bond prices, but interest rates are one of the big factors that drive the value of bonds. Of course, the changing prices of bonds matter only if you need to sell before maturity. If you can hold your bond to maturity, you will get your original investment back—so long as the issuer has the money to pay you.

Government bonds pay less than junk bonds (bonds rated lower than BBB) because investors believe the U.S. government will absolutely pay the bond off at maturity. A buyer of junk bonds insists on a higher annual payment (yield) to compensate for the risk that a weaker lender will be unable to make all the interest payments or return the cash at maturity.

Investors purchase bonds for their coupon or fixed-income stream because it never changes for the life of the bond. By definition, it fails to keep pace with inflation. In addition, the initial investment made to purchase the bond also fails the inflation test because it never appreciates in value.

If inflation averages just 4 percent per year, the initial investment of $10,000 is worth only $4,604 twenty years later. That means the original bond investment has declined 54 percent in purchasing power when it is returned at maturity year. The value of the fixed-income stream from the bond also decreases in value because of inflation. The bond income declines by more than 50 percent after adjusting for inflation. And last but not least, the interest income from a bond or savings vehicle is included in taxable income. Not only will you pay high ordinary income tax rates on the interest you earn, but the bond interest you earn may possibly also shift you into a higher tax bracket where you will pay more on each dollar of income you earn.

Although investors often shy away from stocks because of volatile price changes, they don't seem to realize how volatile bond prices can be. When interest rates rise, bond prices fall. And with interest rates already at historic lows, investors need to watch out for rising interest rates or they may once again notice frightening declines in the value of their accounts.

As an investor in dividend-paying stocks, you not only get to keep more of what you earn from dividends because of lower taxes, but also it's likely your dividend income and value will increase over time to help you with inflation. These exciting fundamental benefits are also available in dividend-paying stocks for growth—the topic of the next chapter.

ENDNOTE

1. Using the S&P 500 Index as a proxy for growth stocks.

CHAPTER 5

Advantages for Growth Investors

Don't gamble; take all your savings and buy some good stock and hold it till it goes up, then sell it. If it don't go up, don't buy it.

—Will Rogers

For many investors, current income is not an important consideration in building their portfolios. They may have sufficient income from other sources, including employment. For them, building and growing the overall value of their portfolios may be the primary focus of their efforts. Why should these "growth investors" concern themselves at all with a strategy built around investing in dividend-paying securities?

As we've already seen, one of the classic advantages of dividends is their large contribution to the long-term performance that has made stocks so attractive to investors. We've also seen how reinvesting those dividends can compound the growth of a portfolio. The attraction dividend-paying stocks hold for investors looking for a steady and rising stream of income to support their lifestyles is pretty clear.

The goal of a growth investor, on the other hand, is to increase the overall size of the portfolio so that it will be large enough to meet a future need. That need may be a lump sum to pay for college expenses or a much larger account from which to draw retirement income. In either case, the object of the game is to make the pot of money bigger in the time available. The key to winning this game lies in understanding that *total return* is what counts.

Total return is made up of two parts: price appreciation and income. A security that goes up in price by 5 percent and pays 5 percent in income adds as much to the financial pot as one that goes up by 10 percent in value but pays no income. Still, like the customer who insists on having his pizza cut into six slices because he doesn't think he can eat eight, some investors want their returns delivered only as appreciation.

Stocks that pay dividends do tend to be more mature companies, with characteristically slower growth rates. This is sometimes taken to mean they have low total-return prospects. More accurately, they offer a different path to total return, and that path can lead to an excellent outcome. Flashy price gains are exciting; steady and reliable income can seem boring by comparison. To the extent those flashy gains come at the expense of increased volatility in annual returns, chasing them could lead you down the road to disaster.

THE PERFORMANCE ILLUSION

Which would you rather have, a portfolio with an average annual return of almost 34 percent, or one with an average annual return of just 5 percent? Let's look at a couple of examples that show why sometimes less is more.

Example 1: In Exhibit 5.1, we assume an initial investment of $100,000. Year 1 is terrific, and the portfolio gains 100 percent—a classic double. Year 2 begins with $200,000 in the kitty. Unfortunately, things don't work out quite so well that year, and the portfolio suffers a 99 percent loss. The account is down to $2,000 at the start of the third year, but that year's performance is outstanding again—another 100 percent gain. Unfortunately, that brings the portfolio back up to only $4,000 by the end of the year. The average annual return for the three years is 33.67 percent, but the account has lost 96 percent of its starting value!

Example 2: Exhibit 5.2 assumes a far less volatile approach. Starting with the same $100,000, the return in year 1 is a very respectable, if not as spectacular, 15 percent. Adding the $15,000 gain to the account balance brings us to $115,000 at the start of year 2. Again, year 2 is disappointing, more than wiping out the prior year's gains with a 15 percent loss. The account is now down to $97,750. Once again, the return in year 3 matches the first year's return, enough to lift the

EXHIBIT 5.1

The Performance Illusion: High Average Return

	Starting Account Value	% Return	$ Gain or (Loss)	Ending Account Value
Year 1	$100,000.00	100.00%	$100,000.00	$200,000.00
Year 2	$200,000.00	−99.00%	($198,000.00)	$2,000.00
Year 3	$2,000.00	100.00%	$2,000.00	$4,000.00
	Average Annual Return: **33.67%**		*Change in Value:*	**($96,000.00)**
	Percentage of Initial Investment Gained or (Lost) after 3 Years: −96.00%			

EXHIBIT 5.2

The Performance Illusion: Low Average Return

	Starting Account Value	% Return	$ Gain or (Loss)	Ending Account Value
Year 1	$100,000.00	15.00%	$15,000.00	$115,000.00
Year 2	$115,000.00	−15.00%	($17,250.00)	$97,750.00
Year 3	$97,750.00	15.00%	$14,662.50	$112,412.50
	Average Annual Return	**5.00%**	*Change in Value*	**$12,412.50**
	Percentage of Initial Investment Gained or (Lost) after 3 Years: 12.41%			

account balance back into positive territory, reaching $112,412.50 at the end of the third year. The average annual return is just 5 percent, but the account balance is more than 12 percent higher than it was when we started!

Which return would you rather have? Of course, to illustrate the dangers of a high-volatility approach to investing, these two examples include an extreme case. Surely no one would ever face the kind of volatility shown in the 100 percent up and 99 percent down example—but they might come close.

Exhibit 5.3 shows the actual results of the NASDAQ Composite Index (NASDAQ) over five years beginning in 1999 and ending on December 31, 2003. (The NASDAQ Composite Index is a market-value weighted index of all common stocks listed on NASDAQ. You cannot invest directly in an index, although a number of investments you can use attempt to replicate index performance.)

The truly remarkable 86 percent return posted by the NAS-DAQ in 1999 was followed by the truly gruesome Y2K bear market

EXHIBIT 5.3

NASDAQ Composite Index

	Starting Index Value	% Return	Point Gain or (Loss)	Ending Index Value
1999	2192.69	85.59%	1876.62	4069.31
2000	4069.31	−39.29%	−1598.79	2470.52
2001	2470.52	−21.05%	−520.12	1950.40
2002	1950.40	−31.53%	−614.89	1335.51
2003	1335.51	50.01%	667.86	2003.37
	Average Annual Return:	*8.74%*	*Change in Index:*	*($189.32)*

Percentage of Initial Index Points Gained or (Lost) after 5 Years: −8.63%

EXHIBIT 5.4

The Y2K Bear Market

Index	Closing High	Date Hit	12/31/2003	Decline	Points from 2000 High	Gain Needed to Recover
NASDAQ	5048.62	03/10/2000	2003.37	−60.32%	3045.25	152.01%
S&P 500	1527.45	03/24/2000	1111.92	−27.20%	415.53	37.37%
DJIA	11722.98	01/14/2000	10453.92	−10.83%	1269.06	12.14%

mauling over the next three years. From the start of 2000 to the end of 2002, the NASDAQ shed an amazing 2,733 points—more than 67 percent of its value. The year 2003 brought welcome relief, but even after a 50 percent rise, the NASDAQ was *still more than 8.6 percent below where it had stood five years earlier.*

An investor unlucky enough to have missed out on the gains over this time span—either by coming late to the party or bailing out before the rebound—would have suffered a massive financial setback. At the end of 2009, the NASDAQ was still more than 3,000 points, or 60 percent, below its all-time closing high in 2000.

Exhibit 5.4 shows the damage the Y2K bear market visited on three major U.S. stock market indices. The S&P 500 and DJIA did not soar nearly as high as the NASDAQ during the technology/telecom/Internet boom of the 1990s, and they suffered much less damage during the bust that followed.

The second major bear market experience in 10 years also demonstrated that dramatic market declines may be more frequent events than many investors had come to expect. From their October highs in 2007 to their lows in 2009, the DJIA, S&P 500, and NASDAQ plummeted 54 percent, 57 percent, and 55 percent, respectively. Once again, volatility came with a terrible cost to accumulated capital that even subsequent dramatic gains could not fully recover. Exhibit 5.5 shows that despite a rally from their March 2009 lows of 79 percent for the NASDAQ, 65 percent for the S&P 500, and 59 percent for the DJIA, all three indices ended 2009 nearly 20 to 30 percent below their 2007 highs—confirming once again the false promise of the performance illusion. And, as Exhibit 5.6 shows, after almost 10 years, these major market indices still languish far below their levels of early 2000. If extreme volatility isn't necessarily a once-in-a-lifetime event, finding a less perilous way to travel toward our long-term investment goals would seem to make a lot of sense.

The purpose of these scenarios is not to trash the notion of investing for capital appreciation. We like capital appreciation and hope to get some whenever we add a stock to a portfolio. We *are* trying to illustrate, though, that there are consequences to taking risks. The easy success of the late 1990s bull market lulled many investors, including many professional investors, into believing

EXHIBIT 5.5

The Performance Illusion Revisited

Index	Index High Oct 2007	Index Low 3/9/2009	% Change	12/31/2009	Recovery from Low	% Below 2007 High
NASDAQ	2,803.91	1,268.64	−55%	2,269.15	79%	−19%
S&P 500	1,565.15	676.53	−57%	1,115.10	65%	−29%
DJIA	14,164.53	6,547.05	−54%	10,428.05	59%	−26%

EXHIBIT 5.6

The Price of Volatility: 10 Years Later

Index	Closing High	Date Hit	12/31/2009	Decline	Points from 2000 High	Gain Needed to Recover
NASDAQ	5,048.62	03/10/2000	2,269.15	−55.05%	2,779.47	122.49%
S&P 500	1,527.45	03/24/2000	1,115.10	−27.00%	412.35	36.98%
DJIA	11,722.98	01/14/2000	10,428.05	−11.05%	1,294.93	12.42%

risk had lost its bite. Why not shoot for a 30 percent return? If you don't get it, you'll probably just have to settle for 20 percent. But that's not how it works in the real world—at least not in the long run. The experience of the NASDAQ versus the DJIA during the decade of the 2000s isn't a fluke. Higher returns have long been associated with higher risks.

Think of trying to reach a certain annual return goal as trying to jump across a trench that's as *deep* as it is *wide*. If the trench is only one foot wide, you simply step over. You have an extremely high likelihood of success. Even if you miss, you can just step out of the little one-foot-deep hole you're in and move on. With a three-foot trench, you'll have to stretch a bit. If you misstep, you might twist an ankle, and you'll probably get your clothes dirty climbing out of the three-foot-deep hole. For a six-foot trench, you'll want to get a running start, and if you don't make it, you could hurt yourself. If you're going to try leaping across a 25-foot gorge, you'd better be able to jump like Carl Lewis. Fail in the attempt, and it will be like falling from a two-story building.

As many investors learned to their dismay over the last few years, performing the investment equivalent of leaping from rooftop to rooftop collecting bags of money can be exciting but very hazardous to your financial health.

How do you cross the gulf between where you are and where you need to go? How can you get from here to there if trying for a big jump in appreciation is too risky for you? Let dividend income help you bridge the gap.

DIVIDENDS AT WORK

Dividends provide a stream of new investment capital with which to build your portfolio and grow your wealth. Systematic liquidation of capital may be "dollar lost averaging," but the systematic addition of new investment capital, or "dollar cost averaging," is a time-honored system long recognized as a successful method for building a portfolio. Dividends tend to be paid quarterly, and on varying dates, so they provide an ideal source of cash flow with which to implement this strategy. Even a small portfolio can use the process of reinvesting dividend payments to build up existing stock positions or to add new holdings to the account.

Example: Dividend income can also help to cushion the fall when stock prices drop. Imagine that you own two stocks. You purchased 100 shares of Stock A today at $10 per share, and 100 shares of Stock I, also at $10 per share. Stock A is attractive for its appreciation potential, while Stock I is a more mature company with less promise for future growth. Stock I pays a 5 percent dividend, but Stock A plows all its cash back into growing its business. Let's say that a year from now, due to a generally sluggish economy, both stocks have seen their price fall by 5 percent. Your $1,000 investment in Stock A will have fallen in value to $950, but the $50 in dividend payments you received from Stock I over the course of the year will have made up for its losses, and you'll still be at breakeven on your investment in that position.

Over and above this cushioning effect, there's evidence to suggest stocks that pay dividends don't tend to suffer as much in falling markets as other stocks do.

The results in Exhibit 5.7 show how stocks with different dividend yields fared during the Y2K bear market. To smooth out the effects any one stock may have had on the outcome, we ranked the S&P 500 industry groups in order of their yield. We then measured their percentage change in value over the three-year period from 2000 through 2002. (Data were derived using Thomson Baseline, a product of Thomson Reuters.)

There were 11 industry groups with no dividend yield, and over the three-year period measured, they fell by nearly 31 percent. We compared that group to a group of the 11 highest-yielding

EXHIBIT 5.7

The Dividend Effect: S&P 500 Industry Performance, Three-Year Bear Market, 2000–2002

Measurement Standard	Average Yield	Average Change
11 industries with 0% yield	0.00%	−30.80%
11 highest yielding industries	3.99%	−14.20%
3-Year Dividend Advantage:	11.97%	16.60%
Measurement Standard	**Average Yield**	**Average Change**
Yields less than S&P 500 yield	0.53%	−9.45%
Yields greater than or equal to S&P 500 yield	2.46%	−6.43%
3-Year Dividend Advantage:	5.79%	3.02%

industries. They fell too, but by less than half as much—an average of only 14.2 percent. Not only did the stocks in the highest-yielding industries hold up better by more than 16 percent, they also produced an average annual dividend of almost 4 percent to help cushion that decline. Over the course of three years, this nearly 12 percent in income from dividend yield offsets a big chunk of the 14 percent price decline.

Since many of the zero-yielding industries fall into the especially hard hit technology and telecommunications categories, we expanded the comparison to see if the dividend advantage persisted across a broader array of industries. Those industries with yields less than the S&P 500's then yield of 1.5 percent were compared to those whose yields were 1.5 percent or higher. The average decline of the higher-yielding industries was only about two-thirds the decline of the others. Add the almost 2 percent extra annual dividend return the high-yielding industries provided for each of the three years, and the dividend advantage is especially striking.

In both sets of comparisons, not only did the industries with the higher yields hold up better in a falling market, but the dividends paid over the course of those three years were almost enough to offset their losses.

This doesn't mean every industry or every stock with a high yield will hold its value better in a falling market than every industry or stock with a lower yield. If it were that simple, the information in the chapters that follow about researching your choices and managing your risks would be unnecessary. We think it does show, however, that dividends should be an important factor in your pursuit of a successful low-volatility approach to building your wealth.

THE KINDNESS OF STRANGERS

Assuming your stock has risen in price since the day you bought it, how do you benefit from this increase in your wealth? You could borrow against your shares, but then you're really using someone else's money, and the stock is just collateral. You still have to repay the loan, plus interest, somehow. If you ever want to *spend* the money, you have to sell the stock. In order to sell your shares, you have to find someone to buy them. The vast majority of stock transactions are simply trades by investors selling the same stocks back and forth among themselves. Prices change as their opinions change about what each share is worth to them. They rise as a buyer tries to entice an owner to sell, and they fall as sellers try to attract a buyer.

Dividend income, on the other hand, does not depend on the kindness of strangers in the same way that appreciation does. Dividends are driven primarily by the ability and willingness of a company to share its profits with its shareholder owners. They are tied more closely to the business itself and are less subject to the emotional response of investors to world or market events. What is a baseball card worth? That depends on the career of the ballplayer on the card and the card's rarity, but—most important—it depends on what a collector is willing to pay for it. What's the value of a painting? Vincent van Gogh survived on handouts, but his *Irises* sold at auction in 1987 for $53.9 million. Whether it's a baseball card, a famous painting, or a growth stock, the only way an investor can benefit from its appreciation is to find someone who will buy it.

Investors holding stocks for the income they provide, on the other hand, enjoy an ongoing advantage that "pure growth" investors don't—they get to keep their shares! Obviously, once you've sold your shares, it's somebody else's stock. You no longer have a stake in the fortunes of the company. Any benefits and profits that follow—as well as the future appreciation in share price—are of no further value to you. Of course, you don't necessarily have to sell all your stock at once and can therefore continue to enjoy some of the good fortune that may continue to visit the company whose shares you're selling.

The simple fact remains, though, that as you sell your shares, you have less of an ownership interest than you did before. By periodically liquidating your holdings, you are systematically reducing your ownership in the very thing that is your store of investment wealth. Appreciation has its advantages too, and, fortunately, dividend investors can enjoy the appreciation in the value of their shares while they continue to collect the ongoing income from their holdings.

When the time eventually comes to take income from your portfolio to support your lifestyle, either in retirement or to help defray major expenses such as education costs, the investments do not have to be sold to create cash flow. The dividends are already flowing cash to you. You simply have to adjust how much of it you're reinvesting and how much of it you can afford to spend.

INVESTOR RISK

Investors are justifiably wary of the various risks that can beset a portfolio. In addition to the eroding effects of volatility, there's business risk, currency risk, market risk, interest rate risk, and inflation risk. Perhaps the most insidious risk of all, though, is the one that's the hardest to protect yourself from—*investor risk*. Investor risk is the risk we face just by being human.

It's easy to understand the concept that to be successful as an investor you should buy low and sell high. But if you invest over a long enough time period to see both rising and falling markets, you'll see just how hard it can be to bring yourself to actually do this. Buying at highs and selling at lows is the opposite of success and can cause your portfolio irreparable harm, but it's extraordinarily common. Had you asked those investors who were rushing into Internet or other high-flying stocks in early 2000, after the NASDAQ had just jumped more than 85 percent in 1999, if they thought they were buying high, you probably would have heard all kinds of reasons why this time was different. There was a "new paradigm"; the old rules of valuation no longer applied. Had you asked many of these same investors in early 2003 if they felt they were selling low after three years of crushing stock market declines, you would likely have heard that the market was going to keep falling, the world had changed, and prospects looked bleak for as far as the eye could see.

Investors were once thought to be "rational," efficiently processing all known market data and making decisions on the basis of the logical pursuit of their own best interests. An entire branch of study called *behavioral finance* has sprung up to study the question of how investors *really* behave, and the short answer is that it's rarely rational. Nature has "wired" us to react in certain ways so we can quickly process information, understand patterns (like those that occur in nature), and make good, quick survival decisions. Unfortunately, many of the same ways of thinking that have proven so helpful to our survival as a species can get us killed as investors.

Emotional responses, uneven reactions to risk and reward, looking for patterns where none may exist, believing our recent experience will persist, and overconfidence in our initial judgments are just some of the natural tendencies that can lead us astray. Rather than trying to overcome our nature—to overcome the thinking processes and habits that have been woven into our very beings for millennia—we can try to invest in such a way as to reduce this investor risk and increase our odds of financial survival.

The markets will continue to rise and fall, but if your account doesn't fall so much that it triggers your primal urge to sell, you'll still be invested for the rebound. Even the most robust market recovery doesn't help the investor who has already sold everything before it starts. To reap the long-term performance advantages of being an investor, you have to find a way to stay invested for the *long term*. To the extent a lower volatility, dividend-based portfolio provides you with an investment experience you can live with *in all kinds of markets,* your portfolio is more likely to evolve into a fortune—and less likely to face extinction.

CHAPTER 6

Why Conventional
Approaches Fail Investors

The enemy of the conventional wisdom is not ideas but the march of events.

—John Kenneth Galbraith

For the last 30 years or so, investment pros have told investors to create buy-and-hold passive asset allocation portfolios focused on growth stocks to obtain the highest returns over the long run, while ignoring short-term loss of capital. These concepts are based on the investment theory developed by academics during the 1950s, 1960s, and 1970s. Unfortunately, many of these investment approaches have failed to deliver an acceptable outcome for investors. As a result of following conventional approaches, many investors find themselves with diminished capital after years of saving carefully to secure a comfortable financial future. Many approaching retirement face the unpleasant reality of never being able to retire. And a growing number of already retired investors find themselves without enough income to pay their bills and now need to return to work.

HOW DID WE GET HERE?

Extreme market events, like the Great Depression, tend to have a significant influence on the development of subsequent investment theory. Harry Markowitz won a Nobel Prize in Economic Sciences in 1990 for his vast body of work covering nearly 40 years, including his development of the basis for modern portfolio theory (MPT). MPT focused on diversification of asset classes to reduce volatility and risk while maximizing return. His greatest contribution was establishing a formal risk/return framework for investment decision making. Markowitz gave investors a mathematical approach to asset selection and portfolio management. He suggested that investors incorporate asset risk, return, correlation, and diversification to determine the probable returns for an investment portfolio. By combining asset classes with low historical price correlation, he theorized a portfolio would have less volatility risk and provide higher average returns than a portfolio with a collection of assets whose prices tend to behave in the same way (high correlation).

Many other theories followed and built upon Markowitz's foundation. During the late 1960s and 1970s, the U.S. economy was in the grips of a recession, which deepened due to the Middle East oil embargo. Inflation was rampant even though economic output was falling. As you might imagine, investors did not fare well as the U.S. stock market faltered along with the economy. The 1973–1974 bear market caused many investors who had lingering memories of the Great Depression to bail on their mutual fund and stock positions. Hard hit by massive liquidations, many mutual fund companies and money managers looked for new approaches to help keep investors invested.

Academics went back to the drawing board in an attempt to find out why some investors failed while others seemed to win. They studied the approaches used by institutional pension fund managers. They found that institutional managers focused on a portfolio's asset allocation model rather than timing the buying and selling of individual investments. Researchers found that the majority of returns generated by the passive allocation approach were determined by the allocation of assets, as Markowitz suggested. Mutual fund companies and investment managers embraced the passive allocation process as the solution to investors bailing during bear market trends. In the early 1980s, their marketing campaigns strongly suggested that investors seek to replicate the passive institutional asset allocation model.

At the time these studies were conducted, there was also a very strong bias against active management due to the drag on performance caused by the cost of executing trades. For decades, stockbrokers made their income from the commissions charged for trading. At this time, the cost for an individual investor to make trades was approximately 1.0 to 1.5 percent of the total trade value, somewhat less for institutions. With a couple of buys and sells in any year, an active investor could find his trading costs eating up 4 percent or more of any return generated. Today, trading costs have been reduced to a few cents or less per share, due to competitive pressure from online trading and discount brokers like Charles Schwab.

Buy-and-hold theorists suggest that investors can't time the markets. By trying to avoid the down days, they insist that investors will miss the few powerful up days that provide most of the market's return. They believe the positive returns generated during market up-trends will always be sufficient to allow investors not only to recover lost capital, but also to generate a return high enough to help them achieve their financial goals. Yet a careful study of market history debunks this widely held belief and shows that there are very long secular bear market cycles that can produce negative—not positive—returns from price appreciation. As we saw in Chapter 1, over the past century these secular cycles have lasted 17 years on average.

A case in point: In 1928, the closing value of the Dow Jones Industrial Average (DJIA) was 300; then markets collapsed during the Great Depression, and the DJIA did not finish a year with a closing value of 300 again until 1952. Investors following the conventional buy-and-hold approach would have spent 24 years, much of their adult lives, waiting to get back to even. In the face of normal market volatility, where stock markets register an average decline of 20 percent every four years and 40 percent or more every six years, investors need to come to grips with the fact that markets give them more risk and loss of capital than they can tolerate. One of the basic tenets of investing is to buy low and sell high, yet investors do the opposite as they try to practice buy-and-hold in volatile markets.

THE HUMAN FACTOR

We know from our three decades of experience that, unfortunately, investors don't buy-and-hold, and the assumption that institutional investment approaches can be applied to individual investors is flawed. Individual investors are genetically predisposed to lose the buy-and-hold battle. When we invest, we all fight the "human factor," the survival instincts and emotions we described in Chapter 5 as investor risk. These instincts were honed as we hunted for food to survive. If we encountered an animal we could not fight off successfully, we fled. Today we don't hunt for survival, but instead we work and invest our savings to provide the things we need when we can no longer work. Money in today's society is important to our basic survival. When account values fall due to declining markets, our survival instincts kick in, triggering a fear response.

Individuals' risk tolerances vary, but fear will eventually trigger the need to "fight or flee." Because it's impossible to fight the "market," the only course of action is to flee, which translates into selling low after money has been lost. Institutional fund managers react differently to significant declines in account values because it's not their money. They also tie investment success to relative performance against a benchmark. But relative performance to a benchmark holds little value to individual investors if their return is negative. Even institutions are rethinking their investment approaches in the face of the devastating losses they have experienced over the past several years.

IT'S TIME FOR A REALITY CHECK!

Unfortunately, investors have had a brutal education trying to follow conventional buy-and-hold approaches through the secular bear market decline that began in 2008. Now is the time for investors to back away from the conventional approaches they have been taught. Why? Simply because they do not work!

To be sure, some of the conventional investment wisdom developed over the past three decades has merit. Every portfolio design should incorporate the fundamental principle of diversification as developed by Markowitz. However, it's been widely assumed that diversification would sufficiently reduce the risk and losses enough to enable investors to stay invested in down-market cycles. This may hold true in mild market corrections, but in 2008, asset values collapsed across the board, and diversification failed to mitigate investor fear and loss.

DON'T LOSE TOO MUCH CAPITAL

As the examples of the performance illusion in Chapter 5 show, preventing a big loss of capital is more important than generating a big return. Once capital is diminished due to losses, it becomes difficult to get back to even, much less obtain a return high enough

EXHIBIT 6.1

Ten Years of Losses, 2000–2009

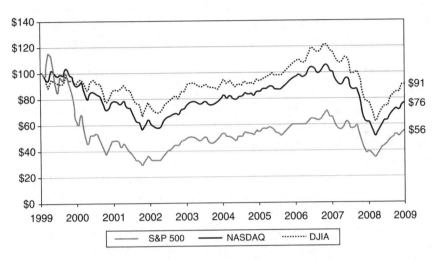

to fund objectives. To break even after the 38 percent decline in 2008, the S&P 500 needed to post a 61 percent return. The conventional assumption that investors can ignore big losses is ridiculous. After 10 years, the popular U.S. stock indexes had not recovered the losses incurred in the 2000–2002 bear market, much less the added declines of 2008. (See Exhibit 6.1.)

Curtailing loss of capital is critical to maintaining the foundation necessary to generate growth and income. Small losses of capital can be overcome by reinvesting the cash flow from dividend income. If you have to lose money, "lose small."

IDENTIFYING CLASSIC INVESTOR MISTAKES

Investors often repeat classic behavioral mistakes that hurt their chances of ever achieving their investment goals. Let's take a look at some examples based on real client stories that catalog just a few of the most important behavioral mistakes to avoid.

Make Hay While the Sun Shines

As markets rise, investors tend to forget that risk is a four-letter word. Greed takes over, and those who once thought themselves in the conservative camp abandon caution in search of higher returns and what looks like easy money to be made. But an investor's tolerance for risk is part of his or her basic personality, and tolerance for risk rarely changes. People are risk takers or risk avoiders by nature. Investors and the markets are said to be rational, but most people are heavily influenced and ruled by their emotions. The primal emotions of fear or greed often cause investors to play the loser's game of buying high and selling low.

Rick found out the hard way that greed leads to heavy losses, not gains. At age 40, Rick was in an unfortunate accident that cost him the use of his legs and prevented him from ever working again. As compensation for his loss of future earnings, he was awarded a lump sum of approximately $4 million. In 1996, Rick's attorney recommended that he seek us out to manage his money. Rick's goals were to set up an investment portfolio that would provide him with current income of $8,000 per month, and an income that would keep pace with inflation over the remainder of his lifetime. Because he depended on income from his assets for his sole support, he wanted to be very careful with his money.

As the stock market advanced unabated, Rick started to listen to the siren song of the easy money to be made. He told us he wanted to get more aggressive with his accounts. The high returns and easy money that the markets were offering were just too good to pass up. He acknowledged that he had previously told us he needed to be conservative, but now he felt he should "make hay while the sun shines!" In other words, he perceived that there was little risk involved in getting more aggressive.

We counseled Rick to stick with his conservative income and growth plan because he could not go back to work to earn back the money he might lose. Rick did not need to chase high returns because his asset base was sufficient to allow him to pursue a lower risk and return strategy. Most important, he would always be okay as long as he kept his capital base intact to produce the income he required. But by 1999, greed's siren song proved too much for him. He abandoned his investment strategies and moved his entire portfolio into high-flying tech stocks just before the speculative bubble burst.

The ensuing "tech wreck" shattered Rick's financial security along with that of millions of other investors. Greed had won again. Rick's more aggressive investment strategy, which looked like a sure path to untold wealth, became the wrecking ball that destroyed his financial security. With losses averaging in excess of 70 percent, Rick's capital base was decimated and, with it, the engine of his income production.

To add insult to injury, the income strategies Rick abandoned actually increased in value. With the huge stock market declines, investors fled to the relative safety that income-producing investments provided. Bond prices increased, as did the prices of many high-yielding, dividend-paying stocks.

I'll Never Invest in Stocks Again; the Markets Are Rigged!

Frank was a reluctant investor. He turned to investing when the interest rates on savings accounts and CDs fell dramatically in the early 1970s. Coinciding with these low rates was a stock market that was starting to move dramatically higher. Equity mutual funds became all the rage with investors; the stock market was finally on a tear after turning in a rather dismal performance in the late 1960s. As his CDs matured, Frank poured more and more of his savings into red-hot "go-go" stock funds.

All was well until the market's growth engine ran out of gas due to the oil embargo. The stock market reversed direction in 1973, and by 1974 many investors, selling into the decline, had lost 50 percent or more of their money. Sick at the loss of his safely hoarded nest egg, Frank swore off stock investing forever. Frank's reaction to his loss is extremely common. Ironically, his decision looked good as the market gyrated between gains and losses for the balance of the decade.

The tremendous inflation caused by the 1970s oil embargo lifted interest rates to all-time highs, and once again Frank was delighted with the interest he earned on his savings accounts and CDs. In 1981, after years of slow economic growth, the U.S. government passed the Economic Tax Recovery Act to jump-start the economy. The stimulus created under this bill started to work its magic, and the economy started to recover. At the same time, the stock market began the biggest bull market run in history. Like Frank, many investors were content to sit on the sidelines for years because they were afraid. The short period of high interest rates lulled investors into a sense of complacency, but with inflation running rampant, the real purchasing power return on these rates was negative.

The market's turning point in 1981 offered investors the greatest opportunity to buy low since the Great Depression. The first few years of a bull market recovery tend to be a fairly bumpy ride for investors as risk factors mitigate, and this time was no different. When did Frank buy? Like many other investors, Frank missed the boat and didn't move back into the market until early 1986. Instead of buying low, he bought high and then sold a short time later as the stock market crashed in October 1987.

So what are the classic mistakes that Frank made? Frank was a saver and not an investor; he didn't fully recognize how much risk he was taking and found out too late that he had a very low tolerance for risk and the loss of capital. In the early 1970s, stock investing looked easy, and Frank decided to join the crowd by investing in stock mutual funds. He made the mistake of buying right before the markets were due for a correction, when prices were high. After his bad experience, Frank sat on the sidelines in savings accounts for years before jumping back into the markets in 1986, after valuations had soared. Each time he invested, he thought risk had abated, because the markets had been going up consistently. His fear of loss and avoidance of risk led to the classic "buy high, sell low" behavior that investors must avoid.

So You Think You're Really Smart!

Judy thought her past business experience and success in redeveloping real estate would allow her to make sound judgments in timing her investments. After all, she had a wide range of business experience to fall back on. Judy made a small fortune in the mid-1990s, and she looked like a genius as the markets soared. Flush with success, she thought investing was easy! The good returns seemed to confirm her judgment, but her big gains turned into even bigger losses during the Y2K bear market of 2000–2002. At the time, her stockbroker told her that she should just "hold on." In the throes of desperation and right before the end of the declines in 2002, she liquidated her portfolio and parked what was left of her money in a money market account.

As the equity markets staged a huge rally in 2003, Judy felt sure the market would falter and then decline. This time would be different; the market wouldn't fool her again, so she left her money in cash. Unfortunately for Judy, the market rally not only continued but also posted one of the best one-year rallies on record. Judy's classic mistake was to believe her prior experience and knowledge in real estate could be applied to becoming a successful stock investor. She also thought investing looked easy. But investing is never easy; it just looks that way during bull markets.

Don't Let Greed Turn Gains into Losses

Neil was sure his high-flying stock would make him rich! In the late 1990s, he invested in one of the tech stock wonders. His $10,000 investment appreciated tenfold to more than $100,000 within a period of 10 months. Instead of cashing in his fantastic gains, he chose to hold onto the stock. The company reports were still favorable, and he was sure the stock's price would go higher. When the tech bubble burst, so did his company. Within months it was out of business. Not only did Neil lose his gain, but because of his greed, he also lost his original investment. In addition to being greedy, Neil made the mistake of thinking his stock would continue to rise in price because it had done so recently. Stocks prices often get ahead of themselves. A stock price can fall quickly once it becomes overvalued and is no longer supported by its fundamentals.

The Investor Who Did Almost Everything Right

Al was a man with an abiding faith in America. He believed in the American economy and the great companies that made up her stock market. He rarely bought a bond for income but instead preferred the rising income streams that dividend-paying stocks offered. He felt certain that if he held his companies forever, he would become financially secure. Al's first investment experience was buying stocks during the latter part of the roaring 1920s. Like many investors at that time, he was introduced to the concept of leverage and buying stocks on margin. The good times didn't last long, and as the market crashed in 1929, he lost everything. Upon reflection, his biggest regret was that he could not hold onto the stocks he bought because of the use of margin. He vowed never to borrow money again—and he never did!

Surprisingly, Al's initial investment experience did not sour him on investing. As the economy recovered from the Great Depression, he carefully saved every penny to buy stocks again. After seeing the high-flying growth stock prices collapse before his eyes, Al decided to focus all of his investments in dividend-paying stocks. He believed dividend income gave him a return he could count on as he waited patiently for his stocks to appreciate in price. He had a childhood friend who became a stockbroker, and Al left it up to him to find good value opportunities to invest in. After

World War II, the U.S. economy and stock markets really took off. Al was able to get in on the ground floor of many of the giant corporations that we know today. He rarely ever sold a stock unless his friend told him the company was in dire trouble. As dividends were paid, they were reinvested into more shares. As the number of shares grew, so did the amount of the dividends paid—causing the value of his holdings to compound tremendously.

After a few decades of helping Al invest, his friend the stockbroker got sick and needed to retire. Without his friend's direction, Al held onto his stocks through "thick and thin." He did not sell into the market corrections of 1973–1974, the crash of 1987, the tech bubble bursting in 2000–2002, or even the frightening market crash of 2008. When people would ask him why he didn't sell during the severe market declines, he would pause and say, "I bought those stocks so long ago, I'm still up. If I sold them now, I wouldn't be able to collect the dividends."

Al was a very successful investor for so many years because he made so few of the classic investing mistakes. He learned early not to use leverage and to take only the investment risks he could tolerate. By focusing on the income and return from dividends, he never worried about price fluctuation. He rarely looked at his account statements to see whether the value was up or down. Through his friend the stockbroker, he learned to buy stocks when they were cheap. The only mistake Al made was to have a little bit too much faith in the companies he bought. Not all of his investments panned out as he hoped they would. A handful of the companies he owned, which were once great investments, stumbled so badly they went out of business altogether.

Even Al Could Not Afford to Buy and Forget the Stocks He Owned!

It simply does not pay to buy and forget about the stocks you own. At least annually, every stock you hold should be reviewed to see if it's a position worthy of remaining in your portfolio. If you wouldn't buy that stock today, then it probably should be sold. Don't be afraid to sell a stock at a loss to protect your remaining capital. Never assume that just because a stock has appreciated dramatically, it will continue to do so forever. Once a stock has become overvalued based on its fundamentals, it should be sold to lock in the gain.

But how do you know whether or not you should buy a particular stock today, and how will you decide when to sell it? In Part 2, we'll dig into the mechanics of building a portfolio focused on dividend-paying stocks that's designed to take the emotion out of investing.

- We'll explore how to avoid the siren song of greed that brought Rick to ruin and instead buy stocks because of their value.
- We'll share ideas about how to more accurately assess your risk tolerance to help you avoid the emotional trap of buying high and selling low that Frank fell into.
- We'll point out sources of the kind of relevant investment information Judy could have benefited from, so you won't have to rely on conventional wisdom or financial news shows to make your investment decisions.
- We devote an entire chapter to showing you how to safeguard your capital by using a stop loss system, so you'll be less likely to watch the price of a stock you own slide all the way to zero like Neil did. You'll also see how setting goals and trailing goal stops could have let Al hold onto his winners and cash in on the others before those gains melted away.

Following the process we outline in this book should help you take the emotion out of investing and avoid many of the classic investing mistakes.

Using the Toolbox: How to Get It Done

CHAPTER 7

Doing Your Homework

I'm living so far beyond my income that we may almost be said to be living apart.

—e. e. cummings

How do you pick great stocks? If you don't have a crystal ball or inside information, the best way you can tell a winning stock from a loser is by analyzing a company's financial statements.

Before you dismiss this simple answer because you find financial statements confusing or boring, you should know that you don't have to become an accountant or financial analyst. Just a nodding acquaintance with the fundamentals will allow you to make better decisions about which stocks you should investigate and which stocks you should own as part of your dividend-focused portfolio.

Financial statements are an important source of information regarding a company's profits or losses, assets and liabilities, and sources of funds used to operate its business. We will just concentrate on the basics: the balance sheet, income statement, and statement of retained earnings. (See Exhibit 7.1.)

The balance sheet gives you an overall picture of a company's assets, liabilities, and equity at the end of an accounting period (e.g., quarterly or year end). The income statement and the statement of retained earnings tell you how much revenue, expense, and profit the firm generated over a specific period of time (e.g., its fiscal year). Together, these statements provide you with all of the

EXHIBIT 7.1

Financial Statement Analysis

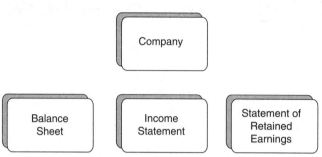

financial data you need to perform a ratio analysis to determine if you might want to buy a stock.

Since financial transactions occur continuously, this information rapidly becomes dated. Be sure you are looking at the most recent statements, and continue to review the updated statements of those stocks you decide to hold.

THE BALANCE SHEET

The balance sheet details what the business owns (assets) and what it owes (liabilities). It also shows what the owners have invested in the firm (equity). When a company is formed, investors capitalize the company by investing cash in exchange for stock (ownership) in the company. The money raised from this initial funding is used to acquire property, plant, and equipment; to fund product research and development; and to hire employees. Any of the original investment left after start-up expenses is retained as cash (current assets) to fund operations. (See Exhibit 7.2 for a sample consolidated balance sheet.)

Assets

The asset section of the balance sheet is broken down into four parts:

- *Current assets* can be readily turned into cash, including bank deposits and accounts receivable (since a company might not be able to collect all of its accounts receivable, a provision is usually made for doubtful accounts).

EXHIBIT 7.2

Sample Consolidated Balance Sheet

Assets	December 31, 2009
Current Assets	
Cash and Cash Equivalents	$450,000
Accounts Receivable, Less Allowance for Doubtful Accounts (2002, $50,000, 2001, $25,000)	$1,450,000
Inventory	$1,639,000
Total Current Assets	**$3,539,000**
Investments	**$500,000**
Property, Plant, and Equipment	
Land	$600,000
Building	$1,250,000
Machinery and Equipment	$1,580,000
Total Fixed Assets	**$3,430,000**
Less accumulated depreciation	$751,000
Net Fixed Assets	**$2,679,000**
Total Assets	*$6,718,000*
Liabilities	
Current Liabilities	
Current Maturing Long-Term Debt	$50,000
Accounts Payable and Accrued Liabilities	$1,050,000
Taxes Due	$195,000
Total Current Liabilities	**$1,295,000**
Long-Term Debt	$500,000
Total Liabilities	**$1,795,000**
Shareholder Equity	
Common Stock ($1.00 per value; 1,000,000 Shares Authorized; Shares Outstanding: 750,000 in 2002; 750,000 in 2001)	750,000
Additional Paid-In Capital	**$500,000**
Retained Earnings	**$3,673,000**
Total Shareholder Equity	**$4,923,000**
Total Liabilities and Net Worth	*$6,718,000*

- *Investments* can be converted into cash but might have some market risk associated with their sale, such as a portfolio of readily tradable stocks or bonds.
- *Fixed assets,* such as property, plant, and equipment, are permanent assets used to produce the product or services of the business and usually have a very long life. Most

values, such as the value of real estate, are carried at purchase price or book value and usually understate the real value of the asset.

- *Accumulated depreciation* is an accounting adjustment for the depletion or obsolescence of long-life fixed assets that allows the company to build a reserve to replace depleted or outdated assets.

The sum of these is listed as *total assets*.

Liabilities

The company might need to borrow money to fund operations, to buy equipment, or to expand its facilities. Borrowed funds are recorded in the liability section of the balance sheet and are segregated into current liabilities, those funds that have to be paid back within a year, and long-term debt.

Current liabilities might include the following:

- *Accounts payable,* which are debts that are usually due in 30 days, such as money owed to the company's suppliers.
- *Taxes due,* which include payroll taxes owed to state and federal agencies for workers' wages and for taxes due on the profit of the company. These taxes are usually due within 30 days or less and often have to be paid within a few days of the due date.

Long-term debt differs from current liabilities in that it is usually paid back over a longer period of time. It can take the form of an equipment loan or mortgage against property.

The sum of all debt is calculated as *total liabilities*.

Equity

The capital invested by the owners of the company is reflected in the equity section of the balance sheet as follows:

- *Shareholders equity* reflects the initial investment in the company by shareholders in exchange for shares at a stated par value.
- *Additional paid-in capital* is the money raised from the sale of additional shares after the initial offering of shares to investors during a company's start-up phase. These secondary share offerings are authorized by a company

hoping to sell additional shares at higher prices in the open market at some time in the future.

- *Retained earnings* are any profits not paid out as dividends.

The combination of these equity entries comprises the *total investment* held by owners in the company.

THE INCOME STATEMENT

The *income statement* is a summary of a firm's revenues and expenses and accounts for the level of profit or loss the company has earned over the period. *Sales* is the first entry on the statement and shows all revenues generated from the sale of the company's products for the period. The costs of the raw materials that go into the product along with the cost of converting the raw materials into a finished product are accounted for in *cost of goods sold*. (See Exhibit 7.3 for a sample consolidated income statement.)

The difference between the revenue generated and the cost of goods is accounted for as *gross profit*. Depending on the industry, you generally would like to see a company have a gross profit of at least 50 percent, but the higher the better.

All employee costs to sell, market, manage, and administer, as well as costs for plant and equipment, are categorized as *selling and administrative expenses*. These expenses are deducted from gross

EXHIBIT 7.3

Sample Consolidated Income Statement for the Year Ending December 31, 2009

	December 31, 2009
Sales	$18,475,000
Cost of Goods Sold	$6,750,000
Gross Profit	$11,725,000
Selling and Administrative Expenses	$8,385,000
Operating Income (Profit)	$3,340,000
Other Income	$10,000
Income Before Interest, Depreciation, and Taxes	$3,350,000
Interest Expense	$24,000
Depreciation	$66,000
Taxes	$1,072,000
Net Income	$2,188,000
Earnings per Share	$2.92

profit to determine *operating income.* If the company has other income (e.g., interest and dividends), it is added to operating income before deducting interest expense, depreciation, and taxes to arrive at *net income.* Shareholders are generally concerned with *earnings per share,* which is calculated by dividing net income by the number of shares outstanding.

The profit and loss accounting is not complex—far from it. You probably learned it at a young age, much like Michael and Robert in the example that follows.

Example: Michael and Robert started their first business venture when they were six years old. On warm sunny days, the boys would open a lemonade stand and sell their ice-cold world-famous drinks to passersby. They charged 25 cents per eight-ounce cup and on a good day would sell 32 cups of lemonade for a total sale of $8.

The cost to manufacture the product was relatively modest: four cans of concentrated lemonade mix at 50 cents each and a package of 32 paper cups for $1—and the water was free. So their *cost of goods sold* totaled just $3.That meant $5 in *gross profit.*

Michael and Robert didn't have any selling or administrative expenses, and their mom and dad were kind enough to let them set up the family card table in front of the grocery store. Since they didn't have to pay rent or incur any equipment costs, their *operating income* was also $5. And because it was a cash business and didn't incur *interest expense* or *taxes,* their net income was also $5. The brothers shared equal ownership in their fledgling enterprise, so the *earnings per share* were $2.50.

STATEMENT OF RETAINED EARNINGS

The *statement of retained earnings* indicates the amount of the company's earnings (net income from the current income statement) and adds this amount to the previous retained earnings from the balance sheet. When a company earns a profit, management must decide either to

1. Pay out all or part of the earnings to shareholders as dividends; or
2. Retain the earnings to finance the purchase of assets, retire debt, or grow the other resources of the company.

EXHIBIT 7.4

Sample Consolidated Statement of Retained Earnings for the Year Ending December 31, 2009

	December 31, 2009
Retained Earnings Beginning of Year	$2,185,000
Net Income	$2,188,000
Less Cash Dividends	$700,000
Balance Retained Earnings End of Year	$3,673,000

The retained earnings on the balance sheet are the sum of undistributed earnings of the company that have accumulated over time. The statement of retained earnings indicates the amount of retained earnings accumulated at the beginning of the year and then adds the net income for the period. If management declares a cash dividend, it is deducted from retained earnings to arrive at the balance of retained earnings for the end of the year, which is carried forward to the balance sheet. (See Exhibit 7.4.)

Although our example of a lemonade drink business oversimplifies the complexity involved in financial statements, if you keep in mind what information each statement is trying to present, you will find understanding them a snap:

- To find stocks with secure dividend payments, the *balance sheet* will show a company's ability to pay outstanding liabilities either from liquid assets on hand or from the cash flow being generated from operations, which is found on the income statement.
- Year-over-year sales and profit trends are found on the *income statement* and tell you if the company is moving in the right direction and how fast it is growing. From this statement, you will be able to calculate how much sales, cash flow, earnings, and dividends the company is generating per share and use this information to analyze other important performance ratios.
- The *statement of retained earnings* shows you how much net income the company will retain or pay out in dividends for the year—an important factor since you are focusing on dividend-paying stocks.

Armed with this basic understanding, you can now learn how to analyze a company's financial position through the use of a few key ratios. These are the same ratios that we use every day in our stock selection process to build the best *dividend stock*–focused portfolio.

RATIO ANALYSIS

Ratios are widely used not only to evaluate a company but to compare a company's financial position with other companies. The data used to calculate ratios are readily available in each company's annual and quarterly reports. We are going to concentrate our analysis in the following two areas.

Building Block One

Basic financial metrics are formulas that allow you to view any company's results on a per share basis. Once financial data are reduced to the shareholder level, you can easily compare companies that might be very different in size or in different industries.

For example, trying to compare the annual sales of General Motors with the annual sales of a much smaller car company like Porsche might not tell you much, but by comparing sales per share (divide each company's sales by the number of shares outstanding), you have a more meaningful measurement. Generally, the company generating higher sales per share is going to be the better value.

Throughout our analysis we will be using the basic financial metrics shown in Exhibit 7.5.

Building Block Two

Ratio analysis allows you to analyze a company's financial performance against other companies in the same industry, against all stocks in the market, or against industry standards, which are sometimes known as "rules of thumb." Although there is a great number of ratios you can use to analyze a company, we have developed a short list of ratios that will give you the information you need to pick good dividend-paying stocks. (See Exhibit 7.6.)

EXHIBIT 7.5

Basic Financial Metrics

	Formula	Financial Statements or Source
Sales Per Share	Sales/Shares Outstanding	Income statement; Balance sheet
Earnings Per Share	Earnings/Shares Outstanding	Income statements; Balance sheet
Dividends Per Share	Dividends/Shares Outstanding	Retained earnings; Balance sheet
Cash Flow Per Share	Operating Plus Other Income + Depreciation/Shares	Income statements; Balance sheet
Yield	Dividends per share/ Price per share	Dividends per share; Newspaper

EXHIBIT 7.6

Ratios

Ratio	Formula	Financial Statements or Source
Liquidity Ratios		
Quick Ratio	Current Assets − Inventory/ Current Liabilities	Balance Sheet
Debt Ratios		
Short-Term Debt Coverage Ratio	Operating Income/ Short-Term Debt (Current Liabilities)	Income Statement; Balance Sheet
Valuation Ratios		
Price to Sales	Stock Price/Sales Per Share	Newspapers; Sales per Share
Price to Earnings	Stock Price/Earnings Per Share	Newspapers; Earnings per Share
Dividend Ratios		
Dividend Coverage Ratio	Cash Flow Per Share/ Earnings Per Share	Basic Metric Formulas
Payout Ratio	Dividend Per Share/ Earnings Per Share	Basic Metric Formulas
Growth Ratios		
Revenue Growth Rate Ratio	Year-Over-Year Percent Change in Revenues	Income Statement
Earnings Growth Rate Ratio	Year-Over-Year Percent Change in Earnings	Income Statement

CALCULATING BASIC FINANCIAL METRICS

Publicly traded companies publish their financial statements in their annual reports to shareholders. You can obtain an annual report on any public company simply by contacting the company's shareholder services department and requesting the report. To facilitate our explanation, we will review financial statements from the fictional Gourmet Foods, Inc., a relatively small grocery and specialty food store chain that will serve as our example throughout the calculations that follow.

Example: When Bob took over the family business in 1965 at his dad's retirement, they had one grocery store in New York City. The business had always prospered because they sold only the freshest vegetables and highest quality foods. With the advent of grocery superstores, Bob realized that while he could not compete on price, he could compete on quality.

Bob was able to start expanding in the mid–1970s and over the next 15 years added 10 new locations, all in or around metropolitan New York. When he retired in 1984, Bob passed the business on to his children. They reinvented the business again by increasing the emphasis on gourmet foods and added sections in each of their stores with ready-made gourmet dinners for takeout. Not only is their strategy of higher-margin offerings working, but they seem to be executing their business strategy flawlessly.

By reviewing the financial statements of Gourmet Foods, we are able to determine the information that follows. (Exhibit 7.7 shows the consolidated balance sheet.)

- **Sales per share.** Gourmet Foods' sales were $18,475,000 for 2009, the first entry on the income statement, and shares outstanding from the balance sheet were 750,000. By dividing $18,475,000 by 750,000, we get *sales per share* of $24.63.
- **Earnings per share.** Gourmet Foods' *earnings per share* of $2.92 in 2009 were calculated by dividing net income (income statement) by outstanding shares (balance sheet).
- **Dividends per share.** By dividing $700,000 in dividends paid in 2009 (statement of retained earnings) by 750,000 shares outstanding from the balance sheet, we find that Gourmet Foods had *dividends per share* in 2009 of 93 cents.

EXHIBIT 7.7

Gourmet Foods, Inc., Consolidated Balance Sheet for the Years Ending 2008 and 2009

Assets	December 31, 2009	December 31, 2008
Current Assets		
Cash and Cash Equivalents	$450,000	$185,000
Accounts Receivable, Less Allowance for Doubtful Accounts (2002, $50,000; 2001, $25,000)	$1,450,000	$850,000
Inventory	$1,639,000	$1,150,000
Total Current Assets	**$3,539,000**	**$2,185,000**
Investments	**$500,000**	**$375,000**
Property, Plant, and Equipment		
Land	$600,000	$600,000
Building	$1,250,000	$1,250,000
Machinery and Equipment	$1,580,000	$1,180,000
Total Fixed Assets	**$3,430,000**	**$3,030,000**
Less Accumulated Depreciation	$751,000	$685,000
Net Fixed Assets	**$2,679,000**	**$2,345,000**
Total Assets	***$6,718,000***	***$4,905,000***
Liabilities		
Current Liabilities		
Current Maturing Long-Term Debt	$50,000	$50,000
Accounts Payable and Accrued Liabilities	$1,050,000	$875,000
Taxes Due	$195,000	$145,000
Total Current Liabilities	**$1,295,000**	**$1,070,000**
Long-Term Debt	$500,000	$400,000
Total Liabilities	**$1,795,000**	**$1,470,000**
Shareholder Equity		
Common Stock ($1.00 par value; 1,000,000 shares authorized; shares outstanding: 750,000 in 2009 750,000 in 2008)	750,000	750,000
Additional Paid-In Capital	**$500,000**	**$500,000**
Retained Earnings	**$3,673,000**	**$2,185,000**
Total Shareholder Equity	**$4,923,000**	**$3,435,000**
Total Liabilities and Net Worth	***$6,718,000***	***$4,905,000***
Note (Closing Stock Price 12/31)	*$45.00*	*$37.50*

Current assets are assets that are liquid

Current liabilities are short-term debts the firm must pay within a year

The owner's investments feflected as shareholder equity

- **Cash flow per share.** The *cash flow per share* of $4.55 in 2009 was calculated by taking income of $3,350,000 (sum of operating income and other income), adding depreciation of $66,000 (income statement), and then dividing by the 750,000 shares outstanding (balance sheet).

- **Yield.** Gourmet Foods' stock had a *dividend yield* on December 31, 2009, of 2.07 percent. The dividend yield is calculated by dividing the dividend per share of 93 cents at the close of 2009 by the stock price of $45 per share. We included the December 31 stock prices on the balance sheet to facilitate our analysis, but you should look for a stock's price in your daily newspaper or on the Internet. While most companies don't change their dividend payouts frequently, stock prices do change all day long, so yield must be calculated at least daily or at least each time you analyze a stock.

Now let's begin our analysis of the ability of Gourmet Foods to meet its maturing loan obligations and current cash flow needs by computing its liquidity and debt coverage ratios.

QUICK RATIO

The *quick ratio* is an important liquidity ratio that is computed by removing inventory from current assets and then dividing the remainder by current liabilities. All three data points—current assets, inventory, and current liabilities—are found on Gourmet Foods' balance sheet (Exhibit 7.7). Since inventories are typically the least liquid of a company's current assets and are likely to produce a loss if liquidated, it is prudent to look at the firm's ability to cover short-term liabilities without relying on them. The rule of thumb is that a company with a quick ratio of 1.0 or better indicates that it could cover all current liabilities with the liquid assets it has on hand, thereby reducing any need to cut its dividend.

Gourmet Foods' quick ratio for 2009 is 1.47, more than the standard rule of thumb you would like to see. If the ratio was less than 1, you would want to assure yourself that the company is generating enough cash flow from operations to cover both normal expenses and any short-term debt obligations that come due.

The higher the quick ratio, the better we like the company.

DEBT COVERAGE RATIO

The *short-term debt coverage ratio* allows you to quickly see if the company's short-term debt obligations can be easily paid by using the cash that is being generated from company operations. This ratio is calculated by dividing income from operations (see the income statement in Exhibit 7.8) by current liabilities or short-term debt (balance sheet). This ratio should equal at least 2.0.

Gourmet Foods' short-term debt coverage ratio equals 2.58 for 2009. This means that the company is generating more than twice the cash flow it needs from operations to pay off all of its short-term obligations. Taken alone, this ratio would indicate that the dividend is pretty secure and would also indicate that there is sufficient operating income to offset a slightly lower liquidity position if that was indicated by the company's quick ratio.

Leverage allows a company to grow faster and so might enhance the return on investor capital, but it will also increase risk. Since too much leverage strains the company's ability to pay back the debt, creditors and dividend investors prefer companies with moderate debt levels. Greater asset coverage cushions a company

EXHIBIT 7.8

Gourmet Foods, Inc., Consolidated Income Statement for the Years Ending 2008 and 2009

	December 31, 2009	December 31, 2008
Sales	$18,475,000	$16,627,500
Cost of Goods Sold	$6,750,000	$6,205,000
Gross Profit	$11,725,000	$10,422,500
Selling and Administrative Expenses	$8,385,000	$7,546,500
Operating Income (Profit)	$3,340,000	$2,876,000
Other Income	$10,000	$7,500
Income before Interest, Depreciation, and Taxes	$3,350,000	$2,883,500
Interest Expense	$24,000	$15,000
Depreciation	$66,000	$30,000
Taxes	$1,072,000	$922,720
Net Income	$2,188,000	$1,915,780
Earnings Per Share	$2.92	$2.55

Earnings per share measures the firm's profit for each share owned.

during negative cash flow periods and should allow the company to maintain its dividend payment even during tough times.

Income from operations is an important measure of the ability of Gourmet Foods to generate positive cash flow from normal operations without liquidating other assets to fund expenses and dividend payments. In addition to operating income, Gourmet Foods earned $10,000 in interest income on cash balances during 2009. Other income items can include sale of assets (e.g., products, patents, or even an entire operating division or subsidiary). These are one-time income events and can distort an investor's perception of the company's ability to generate income. That is why we use operating income in our formulas as a much more reliable indication of cash flow. Other income for a company might be akin to your winning a $10,000 windfall from a lottery—it can be spent or reinvested when received, but you can't count on it happening again to cover next year's bills.

VALUATION RATIOS

Since our focus as investment managers is on finding dividend-paying stocks that are good values, we also look at *valuation ratios* in an effort to buy stocks at an attractive price. We have a value focus and would rather buy stocks at a low price today, so we can sell them at a higher price later. This helps us avoid the classic mistake many investors make of buying high and selling low.

While investors were rushing to buy stocks during the buildup in valuations and prices during the bubble phase of the market (1998–1999), we could not find many stocks with compelling value to buy. One of the lessons we have learned over the years is that free cash in the portfolio is often best left *un*invested unless you can find stocks that are attractive.

We look to buy stocks that are cheap not only by historical standards but also by comparison to other stocks. Typically, value stocks have less downside risk because they are already down. They also tend to have more upside potential; often there is nowhere to go but up.

If you can find a stock that is a good value, it usually means the stock has fallen from the market's grace. Maybe the company is struggling with its product mix or has had labor problems, or there might be a new competitor. At any rate, investors have abandoned the stock, its price has fallen, and the immediate prospects for a turnaround are a bit murky. If the company's business and stock price seem to have stabilized, you might want to consider buying it.

There are two important ratios that can help you identify companies with good value characteristics.

- **Price-to-sales ratio.** We rank companies with low *price-to-sales ratios* higher than those companies whose stock is pricey relative to the sales being generated. You calculate the ratio by dividing the current stock price ($45) by sales per share ($24.63). Gourmet Foods' price-to-sales ratio is 1.83 for 2009, which is lower than the 2.00 rule of thumb ratio we use to indicate good value.

- **Price-to-earnings ratio (P/E).** Also known as the *price-to-earnings multiple,* this ratio tells you how expensive the stock is from a price standpoint given the earnings the stock is generating. Historically, stocks are a good value when the ratio or multiple is around 14.00, but we will consider stocks that have P/E of less than 20.00—the lower the ratio, the better. You calculate the ratio by dividing the stock's price by the earnings per share being generated. Gourmet Foods' price-to-earnings ratio is 15.41, which is below our rule of thumb P/E ratio of 20, so we would consider Gourmet Foods a decent value based on this ratio.

Gourmet Foods, Inc., has passed both of our value screens, but it might not rank as high as some other companies that we screen on a daily basis.

DIVIDEND RATIOS

As previously stated, when a company earns profits, management must decide whether to retain earnings for growth or pay a portion of the profits out to stockholders in the form of cash dividends.

Two additional important ratios will help further determine the security of the dividend income stream and, thus, the attractiveness of a stock.

- **Dividend coverage ratio.** This ratio shows how secure the dividend is based on the cash flow being generated by the company. Instead of applying the cash flow to analyze whether the company can meet its debt obligations, we analyze this ratio to assess how easily the company can keep making its dividend payments. To calculate this ratio, you divide cash flow per share by dividend per share. The higher the dividend coverage from cash flow, the better we like it.

Gourmet Foods has a *dividend coverage ratio* of 489 percent, significantly more than our minimum rule of thumb of 120 percent.

- **Dividend payout ratio.** This ratio tells you how much profit the company is paying out to shareholders in dividends. Once again, the higher the better, as long as the ratio does not exceed 100 percent. Since a company can pay dividends only from current or retained earnings, it is a warning sign if a company is paying dividends that exceed current earnings.

Gourmet Foods' *dividend payout ratio* is 32 percent and is calculated by dividing its dividend per share ($0.93) by earnings per share ($2.92). We tend to look for companies that have payout ratios of at least 50 percent, which to us indicates that the company is committed to rewarding shareholders through dividend payouts.

The retained earnings figure on a company's balance sheet is the sum of all undistributed profits that have not been paid out as dividends but instead have been reinvested to finance operations, purchase fixed assets, or pay down debt. To understand how those earnings are used, you must consult the firm's statement of retained earnings. (See Exhibit 7.9.)

Gourmet Foods generated $2,188,000 in net earnings, and management declared dividend payments of $700,000 for 2009, retaining

EXHIBIT 7.9

Gourmet Foods, Inc., Consolidated Statement of Retained Earnings for the Years Ending 2008 and 2009

	December 31, 2009	December 31, 2008
Retained Earnings Beginning of Year	$2,185,000	$829,220
Net Income	$2,188,000	$1,915,780
Less Cash Dividends	$700,000	$560,000
Balance Retained Earnings End of Year	$3,673,000	2,185,000

A balance between dividend payments and retained earnings shows prudent management.

the balance of their earnings to grow the company. The company maintains a conservative *payout ratio* of 32 percent, which allows management to consider increasing dividends as earnings increase.

GROWTH RATIOS

Year-over-year growth and shrinkage in revenue and earnings are good indications of a positive or negative trend developing. The importance of confirming a positive trend when analyzing value stocks cannot be overstated. Remember, it would not be a value stock if there weren't something wrong. Without confirming a positive trend, you could invest in a stock that will continue to slide, eventually cut its dividend, and maybe even go bankrupt.

Two growth ratios will help you identify these trends.

- **One-year revenue growth ratio.** This ratio measures the one-year percentage change in revenue growth. It is calculated by subtracting last year's revenue from the current year's revenue to find the difference, then dividing that difference by last year's revenue to find the percentage change. Gourmet Foods' *revenue growth rate* for 2009 is 11.11 percent, indicating that revenue has improved by slightly more than our 10 percent rule of thumb.

- **One-year earnings growth ratio.** This ratio measures the one-year percentage change in earnings growth. It is calculated by subtracting last year's earnings from the current year's earnings to find the difference, then dividing that difference by last year's earnings to find the percentage change. Gourmet Foods' *earnings growth rate* was 14.21 percent in 2009, which was also greater than our 10 percent rule of thumb for earnings growth rate. With both revenue and profits rising, Gourmet Foods' stock price should reflect this positive trend and move higher.

One ratio by itself does not tell a story, but several taken together provide a much clearer picture of a firm's strengths and weaknesses. A summary of Gourmet Foods' financial ratio analysis is shown in Exhibit 7.10.

While the preceding ratio analysis gives a reasonably good picture of Gourmet Foods, it is missing the important component

EXHIBIT 7.10

Gourmet Foods, Inc., Financial Ratio Analysis

Ratio	Formula	2009	2008	Rule of Thumb	Preference
Liquidity Ratios					
Quick Ratio	Current Assets – Inventory/				
	Current Liabilities	1.47	0.97	> 1.0	Higher
Debt Ratios					
Short-Term Debt	Operating Income/				
Coverage Ratio	Short-Term Debt				
	(Current Liabilities)	2.58	2.69	> 2.0	Higher
Valuation Ratios					
Price-to-Sales	Stock Price/Sales Per Share	1.83	1.69	< 2.0	Lower
Price-to-Earnings	Stock Price/Earnings				
	Per Share	15.41	14.71	< 20	Lower
Dividend Ratios					
Dividend Coverage	Cash Flow Per Share/				
Ratio	Dividend Per Share	489%	517%	= or > 120%	Higher
Payout Ratio	Dividend Per Share/				
	Earnings Per Share	32%	29%	< 100% > 50%	Higher
Growth Ratios					
Revenue Growth	2009 revenue – 2008				
Rate Ratio	Revenue/2008 Revenue	11.11%		> 10.00%	Higher
Earnings Growth	2009 Earnings – 2008				
Rate Ratio	Earnings/2008 Earnings	14.21%		> 10.00%	Higher

of time. (In our limited example, we have only two years of financial statement results, 2008 and 2009, for Gourmet Foods.)

TREND ANALYSIS

All of the preceding ratios are snapshots of the company's financial condition at a point in time, but there are trends in motion that need to be identified so you can understand whether the company's position is improving or deteriorating.

Gourmet Foods' year-over-year trend analysis is shown in Exhibit 7.11. It indicates a generally positive trend with an increasing growth in sales, earnings, cash flow, and dividends per share. The leverage, value, and dividend ratios are all positive or well within acceptable ranges, with the exception of the quick ratio. Based on our analysis, the dividend looks to be secure, and Gourmet Foods would be a good buy.

EXHIBIT 7.11

Gourmet Foods, Inc., Trend Analysis

Basic Financial Metrics	Formula	2009	2008	Increase / (Decrease)
Sales Per Share	Sales/Shares Outstanding	$24.63	$22.17	11.10%
Earnings Per Share	Earnings/Shares Outstanding	$2.92	$2.55	14.51%
Dividends Per Share	Dividends/Shares Outstanding	$0.93	$0.75	24.00%
Cash Flow Per Share	Operating + Other Income + Depreciation/Shares	$4.55	$3.88	17.27%
Yield	Dividend Per Share/ Price Per Share	2.07%	2.00%	3.50%
Ratios	**Formula**	**2009**	**2008**	**Increase / (Decrease)**
Quick Ratio	Current Assets − Inventory/ Current Liabilities	1.47	0.97	51.55%
Short-Term Debt Coverage Ratio	Operating Income/ Short-Term Debt (Current Liab.)	2.58	2.69	−4.09%
Price-to-Sales	Stock Price/Sales Per Share	1.83	1.69	8.28%
Price-to-Earnings	Stock Price/Earnings Per Share	15.41	14.71	4.76%
Dividend Coverage Ratio	Cash Flow Per Share/ Dividend Per Share	489%	517%	−5.42%
Payout Ratio	Dividend Per Share/ Earnings Per Share	32%	29%	10.34%

Caution: A Parting Word about a Standard Rule of Thumb

Although convenient, rules of thumb should not be adhered to in isolation. For example, electric utilities normally have current liabilities that exceed their current assets, yielding a quick ratio of less than 1. However, investors are not concerned because utilities have strong cash flow from operations, and their accounts receivables are from electricity users who must pay their bills if they want to continue to receive electricity. If your rule of thumb were rigid, a low quick ratio would be a signal for you to avoid the company and discard promising stocks individually or even across an entire industry.

Ultimately, by integrating these ratios into a single analysis for any given company, you should be able to confidently select dividend-paying stocks that will help you to accomplish your investment goals and to build your wealth slowly over time through compounding dividends and price appreciation.

YOU'RE NOT DONE YET

Being able to recite a list of key information critical to stock selection isn't a kind of magic incantation for success. You have to actually find that information for every stock on your list. And because the information is constantly changing, you also have to keep your analysis up to date—preferably quarterly.

How much time your research effort will take depends on how you do it. Visiting the library and writing or calling for annual reports will certainly work, but you'll spend a lot of time gathering data. If you're able to automatically download the information you want directly into a spreadsheet or database, that part of your research can happen in minutes every day—while you're sleeping.

It's hard to imagine anything that has done more to ease the burden of securities research for the individual investor than the development of the Internet. The amount and quality of information you can easily access from the comfort of your own home truly boggles the mind. Need an annual report? Click. Access to government filings? Click. Prices, charts, analysis, commentary? Just click again. Information that once took vast amounts of time and dedication to assemble now rushes to your fingertips down the information superhighway.

Technology can certainly help you cast a wider net in your search for winning stocks, but your ultimate success as an investor will most likely be determined by how you use the information you find, rather than by how you find it.

There are three fundamental ways in which the information you're looking for will vary.

1. **Cost.** A surprising amount of information is available for free, either directly from companies themselves, from government agencies like the Securities and Exchange Commission (SEC), or certain Web sites. Brokerage firms often make some form of research available to their customers. Subscription services vary dramatically in price, from the cost of a daily newspaper to thousands of dollars per month for comprehensive data and analysis services.

2. **Format.** Information is available in print or electronic format. Newspapers, magazines, and annual reports are familiar in print. Electronic versions of all these publications are commonly available, as are hosts of software applications and Web sites.

3. **Content.** Financial statements, balance sheets, and company reports provide a rich source of data items, but you probably will have to compute the ratios yourself. Many third-party information services provide exactly this kind of processed information already calculated for you. Key financial ratios, earnings trends, and per share data are commonly listed, along with analysis and commentary, including rating services and lists of specific security recommendations. The amount of information is usually commensurate with its cost.

The cost, format, and content of all kinds of information sources are rapidly evolving, and any attempt at a comprehensive listing would be almost instantly obsolete. By pointing out a few alternatives across the spectrum of choices, we hope to show you a sample of the kind of information that's available. How you choose to proceed will depend on your level of interest, resources, preferences, and expertise with computers.

Printed Materials

Most newspapers include business sections, but their coverage varies widely, and their stock and mutual fund listings are often incomplete and list little more than the prior day's price. For business news, the *Wall Street Journal* and *Investor's Business Daily* are popular daily papers.

Barron's

An excellent place to start gathering information and to keep up to date on important market news is *Barron's*, a weekly financial newspaper. In *Barron's* Market Week section, you'll find robust stock listings with more than just the recent price, including:

- Ticker symbols (important for obtaining information and placing accurate transaction orders)
- Dividend yield expressed as a percentage of the current stock price, and the dividend amount in dollars per share
- The price/earnings ratio (P/E), an important valuation measure
- Per-share earnings information, including last year's earnings, this year's earnings, and next year's projected earnings

- Trading volume
- The 52-week high and low price for the security
- A host of "stock ticker code symbols" to alert you to everything from bankruptcy to stock splits

The listings also show a ♣ symbol next to stocks that participate in *Barron's* Annual Reports Service. Free annual reports and, where available, quarterly reports can be ordered 24 hours a day, including weekends, at www.barrons.ar.wilink.com or by calling 800–965–2929. If you're looking for an inexpensive way to get your research project started, for the price of a single week's paper you can obtain hundreds of free annual reports from the companies that catch your eye in the listings.

A similar service, *Barron's* Fund Info Service, is available for mutual funds. (Visit www.barrons.fundinfo.wilink.com or call 888–201–3503.)

Barron's is a lot more than just its stock tables. Every week it's full of interviews, opinions, research, and articles on the markets (stock, bond, real estate, commodity, and foreign), the economy, technology, mutual funds, and interesting companies. For the dividend investor, *Barron's* Market Lab section contains a table listing the week's dividend payments. A regular column, "Speaking of Dividends," carries news and views about what's going on in that corner of the investment world.

Annual Reports

A company's annual report is a good source for many of the data items you'll need, as well as for commentary about the company. It usually includes a letter from the top executive to shareholders with his or her view of the major events affecting the company, and his or her view of the company's prospects going forward. You'll also typically find descriptive information about the company and its business (or businesses), plus a section that provides all the financial statements, including consolidated income statements, balance sheets, cash flow statements, statements of shareholders' equity, footnotes, and a report of the independent auditors.

Reading the annual report is a great way to familiarize yourself with a company. Keep in mind, though, that companies try to put their best foot forward in their reports to shareholders, so the commentary is likely to cast the company's position in the best possible light. A call or letter to a company's investor relations department is usually all that's needed to have a free copy of the most recent annual report sent your way.

For a presumably less biased view of a company's condition and prospects, you can turn to one of several stock rating publications:

- The Value Line Investment Survey provides financial information and key ratios on approximately 1,700 stocks and rates their attractiveness on a scale of 1 to 5 for both safety and timeliness. A sample report is shown as Exhibit 7.12.
- Standard & Poor's Stock Reports offer commentary and buy/hold/sell recommendations based on its STARS rankings for approximately 5,000 publicly traded companies listed on the New York, American, NASDAQ, and regional stock exchanges.
- Morningstar made its name ranking mutual funds but has expanded into stock research through its Stock Analyst Reports on approximately 1,700 stocks.

If you use a brokerage firm, it may also have a variety of stock research and recommendation information available to you. Check with your representative to find out what's offered and at what cost.

Internet Sources

Each of the business newspapers and stock rating services just described is available in an online Internet version. You can generally also obtain information directly from an interesting company's Web site. Simply run a search on the company name, go to the company's home page, and look for the "investor relations" section. Companies' Web sites vary widely in terms of their ease of use and content, but most will include:

- The most recent annual and quarterly reports (the quarterly report may be referred to as the "10-Q")
- Recent news releases and access to a news release archive
- A calendar of events, including planned shareholder meetings
- Notes and commentary from recent analyst meetings, speeches, or other presentations

EXHIBIT 7.12

Value Line Investment Survey Report on Marathon Oil

MARATHON OIL NYSE-MRO

RECENT PRICE	34.86	
P/E RATIO	11.5	(Trailing: 10.7 / Median: 15.0)
RELATIVE P/E RATIO	0.60	
DIV'D YLD	2.9%	

VALUE LINE

TIMELINESS	4	Lowered 2/6/04
SAFETY	2	Raised 6/20/03
TECHNICAL	2	Raised 2/20/04
BETA	.85	(1.00 = Market)

High: 20.6 / Low: 16.4 | High: 19.1 / Low: 15.6 | High: 21.5 / Low: 15.8 | High: 25.5 / Low: 17.3 | High: 38.9 / Low: 23.8 | High: 40.5 / Low: 25.0 | High: 33.9 / Low: 19.6 | High: 30.4 / Low: 20.7 | High: 33.7 / Low: 25.0 | High: 30.3 / Low: 18.8 | High: 33.6 / Low: 19.8 | High: 36.3 / Low: 31.7

LEGENDS
5.0 x "Cash Flow" p sh
---- Relative Price Strength
Options: Yes
Shaded area indicates recession

2007-09 PROJECTIONS

	Price	Gain	Ann'l Total Return
High	55	(+50%)	14%
Low	40	(+15%)	6%

Target Price Range 2007 | 2008 | 2009

Price scale (right): 80, 60, 50, 40, 30, 25, 20, 15, 10, 7.5

Insider Decisions

	A	M	J	J	A	S	O	N	D
to Buy	0	0	0	0	0	0	0	0	0
Options	0	0	0	0	0	0	0	0	0
to Sell	0	1	0	1	0	0	0	0	0

Institutional Decisions

	2Q2003	3Q2003	4Q2003
to Buy	202003 203	302003 179	402003 222
to Sell	153	177	160
Hld's(000)	247627	245881	243434

Percent shares traded: 9 / 6 / 3

1988	1989	1990	1991	1992	1993	1994	1995	1996	1997	1998	1999	2000	2001	2002	2003	2004	2005	© VALUE LINE PUB., INC.	07-09
38.41	47.98	57.43	53.90	44.60	41.74	44.49	48.26	56.81	54.25	71.56	78.02	96.86	91.60	88.65	118.16	111.85	109.30	Sales per sh A	128.60
3.94	5.53	5.87	4.14	2.70	2.99	2.79	3.61	4.22	4.49	4.09	4.44	7.65	8.25	5.69	7.05	6.90	6.70	"Cash Flow" per sh	8.15
.05	1.49	1.94	.78	d.07	.46	.30	.75	1.81	2.20	1.09	1.40	4.20	4.26	1.81	3.26	3.15	2.90	Earnings per sh B	4.00
1.09	1.22	1.22	.70	1.22	.68	.68	.68	.70	.76	.84	.84	.88	.92	.92	.96	1.00	1.00	Div'ds Decl'd per sh C■	1.20
3.36	4.04	3.93	3.70	4.16	3.18	2.63	2.23	2.61	3.59	4.12	4.42	4.62	5.30	5.08	6.10	6.30	6.10	Cap'l Spending per sh	5.95
	13.25	13.92	12.40	11.36	10.58	11.03	9.99	11.62	12.53	13.98	15.39	15.72	15.97	16.40	19.57	21.70	23.55	Book Value per sh	30.20
259.03	255.58	254.51	259.28	286.61	286.58	286.73	287.40	287.50	288.80	308.50	311.80	308.30	309.40	309.87	310.42	310.75	311.00	Common Shs Outst'g D	311.00
						58.1	23.9	11.7	14.1	30.5	20.3	6.2	6.8	14.0	8.0	Bold figures are Value Line estimates		Avg Ann'l P/E Ratio	12.0
		14.8	34.4	35.8	38.8	3.81	1.60	.73	.81	1.59	1.16	.40	.35	.76	.46			Relative P/E Ratio	.80
		1.10	2.20			3.9%	3.7%	3.3%	2.5%	2.5%	3.0%	3.4%	3.2%	3.6%	3.7%			Avg Ann'l Div'd Yield	2.5%
		4.3%	2.6%	6.0%	3.7%														

CAPITAL STRUCTURE as of 12/31/03
Total Debt $4357 mill. Due in 5 Yrs $1494 mill.
LT Debt $4085 mill. LT Interest $295 mill.
(Total interest coverage: 6.7x) (40% of Cap'l)

12757							13871	16332	15668	22075	24327	29861	28340	27470	36678	34750	34000	Sales ($mill)	40000
9.0%						9.0%	10.9%	10.5%	11.5%	9.7%	8.7%	12.6%	14.9%	9.4%	9.5%	9.5%	9.5%	Operating Margin	10.0%
721.0						721.0	817.0	693.0	664.0	941.0	950.0	1052.0	1236.0	1201.0	1175.0	1175	1190	Depreciation ($mill)	1300
86.0						86.0	224.1	520.0	633.5	321.0	434.0	1308.0	1318.0	563.0	1012.0	975	895	Net Profit ($mill)	1235
38.1%						38.1%	43.8%	32.9%	33.7%	29.0%	34.0%	38.6%	36.5%	40.9%	36.6%	37.0%	37.0%	Income Tax Rate	37.0%
.7%						.7%	1.6%	3.2%	4.0%	1.5%	1.8%	4.4%	4.7%	2.0%	2.8%	2.8%	2.6%	Net Profit Margin	3.1%
25.0						25.0	d137.0	d96.0	d244.0	366.0	953.0	973.0	943.0	820.0	1833.0	1100	900	Working Cap'l ($mill)	1575
3983.0						3983.0	3367.0	2642.0	2476.0	3458.0	3320.0	1937.0	3432.0	4410.0	4085.0	4000	4000	Long-Term Debt ($mill)	4000
3241.0						3241.0	2872.0	3340.0	3618.0	4312.0	4800.0	4845.0	4940.0	5082.0	6075.0	6750	7325	Shr. Equity ($mill)	9395
3.6%						3.6%	6.0%	11.2%	12.2%	5.9%	7.2%	21.0%	16.8%	7.4%	11.3%	10.5%	9.9%	Return on Total Cap'l	10.5%
2.7%						2.7%	7.8%	15.6%	17.5%	7.4%	9.0%	27.0%	26.7%	11.1%	16.7%	14.5%	12.0%	Return on Shr. Equity	13.0%

Leases, Uncapitalized Annual rentals $108.0 mill.
Pension Assets $895 mill. Obligation $1454 mill.
Pfd Stock None

Common Stock 310,648,972 shs.
as of 1/31/04

MARKET CAP: $10.8 billion (Large Cap)

% TOT. RETURN 2/04

	THIS STOCK	VL ARITH. INDEX
1 yr.	57.6	85.3
3 yr.	41.5	37.3
5 yr.	95.8	83.6

107-09 targets: Sales per sh A 128.60; Target Price 2008; Range 2009

												Retained to Com Eq	9.0%
NMF	.9%	9.6%	11.5%	1.7%	3.7%	21.3%	19.8%	5.5%	11.8%	10.0%	8.0%	All Div'ds to Net Prof	30%
NMF	89%	39%	35%	77%	59%	21%	26%	51%	29%	32%	34%		

CURRENT POSITION ($MILL.)	2001	2002	12/31/03
Cash Assets	657.0	488.0	1396.0
Receivables	1772.0	1854.0	2463.0
Inventory (LIFO)	1851.0	1984.0	1953.0
Other	131.0	153.0	228.0
Current Assets	4411.0	4479.0	6040.0
Accts Payable	2431.0	2885.0	3352.0
Debt Due	215.0	161.0	272.0
Other	822.0	613.0	583.0
Current Liab.	3468.0	3659.0	4207.0

ANNUAL RATES of change (per sh)	Past 10 Yrs.	Past 5 Yrs.	Est'd '01-'03 to '07-'09
Sales	8.0%	10.5%	4.5%
"Cash Flow"	8.0%	10.5%	2.5%
Earnings	23.0%	13.0%	4.5%
Dividends	0.5%	4.0%	4.5%
Book Value	4.0%	6.5%	9.5%

Cal-endar	QUARTERLY SALES ($ mill.) A				Full Year
	Mar.31	Jun.30	Sep.30	Dec.31	
2001	7613	7974	7119	5634	28340
2002	5468	7036	7409	7557	27470
2003	9086	8613	9149	9830	36678
2004	8700	8550	8550	8250	34750
2005	8650	8650	8350	8500	34000

Cal-endar	EARNINGS PER SHARE B				Full Year
	Mar.31	Jun.30	Sep.30	Dec.31	
2001	1.64	1.88	.62	.12	4.26
2002	.09	.62	.48	.62	1.81
2003	.92	.76	.94	.64	3.26
2004	.80	.85	.75	.75	3.15
2005	.75	.80	.65	.70	2.90

Cal-endar	QUARTERLY DIVIDENDS PAID C a				Full Year
	Mar.31	Jun.30	Sep.30	Dec.31	
2000	.21	.21	.23	.23	.88
2001	.23	.23	.23	.23	.92
2002	.23	.23	.23	.23	.92
2003	.23	.23	.25	.25	.98
2004	.25				

(A) Excludes excise taxes starting in 2000.
(B) Primary earnings until 1996, then diluted. Excludes nonrecurring gains (charges): '91, ($1.09); '92, (73¢); '93, (58¢); '94, 80¢; '95, ($1.11); '96, 52¢; '97, (61¢); '98, (4¢); '99, 71¢; '00, ($2.81); '01, ($3.12); '02, (15¢); '03 (5¢). Next earnings report due late April
(C) Dividends historically paid near the middle of March, June September, December. Dividend reinvestment plant available.
(D) In millions.

BUSINESS: Marathon Oil Corp. is an integrated oil company. Daily 2003 production: oil, 190,700 barrels; natural gas, 1.1 billion cubic feet. Reserves at 12/31/03: 578 million barrels of oil; 2.8 trillion cubic feet of gas. Est. pretax present value of reserves: $8.8 bill. Acq. Pennaco, '01; Globex Energy, '02. Daily refining capacity 935,000 bbls (62% owned through a joint venture with Ashland). Markets to 5,984 stations. Capital by segment: upstream, 57%; downstream, 41% other, 2%. Employs 28,287. Capital Research owns 13.5% of stock; Barclay's Capital, 10.9% (4/04 Proxy). Chrmn.: Thomas Usher. CEO & Pres.: Clarence Cazelot, Jr. Inc.: DE. Address: 5555 San Felipe Rd., Houston, TX 77056. Tel.: 713-629-6600. Internet: www.marathon.com.

Downtime at Marathon Oil's refineries may keep a lid on near-term profits. Two plants are undergoing scheduled maintenance. As a result, the company won't get the full benefit of high margins on oil products in the first quarter of 2004. Separately, plant upgrades for mandated cleaner-fuel requirements effective in 2006 are progressing. The cost of those installations is steep, but Marathon can handle it, financially, and is taking the opportunity to increase capacity at one refinery by 25%.

Marathon won't benefit from higher oil and gas production for a couple of years, either. The company has done well lately to enhance its asset base with promising international projects in Equatorial Guinea, Norway, and Russia. But it has sacrificed current production levels through the sale of mature properties. On the plus side is that asset sales are providing funds for development and, combined with strong price realizations, are enabling the company to keep its finances in order. Production should be flat through 2005, rendering earnings largely a function of oil and gas prices, as well as refining margins. Those indicators are strong now, supporting the stock price, but are likely to remain volatile, and may well ease at some point between now and the end of next year.

Much improved reserve replacement is a plus for the stock. Marathon Oil added more oil and gas to its reserve base than it extracted for the second straight year in 2003, after having struggled in this area for quite a spell. Prospects are good for strong reserve replacement in 2004, as well. All told, field production is set to rise by a sizable 20%-30% in 3 to 5 years. The progress here provides some upside to the stock, assuming earnings benefit from greater, and higher-margined, production in the second half of this decade. We also figure on oil prices being supportive. **The good-yielding stock has appeal for its risk-adjusted total-return potential to 2007-2009.** The company should be in good shape after a transitional period in 2004 and 2005, based on the premise that projects go ahead as planned. But, for the coming months, the shares are untimely.

Robert Mitkowski, Jr. *March 19, 2004*

© 2004, Value Line Publishing, Inc. All rights reserved. Factual material is obtained from sources believed to be reliable and is provided without warranties of any kind. THE PUBLISHER IS NOT RESPONSIBLE FOR ANY ERRORS OR OMISSIONS HEREIN. This publication is strictly for subscriber's own, non-commercial, internal use. No part of it may be reproduced, resold, stored or transmitted in any printed, electronic or other form, or used for generating or marketing any printed or electronic publication, service or product.

Company's Financial Strength	B++
Stock's Price Stability	85
Price Growth Persistence	70
Earnings Predictability	35

A company's Securities and Exchange Commission filings can be found on the SEC's Web site under EDGAR (http://www.sec.gov/edgar.shtml), where you'll find instructions for using the EDGAR database. There's also the FreeEDGAR Web site (www.freeedgar.com), where you can sign up for free trials of various EDGAR Online subscription services if you'd like to explore the more extensive access to company information they offer. The Reuters Web site (www.reuters.com) offers a company search feature with which you can find a lot of detailed information about a prospective purchase candidate. Under "News and Markets," select "Stocks" and then enter the company's symbol. You'll be offered a choice of views, including Overview, Financials, News, Options, People, Analysts, Charts, and Research. In the Overview, you'll find a current quote, a short description of the company's business, and a few items of financial data, including dividends per share, yield percentage, price/earnings ratio, and earnings per share. The Financials view presents a much more robust collection of data, including revenue and earnings history, analyst estimates, valuation ratios, dividend growth rates, industry and sector comparisons, and much more.

You can also enter a symbol in the Yahoo! Finance section (www.finance.yahoo.com) to find a company profile and links to Quotes, Historical Prices, Charts, Technical Analysis, News & Info, Headlines, Key Statistics, SEC Filings, and Financials, including the Income Statement, Balance Sheet, and Cash Flow Statement.

Most brokerage firms make whatever research is normally available to their customers accessible online as part of their Web sites, often with news, quotes, and other information as well.

The sources and supply of information available on the Internet are rapidly growing and changing. The locations and information described here may differ from what you find as you surf the Internet for data, and you may find sites that don't even exist as this book is being written. The point of this brief inventory is simply to illustrate the enormous amount of information easily accessible online. While the speed and convenience of the Internet can be invaluable, be careful to test the accuracy of the data you're getting against a verifiable source before you rely on it on a regular basis to make your decisions. Bad data can be worse than no data at all.

While some investors enjoy discussing their stock picks in "chat rooms," we recommend that you stick to the numbers—not chat room commentary—in making your investment decisions.

Although you might gain some insights from sharing ideas online, there have been plenty of stories of unscrupulous people using their Internet postings to try to hype, influence, or sell stocks. With all the reputable sources of information available, why gamble your hard-earned money on the advice of an anonymous or unsolicited tipster?

SOFTWARE AND DATA SERVICES

There are software programs and data providers that deliver an almost unimaginable amount of detailed financial data on virtually every publicly traded stock. They include powerful analysis tools and forecasting models, charting capabilities, and interfaces with spreadsheets and other software programs. They are also expensive. Geared primarily toward the needs of the institutional or professional investor, they can still be a great value for these users despite the cost because they make collecting and processing vast amounts of data feasible. Unless your portfolio is of an institutional size, however, it's unlikely that the typical cost of thousands of dollars per month could ever make sense for you.

We used one of these products, Thomson Baseline, to generate the searches, lists, and rankings that appear in this book—all in just a few minutes' time. (Thomson Baseline is a product of Thomson Reuters.)

There are software programs available for the individual investor, but many are geared to helping with technical analysis and/or day trading. As dividend investing becomes more popular, however, it would not be surprising to find new products being introduced that provide automated access to the kinds of ratios and fundamental stock information you need. Attractive features would include the daily download of updated information into your computer and tools to screen and rank the stocks in your universe by the criteria you specify. We haven't found any programs priced for the individual user that fit this description, but they could be out there—or on the way.

While Internet access and computer software can make your research relatively simple and efficient, don't forget the library. Your local library probably has computer facilities for Internet access in case you'd like to explore that venue for your research but don't have a computer or Internet access at home. Depending on their size, many public libraries have extensive collections of business related reference materials, often including copies of the Value Line Investment Survey, Morningstar Stock Analyst and Mutual Fund reports, and Standard & Poor's Stock Reports. You're likely to find a copy of the current week's *Barron's* at the library, as well as a host of other newspapers, business magazines, and books. If you find you have the inclination, aptitude, interest, and time to do so, take the opportunity to pursue further education in the area of stock analysis. Many individual investors become quite skilled at reading and analyzing financial statements, and there are many anecdotes about amateur investors unearthing valuable information that professional analysts have missed.

Once you find the right sources of information for you, it's time to use your data to define the universe of stocks you will be tracking.

CHAPTER 8

Filling Your Toolbox

You can't have everything. Where would you put it?

—Steven Wright

Imagine walking into a home improvement superstore with only a vague idea of what you want to buy. You could spend hours wandering up and down the aisles looking for the right tools.

Investments are the tools you use to achieve your long-term financial goals, and choosing the right tools is critical to your success.

The universe of possible choices is huge. There is a virtual superstore of more than 3,900 companies listed on the New York Stock Exchange, approximately 3,800 listed on the NASDAQ, and thousands more listed on other exchanges in the United States and around the world. In addition to stocks, there are commodities, real estate, bonds, annuities, options, hedge funds, mutual funds, futures contracts, and on and on. One of the beauties of investing for dividends is that you can limit your search to just stocks—and to just those stocks that pay dividends.

CHOOSING THE RIGHT TOOLS

How you conduct your search will play a large part in how many stocks you'll be able to choose from. If you're using a computer, you may be able to access, download, and process thousands of potential candidates. If you're conducting your search by hand, you may be looking through the stock listings in the newspaper with a highlighter. In either case, your goal is the same: to find a manageable list of stocks that meet your initial criteria. Over time, these will become familiar friends. By tracking their fortunes over the years, you can gain a solid understanding of their underlying value and potential future prospects.

As you begin the process of narrowing your universe to a useful list, think about the qualities you find in your candidates in terms of *screens* and *standards*.

A *screen* is any element of a security that would eliminate it from further consideration—for example, the absence of a dividend. The purpose of a screen is to limit your universe of stocks to a manageable list of candidates. The concept of using a screen to narrow our choices is a familiar part of daily life. For example, people with food allergies can't eat certain dishes, no matter how delicious they are. We read books written only in languages we understand, and when we shop for clothing we start by looking for clothes that will fit. After all, it doesn't matter how nice an item is if it's not the right size. Screens help us discard all of the possibilities that, no matter what else they may have to offer, just don't meet our needs. Any stock that fails to pass one of your screens simply won't be on your list of candidates.

Standards are those criteria by which you will compare one security to another when both of them pass your screening process in order to select your preferred choice. The purpose of standards is to help you decide which stocks on your list of candidates to invest in. Returning to our shopping example, once we narrow our choices to those items that are the right size, we can try them on to see which ones fit the best. There are other clothing standards in addition to fit—such as color, style, quality, and price—that we can use to compare our finalists when deciding which ones to buy. The stocks that pass through your screens will be ranked according to a variety of investment standards to help you find those candidates on your list that appear to offer the most promising fit for your dividend portfolio. We will review these standards, and how we suggest using them, in Chapter 10.

Sometimes a measurement you use as a screen to shorten your list will also be used as a standard to rank your choices. The most obvious screen you'll be running your universe through is the size of the dividend yield. If you've set your minimum dividend yield at 2.25 percent, then a stock with a yield of 3 percent and another stock with a yield of 4 percent would both pass the dividend screen you've set and be added to your list of candidates. Later, when ranking your candidates to decide which ones to buy, you can use the dividend yield measurement again—but this time as a standard. On the basis of the dividend yield standard, the 4 percent stock would rank higher than the one with a yield of 3 percent.

How high the dividend yield should be to pass through your screen depends largely on how much income you need to take from your portfolio and how much risk you're comfortable assuming. If you haven't stopped to address these two important factors, now would be a great time to do so. We recommend creating a written investment policy statement (IPS) before committing a single dollar to an investment plan.

THE INVESTMENT POLICY STATEMENT

The purpose of the IPS is to put in writing exactly what you're trying to accomplish with your portfolio, how you plan to get the job done, and how you'll measure your progress along the way. It should serve as the anchor that keeps you from drifting away from your plan to chase the latest hot tip or investment fad. By helping you to stay focused on your long-term goals, it can also keep you from becoming so discouraged by the inevitable setbacks that you give up on investing altogether. An IPS doesn't have to be a complex document, but it should include the following:

- Your risk tolerance
- Your time horizon
- Your need for current income
- Your need for long-term growth
- Your plan of action
- Your schedule for measuring your progress

A great way to measure your risk tolerance is to decide what percentage you're prepared to lose in any given year without abandoning your strategy. Be honest with yourself. Translate the percentage numbers into real dollar amounts. It's one thing to tell yourself you can sit calmly through a 20 percent decline and another to open an account statement that shows one out of every five dollars of your hard earned money seems to have disappeared. Since the markets tend to spend about a quarter of the time falling, sometime during your lifetime as an investor it's virtually certain that you'll be facing losses in your account.

Big return targets, whether for growth or current income, tend to increase the likelihood of big dips in portfolio value. Investors are infamous for selling at market lows in a panic, usually just before the market recovers. The more harrowing the ride, the more likely you are to want to get off. Be sure you don't put yourself on the path to surrender by choosing too dangerous a route. If you're not prepared to accept any declines along the way, then you're not entitled to the superior gains that stocks have traditionally provided. That's fine; just scale back your plans to match the steady but lower long-term returns you'll probably be able to get from fixed investments.

Your time horizon is simply how long you plan to maintain your current investment strategy. It's usually tied to some major expense or event, such as the arrival of college years for the kids or a planned retirement date. For investors already in retirement, the time horizon for an income portfolio could be their life expectancy. The shorter your time horizon, the more conservative your plan should be. As we have seen, markets can go down for several years in a row. While they have always eventually recovered in the past, the markets might not follow your timetable, leaving you short of the necessary funds when it's time to write the check. In general, money you absolutely need to spend within four or five years should not be a part of your investment portfolio.

The total return your portfolio provides is made up of two parts: income and growth. If your portfolio is providing you with the cash you currently need to support your lifestyle, you need income. We believe there are potential pitfalls in relying on the systematic liquidation of portfolio growth ("dollar lost averaging") to fund your current income needs and that these pitfalls are serious enough to offer a strong argument for basing your withdrawals instead on the cash income your investments can generate.

How much money do you need to take from your portfolio today? How much will you need in the years ahead as the cost of living rises? Is your portfolio big enough to produce that much cash?[1] Exhibit 8.1 shows the annual distribution rate required to meet a range of monthly income needs from portfolios of varying sizes. An investor with an $800,000 portfolio can get $1,000 per month by taking cash at just a 1.5 percent annual rate, while someone with $150,000 invested needs to draw cash at an 8 percent rate

EXHIBIT 8.1

Distribution Rate Required to Meet Monthly Income Need

Annual Distribution Rate	$50,000	$100,000	$150,000	$200,000	$250,000	$300,000	$350,000	$400,000	$450,000	$500,000	$550,000	$600,000	$650,000	$700,000	$750,000	$800,000	$850,000	$900,000	$950,000	$1,000,000
							Amount Invested													
0.00%	$0	$0	$0	$0	$0	$0	$0	$0	$0	$0	$0	$0	$0	$0	$0	$0	$0	$0	$0	$0
0.25%	$10	$21	$31	$42	$52	$63	$73	$83	$94	$104	$115	$125	$135	$146	$156	$167	$177	$188	$198	$208
0.50%	$21	$42	$63	$83	$104	$125	$146	$167	$188	$208	$229	$250	$271	$292	$313	$333	$354	$375	$396	$417
0.75%	$31	$63	$94	$125	$156	$188	$219	$250	$281	$313	$344	$375	$406	$438	$469	$500	$531	$563	$594	$625
1.00%	$42	$83	$125	$167	$208	$250	$292	$333	$375	$417	$458	$500	$542	$583	$625	$667	$708	$750	$792	$833
1.25%	$52	$104	$156	$208	$260	$313	$365	$417	$469	$521	$573	$625	$677	$729	$781	$833	$885	$938	$990	$1,042
1.50%	$63	$125	$188	$250	$313	$375	$438	$500	$563	$625	$688	$750	$813	$875	$938	$1,000	$1,063	$1,125	$1,188	$1,250
1.75%	$73	$146	$219	$292	$365	$438	$510	$583	$656	$729	$802	$875	$948	$1,021	$1,094	$1,167	$1,240	$1,313	$1,385	$1,458
2.00%	$83	$167	$250	$333	$417	$500	$583	$667	$750	$833	$917	$1,000	$1,083	$1,167	$1,250	$1,333	$1,417	$1,500	$1,583	$1,667
2.25%	$94	$188	$281	$375	$469	$563	$656	$750	$844	$938	$1,031	$1,125	$1,219	$1,313	$1,406	$1,500	$1,594	$1,688	$1,781	$1,875
2.50%	$104	$208	$313	$417	$521	$625	$729	$833	$938	$1,042	$1,146	$1,250	$1,354	$1,458	$1,563	$1,667	$1,771	$1,875	$1,979	$2,083
2.75%	$115	$229	$344	$458	$573	$688	$802	$917	$1,031	$1,146	$1,260	$1,375	$1,490	$1,604	$1,719	$1,833	$1,948	$2,063	$2,177	$2,292
3.00%	$125	$250	$375	$500	$625	$750	$875	$1,000	$1,125	$1,250	$1,375	$1,500	$1,625	$1,750	$1,875	$2,000	$2,125	$2,250	$2,375	$2,500
3.25%	$135	$271	$406	$542	$677	$813	$948	$1,083	$1,219	$1,354	$1,490	$1,625	$1,760	$1,896	$2,031	$2,167	$2,302	$2,438	$2,573	$2,708
3.50%	$146	$292	$438	$583	$729	$875	$1,021	$1,167	$1,313	$1,458	$1,604	$1,750	$1,896	$2,042	$2,188	$2,333	$2,479	$2,625	$2,771	$2,917
3.75%	$156	$313	$469	$625	$781	$938	$1,094	$1,250	$1,406	$1,563	$1,719	$1,875	$2,031	$2,188	$2,344	$2,500	$2,656	$2,813	$2,969	$3,125
4.00%	$167	$333	$500	$667	$833	$1,000	$1,167	$1,333	$1,500	$1,667	$1,833	$2,000	$2,167	$2,333	$2,500	$2,667	$2,833	$3,000	$3,167	$3,333
4.25%	$177	$354	$531	$708	$885	$1,063	$1,240	$1,417	$1,594	$1,771	$1,948	$2,125	$2,302	$2,479	$2,656	$2,833	$3,010	$3,188	$3,365	$3,542
4.50%	$188	$375	$563	$750	$938	$1,125	$1,313	$1,500	$1,688	$1,875	$2,063	$2,250	$2,438	$2,625	2,813	$3,000	$3,188	$3,375	$3,563	$3,750
4.75%	$198	$396	$594	$792	$990	$1,188	$1,385	$1,583	$1,781	$1,979	$2,177	$2,375	$2,573	$2,771	$2,969	$3,167	$3,365	$3,563	$3,760	$3,958
5.00%	$208	$417	$625	$833	$1,042	$1,250	$1,458	$1,667	$1,875	$2,083	$2,292	$2,500	$2,708	$2,917	$3,125	$3,333	$3,542	$3,750	$3,958	$4,167
5.25%	$219	$438	$656	$875	$1,094	$1,313	$1,531	$1,750	$1,969	$2,188	$2,406	$2,625	$2,844	$3,063	$3,281	$3,500	$3,719	$3,938	$4,156	$4,375
5.50%	$229	$458	$688	$917	$1,146	$1,375	$1,604	$1,833	$2,063	$2,292	$2,521	$2,750	$2,979	$3,208	$3,438	$3,667	$3,896	$4,125	$4,354	$4,583
5.75%	$240	$479	$719	$958	$1,198	$1,438	$1,677	$1,917	$2,156	$2,396	$2,635	$2,875	$3,115	$3,354	$3,594	$3,833	$4,073	$4,313	$4,552	$4,792
6.00%	$250	$500	$750	$1,000	$1,250	$1,500	$1,750	$2,000	$2,250	$2,500	$2,750	$3,000	$3,250	$3,500	$3,750	$4,000	$4,250	$4,500	$4,750	$5,000
6.25%	$260	$521	$781	$1,042	$1,302	$1,563	$1,823	$2,083	$2,344	$2,604	$2,865	$3,125	$3,385	$3,646	$3,906	$4,167	$4,427	$4,688	$4,948	$5,208
6.50%	$271	$542	$813	$1,063	$1,354	$1,625	$1,896	$2,167	$2,438	$2,708	$2,979	$3,250	$3,521	$3,792	$4,063	$4,333	$4,604	$4,875	$5,146	$5,417
6.75%	$281	$563	$844	$1,125	$1,406	$1,688	$1,969	$2,250	$2,531	$2,813	$3,094	$3,375	$3,656	$3,938	$4,219	$4,500	$4,781	$5,063	$5,344	$5,625
7.00%	$292	$583	$875	$1,167	$1,458	$1,750	$2,042	$2,333	$2,625	$2,917	$3,208	$3,500	$3,792	$4,083	$4,375	$4,667	$4,958	$5,250	$5,542	$5,833
7.25%	$302	$604	$906	$1,208	$1,510	$1,813	$2,115	$2,417	$2,719	$3,021	$3,323	$3,625	$3,927	$4,229	$4,531	$4,833	$5,135	$5,438	$5,740	$6,042
7.50%	$313	$625	$938	$1,250	$1,563	$1,875	$2,188	$2,500	$2,813	$3,125	$3,438	$3,750	$4,063	$4,375	$4,688	$5,000	$5,313	$5,625	$5,938	$6,250
7.75%	$323	$646	$969	$1,292	$1,615	$1,938	$2,260	$2,583	$2,906	$3,229	$3,552	$3,875	$4,198	$4,521	$4,844	$5,167	$5,490	$5,813	$6,135	$6,458
8.00%	$333	$667	$1,000	$1,333	$1,667	$2,000	$2,333	$2,667	$3,000	$3,333	$3,667	$4,000	$4,333	$4,667	$5,000	$5,333	$5,667	$6,000	$6,333	$6,667
8.25%	$344	$688	$1,031	$1,375	$1,719	$2,063	$2,406	$2,750	$3,094	$3,438	$3,781	$4,125	$4,469	$4,813	$5,156	$5,500	$5,844	$6,188	$6,531	$6,875
8.50%	$354	$708	$1,063	$1,417	$1,771	$2,125	$2,479	$2,833	$3,188	$3,542	$3,896	$4,250	$4,604	$4,958	$5,313	$5,667	$6,021	$6,375	$6,729	$7,083
8.75%	$365	$729	$1,094	$1,458	$1,823	$2,188	$2,552	$2,917	$3,281	$3,646	$4,010	$4,375	$4,740	$5,104	$5,469	$5,833	$6,198	$6,563	$6,927	$7,292
9.00%	$375	$750	$1,125	$1,500	$1,875	$2,250	$2,625	$3,000	$3,375	$3,750	$4,125	$4,500	$4,875	$5,250	$5,625	$6,000	$6,375	$6,750	$7,125	$7,500
9.25%	$385	$771	$1,156	$1,542	$1,927	$2,313	$2,698	$3,083	$3,469	$3,854	$4,240	$4,625	$5,010	$5,396	$5,781	$6,167	$6,552	$6,938	$7,323	$7,708
9.50%	$396	$792	$1,188	$1,583	$1,979	$2,375	$2,771	$3,167	$3,563	$3,958	$4,354	$4,750	$5,146	$5,542	$5,938	$6,333	$6,729	$7,125	$7,521	$7,917
9.75%	$406	$813	$1,219	$1,625	$2,031	$2,438	$2,844	$3,250	$3,656	$4,063	$4,469	$4,875	$5,281	$5,688	$6,094	$6,500	$6,906	$7,313	$7,719	$8,125
10.00%	$417	$833	$1,250	$1,667	$2,083	$2,500	$2,917	$3,333	$3,750	$4,167	$4,583	$5,000	$5,417	$5,833	$6,250	$6,667	$7,083	$7,500	$7,917	$8,333

to pocket $1,000 per month. If prevailing rates are around 4 percent and you need to take 12 percent to make ends meet, you've got trouble. Your choices are to cut your expenses or shop at the high-yield end of the investment market where risks are greater. As the spread between what's reasonable and what's necessary grows, so does the likelihood of depleting a portfolio.

Those investors who don't need to take current income from their investments, or who have more than enough invested to meet their income needs, can focus on growing their portfolios. You'll still need to know your required rate of return—the total return you'll need to achieve, on average, to take you from where you are right now to where you want to be. Answering the following questions will help you to find your required rate of return.

- How much will your future goals cost once inflation is taken into account?
- How much have you accumulated so far?
- Where is the rest going to come from in the time you have remaining?
- Is there a rate of return you can reasonably expect that will help you get the job done, and can you actually achieve that return while staying within your comfort level?

Without the pressure of monthly withdrawals, investment income can be reinvested to provide for future income goals, inflation protection, or generational wealth creation. As part of your total return equation, the level of income you should be looking for can be matched to the distance in dollars you have to go to reach your goals and the risk you're prepared to assume to get there.

The description of your plan of action can be as simple as "Invest primarily in dividend-paying stocks," or as comprehensive as a complete summary of the details of your investment process. The key is to create a benchmark against which you can measure every investment decision you make to help you keep your plan on track.

Plan on reviewing your progress at predetermined intervals spaced at least one year apart. This is not the same as the process of regularly monitoring your securities. It's a chance to take a fresh look at your circumstances to see whether there have been any material changes in your income needs, time horizon, or risk tolerance. The purpose of this review is to make sure your plan of action still makes sense, given any changes in your situation, and to help you keep your overall investment experience tied to the long-term context of what you hope to achieve. This review is about you, not about the markets. The investment environment is always changing, and your plan of action already takes that kind of change into account. Be careful not to let what's going on right now in the investment markets alter your strategy.

Keep a historical perspective in mind. Big bull market advances don't last forever, and neither do major bear market declines. As long as your process is performing as you would expect under the circumstances and still meets your needs, your IPS should not require a major revision.

SETTING YOUR SCREENS

Now that you've determined your income need and/or required rate of return, you can start your screening process by limiting your candidate pool to those stocks meeting an appropriate minimum dividend yield for you.

Dividend Yield

Even if you don't currently require any income, we recommend requiring a stock to have a minimum yield to pass your screen. This will put you in position to capture the advantages of dividend investing for growth investors described in Chapter 5. Typically, we'd be looking for stocks with yields at least 1.5 times higher than the yield of the S&P 500. There can be times when yields reach unusually high or low levels, during which you may have to adjust your target to something that seems reasonable given the circumstances. At a minimum, though, we would generally recommend considering only stocks with yields at least equal to that of the S&P 500 Index. The highest-yielding stocks have tended to be concentrated in a few industries. This could change, however, as more companies move to take advantage of the improved tax treatment of dividends and boost their payouts to investors. A list of industries sorted by their yield as of March 2010 appears in Exhibit 8.2.

There are, of course, many fine companies that either don't pay a dividend or pay dividends that are too small to pass through this screen. For all the reasons we've already discussed, however,

EXHIBIT 8.2

Dividend Yield, by Industry

Industry Name	Dividend Yield (Indicated Rate)	Industry Name	Dividend Yield (Indicated Rate)	Industry Name	Dividend Yield (Indicated Rate)
CHEMS-COMMODITY	20.9	AUTOMOBILE MFRS	2.0	REGIONAL BANKS	1.0
PHOTOGRAPHIC PRODS	8.4	PAPER PRODUCTS	2.0	MULTI-SECTOR HLDGS	1.0
INTEG TELECOM SVC	6.6	HOUSEWARES & SPECS	2.0	OIL & GAS-EQUIP/SVC	1.0
SERVICES-OFFICE/SUPP	5.3	PUBLISHING	2.0	HC-EQUIPMENT	1.0
SPECIALIZED REITS	5.1	ALUMINUM	1.9	HC-DISTRIBUTORS	1.0
TOBACCO	5.1	PERSONAL PRODUCTS	1.9	ELECTRONIC COMPONENT	0.9
COMMERCIAL PRINTING	5.1	HYPRMKTS & SUPRCNTRS	1.9	CABLE & SATELLITE	0.8
HOME FURNISHINGS	4.9	GAS UTILITIES	1.8	RETAIL REITS	0.8
ELECTRIC UTILITIES	4.8	HOUSEHOLD APPLIANCES	1.8	DIVERSE FIN'L SVC	0.8
INDUSTRIAL REITS	4.6	STEEL	1.8	TIRES & RUBBER	0.8
MULTI-UTILITIES	4.4	RAILROADS	1.8	DEPARTMENT STORES	0.8
THRIFTS&MORTGAGE FIN	4.2	AGRICULTURAL PRODUCT	1.8	INV BANK & BROKERAGE	0.8
DISTRIBUTORS	4.0	IT CONSULTING & SVC	1.8	GOLD	0.8
DIVERSIFIED REITS	3.7	RESIDENTIAL REITS	1.7	CASINOS & GAMING	0.7
SPECIAL CONSM SERV	3.6	INSURANCE-LIFE/HLTH	1.7	OIL & GAS-EXPL/PROD	0.7
IND'L CONGLOMERATES	3.4	OFFICE ELECTRONICS	1.7	HOMEBUILDING	0.7
PHARMACEUTICALS	3.3	MACHINERY INDUSTRIAL	1.7	COMPUTER HARDWARE	0.7
FOOD DISTRIBUTORS	3.3	TRADE COS & DISTR	1.6	HC-SUPPLIES	0.6
CHEMS-DIVERSE	3.2	AUTO PARTS & EQUIP	1.6	COAL & CONSUME FUELS	0.6
WATER UTILITIES	3.2	SPECIALIZED FINANCE	1.6	CONSTRU & ENGINEER	0.6
CONSTRUCTION MATRLS	3.2	REINSURANCE	1.6	INSURANCE-MULTI-LINE	0.6
OIL & GAS-REF NG/MKTG	3.2	RETAIL-FOOD	1.6	HC-FACILITY	0.6
DIVERSIFIED SUPP SER	3.1	WIRELSS TELECOM SVC	1.5	HEALTH CARE TECH	0.5
BUILDING PRODUCTS	3.1	SEMICONDUCTOR EQUIP	1.5	COMMUNICATIONS EQUIP	0.5
PACKAGED FOODS/MEATS	3.0	CHEMS-SPECIALTY	1.5	SECURITY & ALARM SER	0.4
OIL & GAS-STORAGE	2.9	CONSUMER FINANCE	1.5	HOTEL/RESORT/CRUISE	0.3
LEISURE PRODUCTS	2.9	RETAIL-APPAREL	1.5	CONTAIN METAL/GLASS	0.3
OFFICE REITS	2.8	FOOTWEAR	1.5	LEISURE FACILITIES	0.2
OIL & GAS-INTEGRATED	2.8	MOTORCYCLE MFRS	1.5	OIL & GAS-DRILLING	0.2
TRUCKING	2.7	DIVERSIFIED BANKS	1.4	AIRLINES	0.2
HOUSEHOLD PRODUCTS	2.7	FOREST PRODUCTS	1.4	ELECTRONIC EQUIPMENT	0.2
SOFT DRINKS	2.7	DISTILLER & VINTNERS	1.4	EDUCATION SERVICES	0.1
SERVICES-ENVIRONMNTL	2.7	BROADCASTING	1.4	LIFE SCIENCE TOOLS	0.1
ELECTRICAL COMPONENT	2.6	INDPENDENT POWR PROD	1.3	CONSUMER ELECTRONICS	0.1
PAPER PACKAGING	2.6	CHEMS-AGRI/FERTILIZR	1.3	HC-MANAGED CARE	0.1
INSURANCE-BROKERS	2.5	SYSTEMS SOFTWARE	1.3	HC-SERVICES	0.1
RESTAURANTS	2.5	SPECIALTY STORES	1.3	APPLICATION SOFTWARE	0.1
RETAIL-HOME IMPROVE	2.3	MARINE	1.2	AUTOMOTIVE RETAIL	0.0
INSURANCE-PROP/CAS	2.2	ASSET MANAGEMENT	1.2	HOMEFURNISHING RETL	0.0
BREWERS	2.2	ADVERTISING	1.2	RETAIL-INTERNET	0.0
AEROSPACE/DEFENSE	2.2	RESEARCH & CONSLTING	1.2	INTRNET SOFTWR & SVC	0.0
DIVERSE METAL/MINING	2.2	SERVICES-DATA PROC	1.2	COMPU STORAGE/PERIPH	0.0
ELECTRONIC MNFRG SVC	2.2	GENERAL MERCHANDISE	1.2	REAL ESTATE DEVELOP	0.0
MACHINERY CONST/FARM	2.1	MOVIES & ENTMT	1.2	HOME ENTMT SOFTWARE	0.0
INDUSTRIAL GASES	2.1	RETAIL-COMP/ELECTRN	1.2	REAL ESTATE SERVICES	0.0
AIRFRGHT & LOGISTICS	2.1	SERVICES-EMPLOYMENT	1.1	BIOTECHNOLOGY	0.0
SEMICONDUCTORS	2.1	APPAREL & ACCESSORY	1.1	TECHNOLOGY DISTRIB	0.0
S&P 500	2.0	RETAIL-DRUGS	1.1		

Source: Thomson Baseline.

this process will focus on building a dividend-based portfolio. (Feel free to hold onto the names of any particularly compelling stocks you come across, though. One or two might find a place in the tactical portion of your portfolio, as described in later chapters.)

A stock's dividend yield is an easy number to find and is often listed with a stock's price in the newspaper. It's simply the annual dividend per share divided by the share price. It has a familiar feel because it's similar in concept to the *interest rate* offered by other income-producing alternatives like bonds and savings accounts. Of course, there are significant differences between dividend yields and interest rates. As described in Chapter 7, dividends are not guaranteed, and a stock's dividend yield will vary as both its price and dividend payment amounts change. A very high yield could be the result of either an extremely generous dividend—or a big drop in a security's price. Still, yield is an easily understood measure of the rate at which your invested cash is producing income for you.

The overall yield requirement of your portfolio should serve as a kind of "middle ground" as you plan your minimum yield screen. Since higher-yielding stocks tend to have different strengths, weaknesses, and prospects than lower-yielding stocks, you can improve the diversity of your portfolio by allowing for some of each in your candidate list.

Dividend Safety

You don't want to purchase a security on the basis of its dividend only to have the dividend cut or eliminated shortly after your purchase. A company might have valid reasons to cut the dividend—from exploring new investment opportunities to assuring its very survival. Still, cuts are often a sign of trouble.

How can you measure the likelihood that the dividend of a company on your list will be sustained? We look for a *dividend coverage ratio* of 1.2—that is, 120 percent cash flow coverage of the annual dividend amount. This means that for every $1 of dividend, the company has $1.20 of cash flow. In Chapter 7 we explained how to calculate this ratio: we divided the cash flow per share by the annual dividend per share. We don't want the company to have to borrow to pay the dividend, so we want at least that much of a cushion. Be sure to keep track of your ratio for all the stocks that meet the test; this measure becomes a standard later on in the stock selection process.

The Veto List

Stocks on your "veto list" are excluded from consideration even if they meet all of your other criteria. The reason a particular security may not be a comfortable choice for you could be personal or analytical. There are as many reasons to genuinely object to a particular industry or company as there are individuals with strongly held beliefs. Tobacco companies; defense contractors; meat packing plants; big oil companies; chemical companies; drug companies; and companies considered insensitive to women's issues, equal rights issues, and religious issues are common targets of investors' objections.

Perhaps you had a bad experience with a company or one of its products. Your firsthand observation may give you an early insight into problems that are not yet widely understood by other investors.

Maybe you work for a company that appears in your list and already own its stock in your 401(k) or other company-sponsored plan. Even if you don't own any of its stock, you might quite reasonably conclude that your financial future is already tied so closely to your company's fortunes that you don't want to increase your exposure further by buying its shares for your portfolio.

There may be a significant risk to a company's future that's not reflected in its numbers, such as a litigation risk. Asbestos liability has driven companies out of business. A massive judgment in one of the many lawsuits brought against tobacco companies could wipe out your investment. Any circumstance that could allow a single verdict to put a company out of business is a very disconcerting risk.

You may want to temporarily add a company to your veto list if you've recently sold its shares at a loss in a taxable account, so you don't trigger "wash sale" rules by buying it back again within 30 days. (A wash sale occurs when a security is purchased within 30 days of its sale, causing the loss to be disallowed for tax purposes.)

Security Types

While it's possible to make the case for including a broad variety of securities in your portfolio, there are a few types that, while they may meet the other screens we've reviewed, may still not be well suited to your final list of candidates.

Stocks with extremely low prices—generally trading for less than $5 per share—are often called "penny stocks" and would not make our list of serious candidates. There have been too many scandals and scams perpetrated on investors in some of these issues to risk taking a chance here. The market meltdown from October 2007 to March 2009 made penny stocks out of some former blue chip stocks. Some have recovered, but others have become worthless. There are said to be exceptions to every rule, but when there are so many good choices that meet our criteria, we'd rather not spend valuable research time looking among the penny stocks for the exceptions.

A search for high-yielding equities is sure to turn up a lot of *preferred stocks*. Offered extensively by utilities, banks, auto manufacturers, and other mature companies, preferred stocks behave more like bonds than stocks. The dividend rate is set, and owners of preferred stocks rarely participate in the growth of a company the way owners of common stock do. The screening process described in this book is intended to uncover stocks with the prospects for both dividend growth and share price appreciation, so we'll exclude preferred stocks from the candidate list.

Real estate investment trusts (REITs) also usually offer attractive yields, but because of the particular tax rules that apply to them, their dividends do not qualify for the low tax rates other dividends enjoy. To the extent their high yields make their dividends comparable to qualifying stock dividends on an after-tax basis, they may be acceptable. Real estate has been at the center of a market storm that's raged over a significant portion of the time since the change in the tax treatment of dividends took effect, so it's been difficult to tell what part of REITs' performance has been due to their tax disadvantage and what has been due to problems in the sector. We would put this group aside for the time being, until the effect of their tax treatment on their relative appeal becomes clearer. Of course, future changes in tax law could necessitate a reevaluation of the merits of REITs relative to other dividend payers.

Finally, there are two additional types of securities that could present some problems that should be carefully weighed before you decide to include either in your list of investments: small companies and master limited partnerships (MLPs).

Because they have relatively little trading activity in the market, the stocks of very small companies sometimes prove to be difficult to buy and sell. The limited interest in their shares may cause prices to rise as you try to buy and fall as you try to sell. Worse yet, you could find yourself unable to sell the stock of particularly small companies at virtually any price when you decide to get out. Financial information could be hard to find, and the research you're looking for might not exist.

Although they are a kind of partnership and not corporations, a number of MLPs trade on the major stock exchanges, and many offer very attractive yields. Like REITs, however, MLPs are subject to special tax considerations, including rules that may make some of the income they provide taxable in an IRA or pension account.

With the exception of penny stocks, there could be a place in your investment portfolio for any of these security types, but we wouldn't include them in your candidate list of dividend-paying stocks.

ENDNOTE

1. A qualified financial planner can help you with these and other financial calculations and also help to coordinate your investment needs with your tax situation, insurance needs, estate plan, and other important areas of your financial life.

CHAPTER 9

Laying the Foundation

Well begun is half done.

—*Aristotle*

THE BLUEPRINT

To be successful at building just about anything, it's important to start with a good idea of what it's supposed to look like when it's done. The very idea of making a huge investment of time and money to build a house without at least some basic plan or blueprint seems a little silly, and not many people would give such an effort much chance of success. Yet it's amazing how many investors take their life savings and cobble a portfolio together without giving any thought to what its design should look like.

Investing with only the idea of making money is like building a house with nothing more to go on than the notion of "providing shelter." You might end up with something, but it probably won't be what you want or need.

There are a host of considerations to examine before drafting your investment plan:

- How much time do you have before retirement?
- How much money have you saved?
- How much risk are you prepared to assume to achieve your goals?

- How much money will you need to accumulate to achieve your goals?
- How much do you need to add to your portfolio to make up any shortfall?
- Where is that money going to come from?

Caution

Answering these kinds of questions is critical to your long-term success as an investor. We recommend enlisting the help of a trained professional to assist you in finding the answers that apply to your situation and refer interested readers to the Certified Financial Planner Board of Standards, Inc.,[1] for information about finding a CFP practitioner in your area (800–487–1497 or www.cfp.net).

For the purpose of this book, we'll assume that a dividend-based portfolio makes sense in your situation for some portion of your investment assets. What will the dividend portfolio look like when it's finished? It will

- Provide a stream of dividend income sufficient to meet your current income and/or long-term growth goals
- Use securities with different strengths to enhance the opportunity for success while providing diversification to promote safety
- Operate with a system of safeguards to help limit the risk of unacceptable losses

We find a particularly effective way of building a portfolio is to use a "tier" design. By carefully organizing the portfolio into predefined sections, it's much easier to prevent the entire collection from drifting in unintended directions and to keep it on track to produce the intended outcome. Of course, you can vary the design to meet your particular needs and the size of your account, but this template is a good place to start. The model dividend-based portfolio consists of four tiers:

1. Cash
2. Dividend payers
3. Tactical choices
4. Noncorrelating assets

EXHIBIT 9.1

Dividend Portfolio Design

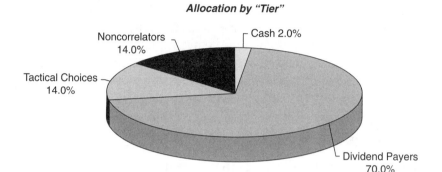

Allocation by "Tier"

The exact size of each tier may vary, depending on how much you have to invest, but Exhibit 9.1 provides a guide to the basic design of the portfolio.

THE CASH TIER

Depending on the size of the account, this tier should be approximately 2 to 5 percent of your dividend-based portfolio. By cash, we mean any cash equivalent that can be used without notice to meet the short-term needs of the portfolio. This function is most often served by the money market or "sweep" cash portion of the brokerage account. It will be available to pay any miscellaneous account costs such as custodial or brokerage fees, wire transfer fees, and trading costs.

Cash provides a place to receive and hold dividends until they can be reinvested or distributed from the account. For income investors, cash can help you create a regular monthly income as opposed to simply taking dividends as they happen to be paid. Since companies tend to pay dividends quarterly, and on varying schedules, an investor taking dividends as they are paid might face months of "feast or famine," not to mention being inundated with many small dividend checks in the mail. A much more manageable approach is to leave enough cash in the account to cover three months' worth of your monthly income need and take regular monthly payments equal to about one-third the total dividend expected to be paid by all the securities you own over the course of the coming quarter.

Cash also helps to provide some latitude as you plan your trading activities. You don't have to worry about a slight miscalculation of the commission cost or a small fluctuation in price as long as you have a little extra cash in the account.

Cash is not intended to serve as your "emergency fund," which is often recommended to be three to six months of your fixed expenses. We assume that store of ready cash is held elsewhere.

THE DIVIDEND PAYERS TIER

This tier contains the securities that have met your screens and produce dividend income. It constitutes the bulk of the portfolio and should represent about 70 percent of the account. We recommend cutting this piece of the pie into five equal slices:

1. Value
2. Growth
3. Quality
4. Yield
5. Overall best

Each of these slices will represent approximately 14 percent of the portfolio. (See Exhibit 9.2.) The number of securities in each slice will depend on the overall size of your account—usually from one to five stocks per slice. (In Chapter 10, we'll review how to choose the right number of stocks for your portfolio.) Each slice

EXHIBIT 9.2

Dividend Portfolio Design: Allocation within the Dividend Payers Tier

Allocation by "Tier"

Noncorrelators 14.00%
Tactical Choices 14.00%
Cash 2.00%
Dividend Payers 70.00%

Dividend Payers

Overall 14.00%
Value 14.00%
Yield 14.00%
Quality 14.00%
Growth 14.00%

should have different standards to help assure that you include stocks with a variety of strengths. Since dividend-paying stocks have a tendency to respond in very similar ways to changes in the economy, interest rates, and the market, using candidates from various industries and with different attributes can enhance diversification and therefore help to reduce your risk.

The standards you use for each slice may be absolute and unforgiving in some instances, such as minimum measures of financial stability, but they should also be considered relative to what's normal in the industries of the securities being ranked. Low-growth companies in mature industries, such as utilities, are likely to have dramatically different characteristics than those of higher-growth companies, such as those in the pharmaceutical sector. Failure to adjust for these differences will almost certainly lead your process to deliver a portfolio concentrated in a single area of the investment landscape. Without awareness of the norms for an industry, you might believe you have found an exceptional value in absolute terms, when in fact you have a company that is expensive by that very standard relative to similar companies in the same industry.

Value

Value stocks tend to be out of favor with investors, often for a very good reason. Maybe business in their particular industry is down, or the regulatory or legal climate is challenging. Sometimes, however, the conditions depressing the stock's price are temporary, or reflect a simple lack of enthusiasm about a group of stocks relative to other more exciting alternatives.

A good value is something you can buy for less than it is actually worth. While that shouldn't be possible in the theoretical world of "rational" investors, experience suggests that investors aren't always rational. They sometimes overpay for a stock (recall any one of the many tragic Internet and tech stories) and sometimes don't understand value when they see it. (As discussed in Chapter 5, Vincent van Gogh couldn't sell his work during his lifetime.)

So how can an investor assess the relative merits of the candidates on his or her list? A good place to start is to remember that each share of stock represents ownership of a piece of a business. This suggests that two things should be very important to a stock buyer: How good is the business I am buying? How big a piece do I get for my money?

To make the point, imagine you've been offered a chance to buy into an ideal vacation property in a great location with all the amenities you could ask for. Although you couldn't afford this on your own, by sharing the cost and use with others, the price comes to about your annual vacation budget. It looks like the perfect investment for you until you find out that, because of the number of total partners, your turn amounts to 1 hour and 20 minutes every March 6 from 3 to 4:20 a.m.! This otherwise great buy is a terrible deal because it costs too much for the piece you're getting.

Many stock "values" have the same kind of problem. If a stock costs just $5 per share, but you're getting only a penny's worth of profit value, it's not a good deal—even if the business is thriving.

One measure investors use in their search for value is a stock's price relative to its 52-week high and low. The thinking is that a stock that traded at $70 per share at its 52-week high and now trades at just $40 per share at or near its 52-week low is a value. While this may be a useful flag for identifying possible values, it could have some serious drawbacks if used alone in your security selection. The stock may cost less today because it's actually worth less, or maybe it was never really worth $70 in the first place, and investors are finally waking up to that fact.

Example: On December 20, 1999, Lucent closed at $72.58. Just over seven months later, on July 24, 2000, it had tumbled to a 52-week low of $44.37, a decline of nearly 39 percent. Surely it represented a great value at this price. Unfortunately for investors who took the plunge on the basis of this perceived "value," Lucent's stock continued plunging. By October 11, 2002, it hit a low of $0.58— exactly $72 lower than its price of nearly three years earlier. For investors who held Lucent stock from $72.58, the loss amounted to 99.2 percent of their investment. Investors who bought at the value price of $44.37 lost "only" 98.69 percent of their money! In either case, that's pretty much all their money, so the 52-week low didn't turn out to be much of a value measure after all. On April 2, 2006, Lucent announced that it would merge with Alcatel. Under the terms of the deal, Lucent shareholders received 0.1952 shares of the merged company for every share of Lucent owned. Based on the price of Alcatel stock at the time of the merger, this turned out to be worth about $2.59 for each Lucent share. That was a nice jump from $0.58 cents, but it would have needed to be about 2,700 percent higher to get an investor back to the $72.58 value. How has

Alcatel-Lucent done since the merger? From the end of 2006 to the close of 2009, the shares have fallen from $14.22 to $3.32, which represents about $0.65 per original Lucent share.

Rather than focus on price alone, we prefer to use measures of value that relate the price of a stock to some measure of how the company is performing as a business. There are many to choose from, but we recommend two tried-and-true favorites: the price-to-earnings ratio (P/E) and the price-to-sales ratio (P/S). As demonstrated in Chapter 7, these ratios measure a stock's price relative to its earnings or its sales. In the simplest terms, they show a prospective investor how many years' worth of one share's earnings (or sales) it would cost to buy a single share of a company's stock.

Example: If a stock had a price of $10 and earnings of $1, it would have a P/E of 10. An investor would have to pay 10 years' worth of a share's earnings to buy a share of stock in this company. A $10 stock with a P/E of 20 is earning only 50 cents per share and, by this measure, would be twice as expensive as the other $10 stock, since it would cost the investor 20 years' worth of earnings to buy it. The lower the P/E, the cheaper the stock—not necessarily in dollar terms, but in terms of this measure of its value.

How could such a large difference in value exist? P/E ratios are based on the current price and current earnings. (Analysts use either the last year's earnings or a forecast of next year's earnings in the calculation.) If a company's earnings are expected to grow quickly over the years, then this higher expected future earnings stream is considered by buyers to be worth a higher price up front.

Exhibit 9.3 shows the implied future prices of two $10 stocks with differing earnings growth rates, assuming they continue to sell at whatever prices keep their P/E ratios unchanged (at 10 for the slow grower and at 20 for the fast grower). The "expensive" $10 fast grower could look pretty cheap 10 years from now when compared to the slow grower, even if it costs twice as much relative to earnings today. Notice that even though the fast grower's earnings don't actually catch up to the slow grower's earnings until year 15, by then the stock is worth twice as much. The faster growth rate and the expected effect on future prices are driving the price, not the actual level of earnings.

EXHIBIT 9.3

Slow Grower versus Fast Grower

Year	Slow Grower		Fast Grower	
	P/E: 10		P/E: 20	
	Growth: 5%		Growth: 10%	
	Earnings	**Price**	**Earnings**	**Price**
0	$1.00	$10.00	$0.50	$10.00
1	$1.05	$10.50	$0.55	$11.00
2	$1.10	$11.03	$0.61	$12.10
3	$1.16	$11.58	$0.67	$13.31
4	$1.22	$12.16	$0.73	$14.64
5	$1.28	$12.76	$0.81	$16.11
6	$1.34	$13.40	$0.89	$17.72
7	$1.41	$14.07	$0.97	$19.49
8	$1.48	$14.77	$1.07	$21.44
9	$1.55	$15.51	$1.18	$23.58
10	**$1.63**	**$16.29**	**$1.30**	**$25.94**
11	$1.71	$17.10	$1.43	$28.53
12	$1.80	$17.96	$1.57	$31.38
13	$1.89	$18.86	$1.73	$34.52
14	$1.98	$19.80	$1.90	$37.97
15	**$2.08**	**$20.79**	**$2.09**	**$41.77**
16	$2.18	$21.83	$2.30	$45.95
17	$2.29	$22.92	$2.53	$50.54
18	$2.41	$24.07	$2.78	$55.60
19	$2.53	$25.27	$3.06	$61.16
20	$2.65	$26.53	$3.36	$67.27

The problem, of course, is that the expected future often has a way of being very different from the future that actually happens. If the lofty expectations priced into a high P/E stock aren't met, the price tends to take a bigger hit than if expectations were more modest.

One of the advantages of the P/E ratio (or simply "multiple," as in "The stock is selling at a multiple of 18") is that it's very easy to find. Many newspapers publish this number daily, right alongside the price.

Since earnings equal revenue minus expenses, earnings improvements can come from rising revenue *or* from cutting costs, closing plants, laying off employees, or changing pension plan assumptions. As we have unfortunately learned, earnings can also be manipulated by underhanded accounting and corporate malfeasance. While any number can be falsified, companies are ultimately in the business of selling something, and if sales are falling, it's a good thing to know.

Sales reside squarely on the revenue side of the ledger, and so, while it's a little harder to find, the P/S ratio provides a good second opinion about the value of a business relative to its ability to make money for its owners. (For a more detailed discussion of the merits of the P/S ratio, see James P. O'Shaughnessy's *What Works on Wall Street*, McGraw-Hill, 2005.)

Growth

The next slice of the dividend payers tier should be focused on stocks with strong prospects for growth. Like all the other slices in the dividend payers tier, this slice should be approximately 14 percent of your account's value. Whether you're investing for growth or income, in order to improve your standard of living you have to be able to outpace inflation. Steady dividends are great; growing dividends are better. Investing in companies with growing businesses can help.

Of course, true growth stocks tend to reinvest their spare cash in an effort to build the business, rather than pay dividends to the shareholders. Perhaps this will change as tax laws and demographic trends provide new incentives for companies at every stage of their evolution to pay dividends in order to attract capital.

To find dividend stocks with relatively strong growth prospects, we once again look at earnings and sales, but this time we're looking for their growth rate over the last 12 months rather than their ratio to the stock's price. Price/earnings and price/sales ratios can point to value, but rising earnings and sales can point to growth. Companies that are growing earnings and sales are likely to show strong stock performance over time, and those that are already paying out a portion of the profits as dividends might be in a position to give the shareholders a raise by regularly boosting the dividend.

We prefer to look at the last 12 months rather than at forecasted growth rates. Forecasts don't always work out—or business could be picking up, and that may not be reflected yet in the data. Even if the forecast is sound, the price may keep falling anyway, so you don't have to be the first one in line to try to catch the falling safe. If the trend is solid and persists, you'll have plenty of time to benefit from a company's superior growth.

Yield

Your screening process should leave you with plenty of stocks with fairly high payouts, so it shouldn't be too hard to find a few stocks for the 14 percent of the dividend payers' tier that offer a generous yield. The object here is to find stocks that not only have high dividends, but that have high dividends with an excellent chance of *actually being paid*. A high yield has some obvious advantages, such as more income for investors who need it, a bigger cushion against price decline, and a potential boost to total return even if share prices stagnate. High yields in this slice also give you the flexibility to allow other stocks with other advantages but lower yields into the rest of the portfolio without compromising your overall income goal.

Since yield equals dividend divided by price, unusually high yields can be the result of either rising payouts or falling prices. A $10 stock that pays a $0.50 annual dividend has a yield of 5 percent (0.50 divided by 10). If the price stays at $10 and the dividendis hiked to $0.75, the yield rises to 7.5 percent. The yield will also rise to 7.5 percent if the dividend stays at $0.50 but the price falls to $6.67.

Prices may be under pressure if investors are expecting the dividend to be cut, or if they're expecting some other bad news to follow shortly. To the extent that this perception is incorrect, a high yield can be another expression of value. In these cases, investors are "paid to wait" for the company to turn its fortunes around. The key is to find high-yielding stocks that

- Are not actually in the process of going out of business, and
- Have the cash flow and financial resources to continue paying the high dividend you're hoping to collect.

To zero in on stocks that fit this profile, we revisit a measure that served as one of the screens, but here we use it as a standard to rank our candidates. We require sufficient cash flow per share to cover 120 percent of the annual dividend; the more cash flow we find to cover the dividend, the more comfortable we are investing in a high-yield stock. We call this measure the dividend coverage ratio. While a dividend cut is still a possibility in these cases, the extra 20 percent cash flow cushion gives us some confidence that an immediate cut isn't likely.

The payout ratio, or the percentage of a company's earnings that are paid out as dividends, should be less than 100 percent. Remember, since earnings can be (and often are) affected by non-cash items, this ratio is not the same as cash flow coverage. It is, however, another indication of a company's likely decision about future dividend payments. While we like to see some room for companies to increase their payout ratio, a reasonably high ratio is not reason enough to discard a candidate, since it can indicate a company's commitment to the policy of paying dividends.

Quality

Although it might not be a strictly accurate name for this slice of the dividend payers tier, quality does capture the overall feel of the securities chosen for this 14 percent slice of the portfolio. The specific quality being evaluated here is financial strength, as measured by how much debt a company has to handle and how that debt service is likely to affect the company's ability to pay—and raise—its dividend.

The need to be able to pay one's bills is a very familiar pressure for many of us. People whose monthly expenses match their monthly incomes can certainly get by, but without any extra left over, they need every dime to keep the wolf away from the door.

An interruption of their income because of a layoff or an uninsured disability, for example, could cause them to start burning through savings. If their income dries up long enough, it could lead to major lifestyle changes or even bankruptcy.

Even if the income eventually resumes, it could take a long time for them to restore their lifestyle and build up their savings again. A neighbor with low expenses relative to her resources may be able to withstand a shock to income without drastically altering her lifestyle. In the same way, companies with manageable debt service and savings on hand may be able to withstand economic shocks or adverse business developments without having to cut the dividend.

Financially strong companies often use their superior staying power to take advantage of hard times by expanding in ways their competitors simply cannot afford to, permanently improving their position in their industry. We look for this kind of quality in companies with a high annual quick ratio. We also look for a high value in something we call the *operating cash flow to short-term debt ratio* (*ops cf/st debt*). As discussed in Chapter 7, the *quick ratio* is calculated by removing inventory from current assets and then dividing by current liabilities. Dividing a company's cash flow from operations by its short-term debt provides ops cf/st debt, the other financial quality ratio.

Overall Best

The final 14 percent slice of the dividend payers tier is probably the most important. In fact, if you have to limit your choices because of the size of your portfolio, these *overall best* selections are the place to start. As you rank your candidates by the various standards for value, growth, yield, and quality, you will probably notice a few stocks near the top of each list, but not high enough to be the best pick in any one slice. These are your "decathletes."

The decathlon is an event, or rather a series of 10 track and field events. Decathletes are often considered to be among the best overall athletes, and yet many famous competitors took home the Olympic gold medal without winning more than a few of the events. Jim Thorpe won four events for his gold in 1912; Bruce Jenner won with just three first-place finishes in Montreal in 1976. In both 1920 (Helge Lovland) and 1960 (Rafer Johnson), the gold medalists finished first in only one event! The key to winning is placing high in all the events, which requires a terrific combination of speed, strength, and agility. (See David Wallechinsky's *The Complete Book of the Olympics*, Aurum Press, 2008.)

Your overall best choices will be solid on the basis of every standard and quality you're looking for. They are the well-rounded securities that, without this slice of the tier, might not find their way into your portfolio at all. Just as the decathlete can win without finishing first in every event, these stocks could bring home the gold for your portfolio.

THE TACTICAL CHOICES TIER

When we think of strategy, we think of careful and often detailed plans designed to position us for long-term success. Tactics, on the other hand, suggest observing changing conditions and adapting plans to capitalize on current opportunities as they unfold. The overall strategy of a dividend investor is to harvest the long-term benefits from a portfolio centered on income-producing stocks. Including a tactical tier in the design allows you the flexibility to profit from changing circumstances. Approximately 14 percent of your portfolio should be allocated to this tier.

Good tactical choices may become obvious to you as you conduct your ongoing screening and ranking process. Or they could come to light in the course of your reading, or surprise you by showing up in completely unexpected ways. In every case, though, you should have compelling evidence that the opportunity you see is likely to be real, and you should have an exit plan to protect your gains once the tactical advantage has run its course.

One segment of the investment universe with many of the "familiar friends" we've followed for years became particularly interesting in October 2002. Utilities had long been thought of as very conservative (and even boring) investments, but ones that provided a consistently high and reliable stream of dividend income. That all changed as the effects of deregulation began to spread through the industry in the wake of the Energy Policy Act of 1992. Utilities began to branch out, introducing telecommunications and energy-trading ventures. Dividend payments often stopped growing as utilities used their cash to fund their transformation from mature companies into growth companies.

The prospect of new growth opportunities initially seemed exciting to investors. (This was the 1990s, after all.) The California power crisis and the fraud that led to the failure of Enron soon changed all that. Investors bailed out of the sector in droves, and stock prices plummeted. For those companies that were able to maintain most of their dividend, these lower prices meant unusually high yields.

From 1984 to 2001, the yield on the Dow Jones Utilities Index (DJU) averaged about 1 percent lower than the yield on the 10-year Treasury bond. Yields for both have risen and fallen, of course, but the DJU yields have generally been below those of the T-bond. By late October 2002, however, the DJU yield exceeded the yield on the Treasuries by more than 2 percent—a big departure from the historical relationship. Of course, the stock market as a whole was hitting bear market lows in October, but it seemed unlikely that all these utilities would go under, leaving us to shiver through that winter in the dark.

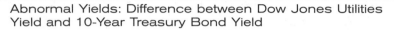

EXHIBIT 9.4

Abnormal Yields: Difference between Dow Jones Utilities
Yield and 10-Year Treasury Bond Yield

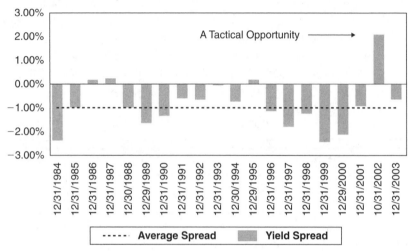

Source: Thomson Baseline.

After hitting a low of 183.66 on October 11, 2002, the Dow
Jones Utility Index moved sharply higher over the next few
months, reaching 255 on June 16, 2003—a gain of 38.8 percent! The
broad market moved higher as well, with the S&P 500 jumping
21 percent over that same time period. Still, the stodgy old DJU
gained nearly twice that much while producing a nice dividend
stream as well. Those hefty gains, together with a rise in interest
rates, brought the DJU yield back below 10-year Treasury yields.
(See Exhibit 9.4)

While the long-term attractiveness of utilities may have
remained, the tactical opportunity seemed to have passed. (In fact,
from June 16, 2003, through December 31, 2003, the DJU appreciated 4.7 percent, a little less than half the 10 percent gain in the S&P
500 over that period.)

The securities chosen for this tier may or may not share the
same basic attributes of your dividend payers. For example, real
estate investment trusts (REITs) often sport a high dividend yield,
but because of their special structure and tax treatment, their dividends do not enjoy the benefit of taxation at the capital gains
rate. Still, we have used REITs as tactical choices when they
seemed attractive. The S&P Energy Sector lagged the broader

market for much of 2003, gaining only 7.6 percent versus the S&P 500's gain of 20.3 percent through the end of November. This group jumped 13.8 percent in December, however, versus a gain of 5.1 percent in the S&P for a gain of 22.4 percent for the year. Your tactical choices might not even pay significant dividends. Small companies tend not to be big on dividends, as they reinvest their cash to support their growth, but as a group they often lead the way out of recession and significant market declines. In 2003, the Russell 2000 (a small-company index) gained 45.4 percent. On the other hand, the S&P Pharmaceutical industry group gained only 6.4 percent in 2003, compared to the S&P 500's gain of 26.4 percent. A similar pattern emerged as stocks climbed out of their depths in 2009. From March 9 to the end of the year, the Russell 2000 soared 82.2 percent versus gains of 64.8 percent for the S&P 500 and 40.2 percent for the Pharmaceutical group.

NONCORRELATOR TIER

If everything in your portfolio is moving in the same direction at the same time, you've probably done something wrong. It might feel great when it's all going up, but when it's all going down—especially if it's all going down year after year—the experience could serve you a bigger helping of investor risk than you're able to digest. The classic solution to the problem of investments that move too much in tandem is diversification.

But if we've already built a portfolio with a little cash, a variety of dividend stocks (with differing value, growth, high yield, quality, and overall strengths), and some interesting tactical choices, aren't we sufficiently diversified? In a word, no. The cash tier at 2 to 5 percent of the portfolio is too small to make a meaningful difference.

Having a collection of dividend stocks certainly helps mitigate the risk of problems with any one of them, but many of the companies that pay high dividends are susceptible to the same risks—and, after all, they're all stocks. There's no requirement that your tactical choices be similar dividend-paying stocks, but there's no prohibition against it either. In fact, as we've seen with the utility example, the dividend stock slice of the market might just be where you happen to find your next opportunity. The only way to be sure you have some of the benefits of diversification to protect your portfolio is to build it in by design. That's the purpose of the noncorrelator tier. The balance of your portfolio would be invested here.

What kind of securities are good choices as noncorrelators? Bonds have traditionally been the third asset in the classic cash, stock, and bond diversified asset allocation mix and deserve some consideration. Keep in mind, though, that as this is being written, interest rates are at generational lows, and as interest rates move higher, bond prices fall. Some stocks that pay high dividends tend to suffer from interest rate hikes as well, since many have high borrowing costs or must compete with higher-yielding bonds to attract capital. For this reason, bonds in general are not necessarily an ideal solution to provide diversification for your dividend portfolio. One possible solution comes in the form of Treasury inflation-protected securities (TIPs).

The principal on these Treasury bonds is adjusted with changes in inflation as measured by the Consumer Price Index (CPI). As inflation rises, so does the principal amount of the bond. The interest payment is based on this adjusted principal amount, so your income stream from TIPs will also rise if inflation heats up. At maturity, you're paid the adjusted principal amount. In the event of deflation, the final payment will not be less than the original par value. Inflation hasn't been a serious problem in the United States for years, but ongoing trade and budget deficits and a falling dollar could result in this not always being the case. In any event, this is supposed to be an "insurance policy" for your portfolio, and it's best to buy your insurance before the house burns down. (For more information on TIPs, visit the U.S. Department of the Treasury's TreasuryDirect® Web site at www.treasurydirect.gov/indiv/products/prod_tips_glance.htm.)

Commodities have also tended to move independently of the stock markets and so may also be a candidate to provide some noncorrelation for your portfolio. Commodities include things you can touch: agricultural products, ranging from grains and orange juice to livestock; precious metals; industrial metals; and other natural resources such as oil and natural gas. Traditionally the province of commodity-producing companies and professional investors, investing in commodities has become more accessible to the individual investor through an increasing number of mutual funds, exchange-traded funds (ETFs), and exchange-traded notes (ETNs) with this specialty.

Although cash equivalents such as money market instruments, certificates of deposit, short-term Treasury bills, and savings accounts aren't glamorous and aren't very likely to help you keep up with inflation over time, they are pretty much oblivious to the swings in the stock market and so can be acceptable noncorrelating anchors for the portfolios of very conservative investors.

One of the significant benefits of including a noncorrelating tier in your portfolio is that it allows you to take advantage of periodic rebalancing. About once a year, bring the amounts invested in your various tiers back into alignment with the targets you've set for them. Unless the performance of all your tiers has been exactly the same, this will mean selling off some of your best performers and using the money to buy more of the laggards. Doing so will not only keep your portfolio from drifting away from your design blueprint but will also assure that at least once a year you're buying low and selling high. You can perform this annual maintenance whenever you want, but set the date to something you won't forget. Some people like to do this at the beginning of the year, so they'll have at least a year before they'll have to pay tax on any gains. Halloween also deserves a mention. Stocks have often hit their lows in October and have a tendency to enjoy seasonal strength from around November through April. Since stocks historically have had higher average returns than bonds and cash, it makes sense if you're due to buy them to buy them while they're on sale in the fall.

See Exhibit 9.5 for a recap of the dividend portfolio design by tier.

EXHIBIT 9.5

The Dividend Portfolio Design

Tier		% of Portfolio	
Cash		**2%**	
Dividend Payers		**70%**	
Weightings		**Standards**	
Value	14%	P/E Ratio	P/S Ratio
Growth	14%	Revenue % Chg	Earnings % Chg
Yield	14%	Yield	CF Div Coverage
Quality	14%	Quick Ratio	Ops CF/ST Debt
Overall	14%	Highest Ranking Across All Standards	
Tactical Choices	**14%**		
Noncorrelators	**14%**		

ENDNOTE

1. Certified Financial Planner Board of Standards Inc. owns the certification marks CFP®, CERTIFIED FINANCIAL PLANNER™, and **CFP** which it awards to individuals who successfully complete initial and ongoing certification requirements.

CHAPTER 10

Building Your Portfolio

Give a man a fish and you feed him for a day. Teach a man to fish and you feed him for a lifetime.

—Chinese proverb

By this point in the process, you have identified your universe of securities to examine, screened out those that don't meet your minimum criteria, and found the information you'll need to evaluate your candidates. You are now ready to do some stock selection to fill in the design you've created for your portfolio.

The first question to answer at this point in the process is: *How many stocks should I buy?* The most obvious limiting factor in determining how many stocks to own is how much money you have to invest. Stock prices vary, of course, but the average of the year-end prices of the stocks in the S&P 500 over the 10 years through 2009 has been around $40 per share. Buying 100 shares of one stock at that price would cost you $4,000, plus commissions.

For adequate diversification, we'd recommend buying no fewer than 10 or 12 issues. Buying 100 shares each of 12 stocks at our average price would require starting with around $50,000, if you're going to invest in individual stocks. If you're still working up to that amount, take a look instead at dividend reinvestment plans (DRIPs), mutual funds, and Exchange Traded Funds (ETFs).

No matter how big your account size, though, we recommend *against* having more than around 35 dividend stocks in your portfolio. Diversification can cut both ways. Fewer, better performing securities may do better for you than just throwing everything into the pot. If you add too many "top picks" to your portfolio, you could end up diluting the benefits of your research. Not only do you risk offsetting the gains of your top performers with the relatively poor results of your also-rans, but even a spectacular winner could do little for you if it's an insignificant speck in a huge portfolio. Balance your need to diversify with your need to capitalize on your research.

In addition, it's critical that you continue to follow developments that could affect the business your stocks represent. Even if you're computer savvy, staying on top of the changing fortunes of the companies you buy into takes time. The more companies you own, the more time it takes. The early rush of enthusiasm you feel as you put your portfolio together for the first time can fade as the reality of the ongoing research and monitoring of your list starts to take hold. Decide which data sources you'll be using and how you will keep your research up to date. Be honest with yourself about how much time this process will take and whether you have that much time and commitment. If you own more stocks than you can keep track of, you could be the last one to hear about some bad news that's just cost you a bundle.

Speaking of costing you a bundle, be sure to factor in your trading costs as you're deciding how many stocks to own. Nobody's going to stop you from buying one share of 100 different companies, but since brokerage firms often charge a minimum commission per trade, you'd probably need some pretty strong performance just to cover your costs. You certainly don't want to spend your first year's dividends paying for a lot of small trades.

Once you know how many stocks you should buy—somewhere between 10 and 35—you are ready to begin your ranking process.

Since each piece of your portfolio has its own standards, you will be ranking your finalist list several times, once for each set of specific measures set for that part of the portfolio. For example, you'll be ranking your list by price/earnings ratios (P/E) and price/sales ratios (P/S) to find your top choices for *value*. We've deliberately limited the number of standards you'll be using to rank your list to two items for each slice of the portfolio to keep the process effective—and manageable.

No matter what kind of ranking system you use, it's important to remember whether the best measurement for a particular standard is a low or high number. A *low* P/E is a good thing when you're looking for value, but all other things being equal, you'll probably be looking for a *high* yield. If you don't keep this in mind as you rank your candidates, you might inadvertently stuff your portfolio full of the most expensive, lowest quality, floundering companies on your carefully crafted list. In each example we use, we'll indicate whether the best data value is high or low.

Here's an example of how the simplest ranking system might look. We'll use all the stocks included in the S&P 500 as our starting point and screen for those that meet the following tests.[1]

- Dividend yield equals 1.5 times the yield of the S&P 500.
- Cash flow per share equals 1.2 times the annual dividend per share (based on the current indicated dividend amount).
- Payout ratio is less than 100 percent.

At the time this search was run, 90 stocks initially passed the screen to qualify for our candidate list. Let's assume there are no social consciousness or veto elements to the screen, but we will exclude seven real estate investment trusts (REITs) from the list, since their dividends don't qualify for preferential tax treatment. This brings the list down to 83 candidates, which appear in alphabetical order in Exhibit 10.1.

CAUTION

Please keep in mind that any companies mentioned here are only examples used to illustrate the process and are *not* portfolio recommendations. The data used are from a specific moment in time, in this case March 2010. By the time you read this, significant changes may have taken place in the condition or circumstances of companies discussed that could alter their ranking in a list or make them completely unsuitable for inclusion in your portfolio. In fact, the screening for the initial edition of this book was done in January 2004 and returned 120 names. Of the 114 non-REIT stocks on that list, only 43 are still on the 2010 list. In the intervening six years, 26 of those stocks have ceased to exist, some through bankruptcy or takeover. The gloomy fate that befell so many of these blue chip, big company, dividend payers reinforces the importance of the ideas discussed in Chapter 11 about safeguarding your capital. Our goal in this chapter is to illustrate the concepts behind

E X H I B I T   1 0 . 1

List of Company Names and Symbols

Company Name	Symbol	Industry	Company Name	Symbol	Industry
Abbott Laboratories	ABT	Pharmaceuticals	Linear Technology	LLTC	Semiconductors
Altria Group	MO	Tobacco	Lockheed Martin	LMT	Aerospace/defense
Amer Electric Power	AEP	Electric Utilities	Lorillard	LO	Tobacco
Ameren	AEE	Multi-Utilities	M&T Bank	MTB	Regional Banks
AT&T	T	Integ Telecom Svc	Marathon Oil	MRO	Oil & Gas-Integrated
Automatic Data Proc	ADP	Services-Data Proc	Marsh & McLennan	MMC	Insurance-Brokers
Bemis	BMS	Paper Packaging	Mattel	MAT	Leisure Products
Block (H & R)	HRB	Special Consm Serv	Mc Donald's	MCD	Restaurants
Bristol-Myers Squibb	BMY	Pharmaceuticals	Merck & Co.	MRK	Pharmaceuticals
Campbell Soup	CPB	Packaged Foods/Meats	Nicor	GAS	Gas Utilities
Caterpillar	CAT	Machinery Const/Farm	Nisource	NI	Mlti-Utilites
Centerpoint Energy	CNP	Multi-Utilities	Northeast Utilities	NU	Electric Utilities
CenturyTel	CTL	Integ Telecom Svc	NYCE Euronext	NYX	Specialized Finance
Chevron	CVX	Oil & Gas-Integrated	Paychex	PAYX	Services-Data Proc
Chubb	CB	Insurance-Prop/CAS	Pfizer	PFE	Pharmaceuticals
Clorox	CLX	Household Products	PG&E	PCG	Multi-Utilities
CMS Energy	CMS	Multi-Utilities	Philip Morris Int'l	PM	Tobacco
Coca-Cola	KO	Soft Drinks	Pinnacle W Capital	PNW	Electric Utilities
Conagra Foods	CAG	Packaged Foods/Meats	Pitney Bowes	PBI	Services-Office/SUPP
ConocoPhillips	COP	Oil & Gas-Integrated	PPG Industries	PPG	Chems-Diverse
Consol Edison	ED	Multi-Utilities	PPL	PPL	Electic Utilities
Dominion Resources	D	Multi-Utilities	Progress Energy	PGN	Electric Utilities
Donnelley (RR)	RRD	Commercial Printing	Progressive	PGR	Insurance-Prop/CAS
DTE Energy	DTE	Multi-Utilities	Public Svc Entp	PEG	Multi-Utilities
Duke Energy	DUK	Electric Utilities	Qwest Communications	Q	Integ Telecom SVC
Dupont	DD	Chems-Diverse	Reynolds American	RAI	Tobacco
Edison Int'l	EIX	Electric Utilities	Sara Lee	SLE	Packaged Foods/Meats
Entergy	ETR	Electric Utilities	SCANA	SCG	Multi-Utilities
Exelon	EXC	Electric Utilities	Sempra Energy	SRE	Multi-Utilities
Federated Investors	FII	Asset Management	Southern Company	SO	Electric Utilities
First Energy	FE	Electric Utilities	Spectra Energy	SE	Oil & Gas-Storage
FPL Group	FPL	Electric Utilities	Sysco	SYY	Food Distributors
Genuine Parts	GPC	Distributors	TECO Energy	TE	Multi-Utilities
Heinz (H.J.)	HNZ	Packaged Foods/Meats	Time Warner Cable	TWC	Cabel & Satellite
Hershey Co (The)	HSY	Packaged Foods/Meats	United Parcel Svc	UPS	Airfrght & Logistics
Home Depot	HD	Retail-Home Improve	V.F.	VFC	Apparel & Accessory
Hudson City Banc	HCBK	Thrifts&Mortgage FIN	Verizon Comm	VZ	Integ Telecom Svc
Intel	INTC	Semiconductors	Waste Management	WM	Services-Environmntl
Johnson & Johnson	JNJ	Pharmaceuticals	Windstream	WIN	Integ Telecom Svc
Kimberly-Clark	KMB	Household Products	Wisconsin Energy	WEC	Multi-Utilities
Kraft Foods	KFT	Packaged Foods/Meats	Xcel Energy	XEL	Multi-Utilities
Lilly (Eli)	LLY	Pharmaceuticals			

the security selection process, not to recommend any particular security. We don't plan to leave you with any "old fish," but hopefully we can share something useful about how we catch them.

We understand that researching and ranking 83 securities may be more work than you care to take on. You can cull your list to a more manageable size by tightening your screens. For example, you can raise the minimum yield required to make the cut. Of course, using too small a list could leave you with little to choose from and keep many excellent possibilities from ever making it into your portfolio.

Now we'll rank our list with the value standards. Exhibit 10.2 shows the value ranking and lists each company's price/earnings

EXHIBIT 10.2

Value Ranking

Value Rank	Company Name	Best data value is:		Low		Low		Low	Symbol	Industry	Dividend Yield
			Low					Value			
		P/E	Rank	P/S	Rank		Score				
1	AMEREN	9.0	4	0.85	16		20		AEE	MULTI-UTILITIES	6.0
1	LOCKHEED MARTIN	10.7	11	0.70	9		20		LMT	AEROSPACE/DEFENSE	3.0
3	QWEST COMMUNICATIONS	11.5	19	0.67	7		26		Q	INTEG TELECOM SVC	6.7
4	PROGRESSIVE	11.1	14	0.80	13		27		PGR	INSURANCE-PROP/CAS	3.8
4	EDISON INT'L	10.4	7	0.89	20		27		EIX	ELECTRIC UTILITIES	3.7
6	PITNEY BOWES	10.5	8	0.89	20		28		PBI	SERVICES-OFFICE/SUPP	6.1
7	DONNELLEY (RR)	12.6	29	0.42	2		31		RRD	COMMERCIAL PRINTING	5.1
8	CMS ENERGY	12.5	27	0.58	5		32		CMS	MULTI-UTILITIES	3.8
9	FIRST ENERGY	10.5	8	0.93	25		33		FE	ELECTRIC UTILITIES	5.6
10	VERIZON COMM	12.4	25	0.78	12		37		VZ	INTEG TELECOM SVC	6.4
28	LILLY (ELI)	8.1	1	1.89	65		66		LLY	PHARMACEUTICALS	5.5
42	MARATHON OIL	19.8	77	0.41	1		78		MRO	OIL & GAS-INTEGRATED	3.0

145

(P/E) and price/sales (P/S) ratios. Each company is ranked from lowest to highest, next to the standard.

In this case, Ameren has the lowest P/E of the top 10 stocks at 9.0 and has a rank of 4 out of the 83 candidates for P/E. Donnelley (R.R.) has the lowest P/S ratio of the top ten at 0.42, which ranks second out of 83 in the P/S rank column. The score column is simply the sum of the two rankings for each stock. Ameren's P/E rank of 4 is added to its P/S rank of 16 to come up with a value score of 20. Donnelley's P/E rank of 29 plus its P/S rank of 2 add up to a value score of 31. Since we're ranking the stocks so that 1 is best, 2 is second best, and so on, the stock with the lowest combined score is the best choice.

For this ranking, Ameren's value score of 20 is tied for the lowest in the list, so it gets the number 1 value ranking, as reflected in the value rank column. Lockheed Martin also has a value score of 20, so it ties Ameren for first place. We'll discuss possible tiebreakers a little later. The lowest P/E among the 83 candidates belongs to Lilly (Eli), but its P/S rank of 65 gives it a combined value score of 66, putting it at number 28 on the value ranking list. Marathon Oil has the best P/S ranking but comes in at number 42 on the value list once its P/E rank of 77 is added to its value score. (For the curious, a complete alphabetical listing appears in Exhibit 10.12 at the end of the chapter showing all 83 stocks with the data used in the sample rankings.)

The same ranking process is repeated using the standards for growth, quality, and yield. Exhibit 10.3 shows the top 10 ranked choices for growth, along with the stocks with the highest rank for each of the criteria.

For the purpose of finding our best growth candidates, we're looking for companies with the highest percentage changes in revenue and earnings per share. The top-ranked stock in the list on the basis of the growth characteristics we're looking for is Hudson City Banc.

Hudson City Bancorp ranks second among the 83 candidates in terms of its revenue percent change, with a change of 34.4 percent. With an EPS percent change of 19 percent, it ranks seventh by this standard. Adding the two ranks gives a growth score of 9, which is the lowest combined score for growth in the list. The highest-ranking stock in terms of EPS percent change is Mattel, but its revenue percent change is only the 54th highest score, so its total score of 55 puts it at number 21 on the list.

EXHIBIT 10.3

Growth Ranking

	Best data value is:	High		High		Low			
Growth Rank	Company Name	Revenue % Change	Rank	EPS % Change	Rank	Growth	Symbol Score	Industry	Dividend Yield
1	HUDSON CITY BANC	34.4	2	19.00	7	9	HCBK	THRIFTS&MORT GAGE FIN	4.4
2	PROGRESSIVE	12.8	6	25.00	4	10	PGR	INSURANCE-PROP/CAS	3.8
3	CLOROX	1.0	16	21.00	6	22	CLX	HOUSEHOLD PRODUCTS	3.2
4	TECO ENERGY	-1.9	21	26.00	3	24	TE	MULTI-UTILITIES	5.0
5	HERSHEY CO (THE)	3.2	15	15.00	11	26	HSY	PACKAGED FOODS/MEATS	3.0
6	LORILLARD	24.5	3	7.00	24	27	LO	TOBACCO	5.3
7	KIMBERLY-CLARK	-1.5	20	16.00	8	28	KMB	HOUSEHOLD PRODUCTS	4.4
8	BRISTOL-MYERS SQUIBB	0.2	18	15.00	11	29	BMY	PHARMACEUTICALS	4.9
9	LILLY (ELI)	7.2	10	10.00	20	30	LLY	PHARMACEUTICALS	5.5
9	ABBOTT LABORATORIES	4.2	12	12.00	18	30	ABT	PHARMACEUTICALS	3.2
11	CENTURYTEL	91.7	1	4.00	30	31	CTL	INTEG TELECOM SVC	8.4
21	MATTEL	-8.2	54	30.00	1	55	MAT	LEISURE PRODUCTS	3.3

Based on the standards of a high quick ratio and high operating cash flow relative to short-term debt, Windstream takes the top spot in this ranking for quality (see Exhibit 10.4). Bemis has the top-ranked quick ratio and comes in at number 4 for quality, while McDonald's comes in at number 8, despite its top score for the ops cf/st debt standard.

The two highest-yielding stocks among our candidates, Windstream and CenturyTel (both telecom services companies), don't make the top 10 on our yield ranking. (See Exhibit 10.5.)

Despite dividend yields hovering around 9 percent, their cash flow dividend coverage ratios are relatively lower than those of other choices on the list. Remember, when we target high yields, we like to see strong cash flow per share to help assure us the dividends aren't likely to be cut or eliminated anytime soon. Qwest Communications has the top yield rank and also the best rank for both dividend yield and cash flow coverage ratio among the top 10 in this example. Note that three of the top 10 choices listed are telecom companies, and six are utilities.

To rank for the overall selections, use the same rank each security earned in the other four lists as the criteria. Add the value rank, growth rank, quality rank, and yield rank numbers together to get the overall score. The stock with the lowest overall score is the top choice, and so forth. (See Exhibit 10.6 on page 151.)

As you rank the list for each of the categories, you will likely find cases in which the total scores for two or more stocks are the same. Two good possibilities for tiebreaker criteria are highest yield or highest score on the overall ranking.

Example: Exhibit 10.2 shows the value ranking generating a couple of ties. The two number 4 ranked choices are Progressive and Edison Int'l, each with a score of 27. Progressive gets to 27 by adding a P/E rank of 14 to a P/S rank of 13, while Edison Int'l reaches 27 by adding a P/E rank of 7 to a P/S rank of 20. Using the higher yield as the tiebreaker puts Progressive ahead of Edison Int'l (3.8 percent versus 3.7 percent), but Edison Int'l could move ahead of Progressive by virtue of using its higher overall rank instead (21 versus 25).

Use whichever tiebreaker rule you prefer, but use it consistently for each tie.

The ranking criteria used for finding your dividend payers might not work for your tactical tier, depending on the kind of securities you

EXHIBIT 10.4

Quality Ranking

Quality Rank	Company Name	Best data value is:				Symbol	Industry	Dividend Yield
		High		High		Low		
		Quick Ratio	Rank	Ops CF/ ST Debt	Rank	Quality Score		
1	WINDSTREAM	1.9	3	47.09	7	10	WIN	INTEG TELECOM SVC	9.1
1	INTEL	1.5	6	64.94	4	10	INTC	SEMICONDUCTORS	3.0
3	LILLY (ELI)	1.3	10	158.23	3	13	LLY	PHARMACEUTICALS	5.5
4	**BEMIS**	**2.9**	**1**	15.19	13	14	BMS	PAPER PACKAGING	3.1
5	MATTEL	1.8	5	18.19	10	15	MAT	LEISURE PRODUCTS	3.3
6	BRISTOL-MYERS SQUIBB	1.8	4	17.60	12	16	BMY	PHARMACEUTICALS	4.9
6	SYSCO	1.2	14	171.99	2	16	SYY	FOOD DISTRIBUTORS	3.5
8	**MCDONALD'S**	1.0	27	**317.73**	**1**	28	MCD	RESTAURANTS	3.4
9	UNITED PARCEL SVC	1.3	9	6.20	20	29	UPS	AIRFRGHT & LOGISTICS	3.0
10	CHEVRON	1.0	24	50.45	6	30	CVX	OIL & GAS-INTEGRATED	3.7

EXHIBIT 10.5

Yield Ranking

	Best data value is:	High		High		Low		
Yield Rank	Company Name	Dividend Yield	Rank	CF Div Coverage	Rank	Yield Score	Symbol	Industry
1	QWEST COMMUNICATIONS	6.7	5	5.50	5	10	Q	INTEG TELECOM SVC
2	VERIZON COMM	6.4	7	4.33	13	20	VZ	INTEG TELECOM SVC
3	FIRST ENERGY	5.6	13	4.72	8	21	FE	ELECTRIC UTILITIES
4	AMEREN	6.0	10	4.03	16	26	AEE	MULTI-UTILITIES
5	DONNELLEY (RR)	5.1	20	4.26	15	35	RRD	COMMERCIAL PRINTING
6	DTE ENERGY	4.7	27	4.49	10	37	DTE	MULTI-UTILITIES
7	CENTERPOINT ENERGY	5.5	15	3.81	23	38	CNP	MULTI-UTILITIES
8	AT & T	6.6	6	3.30	33	39	T	INTEG TELECOM SVC
9	NISOURCE	5.9	11	3.48	31	42	NI	MULTI-UTILITIES
10	AMER ELECTRIC POWER	4.8	25	3.95	19 →	44	AEP	ELECTRIC UTILITIES
24	TIME WARNER CABLE	3.3	60 →	7.58	1	61	TWC	CABLE & SATELLITE
34	WINDSTREAM	9.1	1	2.25	70	71	WIN	INTEG TELECOM SVC

EXHIBIT 10.6

Overall Ranking

Overall Rank	Best data value is: Company Name	Low Value Rank	Low Growth Rank	Low Quality Rank	Low Yield Rank	Low Overall Score	Symbol	Industry	Dividend Yield
1	LILLY (ELI)	28	9	3	24	64	LLY	PHARMACEUTICALS	5.5
2	VERIZON COMM	10	27	43	2	82	VZ	INTEG TELECOM SVC	6.4
3	AMEREN	1	66	18	4	89	AEE	MULTI-UTILITIES	6
4	PROGRESS ENERGY	21	16	40	17	94	PGN	ELECTRIC UTILITIES	6.4
5	CENTURYTEL	34	11	25	31	101	CTL	INTEG TELECOM SVC	8.4
6	DONNELLEY (RR)	7	78	19	5	109	RRD	COMMERCIAL PRINTING	5.1
7	KIMBERLY-CLARK	32	7	26	45	110	KMB	HOUSEHOLD PRODUCTS	4.4
8	SARA LEE	15	31	12	52	110	SLE	PACKAGED FOODS/MEATS	3.1
9	WINDSTREAM	29	47	1	34	111	WIN	INTEG TELECOM SVC	9.1
10	AT&T	17	52	41	8	118	T	INTEG TELECOM SVC	6.6

want to use to take advantage of the opportunity you've found. If you plan to focus on a segment of the broader market, you may want to use *exchange traded funds (ETFs)*. These trade like stocks but replicate the performance of a market or index. Through them you can gain exposure to the performance of an amazing array of investments, from biotechnology to the South African stock market. (See Chapter 12 for a more in-depth discussion of ETFs.)

If you're drawn to individual stocks for your tactical picks, the same standards of value, growth, and financial stability we've reviewed can be useful whether dividends are important to the tactical advantage you're looking for or not.

You may often find yourself looking at your candidate list and wishing some of the stocks in a particular sector or industry ranked higher because you think there could be a tactical opportunity or two in there. In that case, you can use all of your standards to find your best overall choice from among just that short list of similar stocks.

As is the case with your tactical choices, the method you use to evaluate your noncorrelator candidates will depend almost entirely on what type of security you're comfortable using for this portion of your portfolio. Treasury inflation-protected securities (TIPs) can be purchased directly from the Treasury Department through your brokerage account or via mutual funds or ETFs that invest in them for you.

Similarly, you can add some form of commodity exposure in a variety of ways, depending on your asset base and level of interest. The method most likely to feel familiar is through mutual funds, including those that invest in natural resources and gold, or through ETFs. Evaluating cash equivalents to use in this tier requires a comparison of interest rates available, the safety of the issuer, the term of the investment, and the transaction costs or surrender penalties for early withdrawal (if any).

Once you have your rankings in hand, you're ready to start putting together your portfolio. As you select stocks from your ranked lists, here are a few more things to keep in mind.

Your Screens and Standards May Lead You to Concentrate Your Choices in One Particular Industry

This is especially true as your minimum yield requirement rises. After all, there are only so many securities with very high dividend yields, and they tend to be in a few mature industries. It's not uncommon for an entire sector to suffer at the same time because of real or perceived shared risks. For safety's sake, we advise you to not put more than 20 percent of your portfolio in any one industry or sector.

How Should You Handle a Choice You Just Don't Like?

Ultimately, it's your money, and only you are responsible for the investment decisions you make. If you can't bear the thought of owning one of your top-ranked choices, don't buy it. Just remember, many good values are found among the "out of favor" stocks. There may be plenty of good reasons, and lots of news commentary, about why these stocks should be thrown away and forgotten. That's why they're out of favor! Joining the consensus of bias against a stock or industry could lead you away from paying attention to your own research. If you continually veto the results of your process, you may need to ask yourself if you really have a process at all.

Be Patient

Don't give in to the urge to "fill 'er up" and get invested because you've got a list in your hand and money in your account. Sometimes there's just nothing worth buying. Have some minimum standard for all your criteria, such as the minimums discussed in Chapter 7. Any time there are few stocks passing your tests, you should be getting the message that maybe it's not the best time to plunk down your cash.

If You Can't Get Good, Reliable Information about a Company to Use in Your Evaluation, Don't Buy It

You won't be able to rank it accurately against the other possibilities available to you, so you might guess wrong and make a costly mistake. Sure, it could be the next greatest stock in the world, but it's just not worth the risk. There are more viable companies with information readily available than most people would ever be able to research, so there's no need to take a chance on an unknown.

Invest About the *Same Dollar Amount* in Each of the Securities You Select Rather Than Investing in the *Same Number of Shares*

As we've seen, stocks can vary greatly in their price per share. (An extreme example is Berkshire Hathaway, which traded for more than $150,000 per share at times in December 2007.) You won't want to inadvertently put a lot more money into one part of your portfolio by focusing on some set number of shares. Once you've determined how many stocks you'll initially be buying, divide your cash as evenly as possible among them while staying within the guidelines of the overall portfolio design. If you do decide to put extra money into one of your choices, keep this "overweighting" reasonable. Putting twice as much into a favorite candidate as you put into a normal choice might be okay if you're very confident in your ranking process; putting in 10 times as much is probably an emotionally based mistake.

What Happens If the Same Stock Shows Up as a Top Choice in More Than One of Your Ranking Lists?

First of all, this is a good thing; it means you've found a stock with a lot going for it. While you could "double up" on the stock by buying enough of it to cover both slots in your portfolio, for the sake of diversification, we recommend using it for only one of the slots. Move to the next suitable candidate on the list to take its place in the second slot.

We recommend filling the portfolio in the following order: overall, value, growth, quality, and yield in your dividend payers tier, then tactical and, if applicable, noncorrelators. (Of course, cash or its equivalent can appear in as many slots as necessary and in any or all parts of the portfolio whenever no suitable candidates can be found.) An example of using this order to handle duplicate choices appears in Exhibit 10.7, as it would apply to the sample rankings in filling the dividend payers tier.

Exhibit 10.7 assumes that five stocks are required in each slice of this tier, and that all the stocks listed meet the investor's minimum standards. Of course, you may be using fewer choices in your portfolio.

EXHIBIT 10.7

Top Five Available Choices in Each Ranking (without Repeating Selections)

			Dividend Payers		
Overall Ranking			**Company Name**	**Symbol**	**Industry**
1	Lilly (Eli)	→	Lilly (Eli)	LLY	Pharmaceuticals
2	Verizon Comm	→	Verizon Comm	VZ	Integ Telecom Svc
3	Ameren	→	Ameren	AEE	Multi-Utilities
4	Progress Energy	→	Progress Energy	PGN	Electric Utilities
5	CenturyTel	→	Centurytel	CTL	Integ Telecom Svc
Value Ranking					
1	Ameren				
2	Lockheed Martin	→	Lockheed Martin	LMT	Aerospace/Defense
3	Qwest Communications	→	Qwest Communications	Q	Integ Telecom Svc
4	Progressive	→	Progressive	PGR	Insurance-Prop/Cas
5	Edison Int'l	→	Edison Int'l	EIX	Electric Utilities
6	Pitney Bowes	→	Pitney Bowes	PBI	Services-Office/Supp
Growth Ranking					
1	Hudson City Banc	→	Hudson City Banc	HCBK	Thrifts&Mortgage Fin
2	Progressive				
3	Clorox	→	Clorox	CLX	Household Products
4	TECO Energy	→	Teco Energy	TE	Multi-Utilities
5	Hershey Co (The)	→	Hershey Co (The)	HSY	Packaged Foods/Meats
6	Lorillard	→	Lorillard	LO	Tobacco
Quality Ranking					
1	Windstream	→	Windstream	WIN	Integ Telecom Svc
2	Intel	→	Intel	INTC	Semiconductors
3	Lilly (Eli)				
4	Bemis	→	Bemis	BMS	Paper Packaging
5	Mattel	→	Mattel	MAT	Leisure Products
6	Bristol-Myers Squibb	→	Bristol-Myers Squibb	BMY	Pharmaceuticals
Yield Ranking					
1	Qwest Communications				
2	Verizon Comm				
3	First Energy	→	First Energy	FE	Electric Utilities
4	Ameren				
5	Donnelley (R.R.)	→	Donnelley (R.R.)	RRD	Commerical Printing
6	DTE Energy	→	DTE Energy	DTE	Multi-Utilities
7	Centerpoint Energy	→	Centerpoint Energy	CNP	Multi-Utilities
8	AT&T	→	AT&T	T	Integ Telecom Svc

ADVANCED STRATEGIES

For most investors, the methods described in this chapter will provide a powerful process for building a dividend-based portfolio. For those who wish to stretch the boundaries of security selection a bit, here are three possible areas for expansion of the methods already described:

- Additional standards
- Weighting of standards
- Proportional rankings

Additional Standards

As already mentioned, we have limited the selection process to an examination of, and ranking by, only a few basic standards because they are relatively easy to obtain, understand, and compare, and we believe they offer a solid indication of a company's relative prospects for meeting the specific needs of the dividend investor. There are many other viable measures of a company's value, growth prospects, and financial strength than those suggested here. For those enthusiastic investors who are so inclined, further education and research into securities analysis can be a rewarding experience and can lead to a more robust examination of interesting stocks.

Weighting of Standards

It's also possible to use a "weighting" system to try to fine-tune your rankings whenever you are using two or more criteria in your evaluation. The method we have described assumes each characteristic is weighted equally in adding up a stock's score. An alternative would be to give somewhat more weight to one characteristic than another by changing how many points it contributes toward the total score.

For example, if you want to favor stocks with a low P/E over stocks with a low P/S, you can multiply the rank of each stock's P/S by 1.20. By effectively "penalizing" all the P/S scores by raising their rank number by 20 percent (the result of multiplying by 1.20) before adding it to the P/E rank, you will increase the effect of a stock's P/E rank on its overall score. Applying this particular weighting to the stocks listed in Exhibit 10.2 would cause four of the candidates to change their position in the weighted value ranking. The tie between Ameren and Lockheed Martin would be resolved by Lockheed Martin moving into first place alone, and Pitney Bowes and Donnelley (RR) would swap places for fifth and sixth place. The tie between Progressive and Edison Int'l for fourth place would also be resolved, with Progressive now ranking higher instead of simply taking fourth on the tiebreaker of the higher yield. (See Exhibit 10.8.) The same change in the weighted value

EXHIBIT 10.8

Value Ranking: Weighted Scores

	Best data value is:	Low		Low		Low			Simple Value Rank
Weighted Value Rank	Company Name	Weight: P/E	1 Rank	Weight: P/S	1.2 Rank	Value Score	Symbol	Industry	
1	LOCKHEED MARTIN	10.7	11	0.70	10.8	21.8	LMT	AEROSPACE/DEFENSE	1
2	AMEREN	9.0	4	0.85	19.2	23.2	AEE	MULTI-UTILITIES	1
3	QWEST COMMUNICATIONS	11.5	19	0.67	8.4	27.4	Q	INTEG TELECOM SVC	3
4	PROGRESSIVE	11.1	14	0.80	15.6	29.6	PGR	INSURANCE-PROP/CAS	4
5	EDISON INT'L	10.4	7	0.89	24	31	EIX	ELECTRIC UTILITIES	4
6	DONNELLEY (RR)	12.6	29	0.42	2.4	31.4	RRD	COMMERCIAL PRINTING	7
7	PITNEY BOWES	10.5	8	0.89	24	32	PBI	SERVICES-OFFICE/SUPP	6
8	CMS ENERGY	12.5	27	0.58	6	33	CMS	MULTI-UTILITIES	8
9	FIRST ENERGY	10.5	8	0.93	30	38	FE	ELECTRIC UTILITIES	9
10	VERIZON COMM	12.4	25	0.78	14.4	39.4	VZ	INTEG TELECOM SVC	10

rankings can be achieved by multiplying the P/E score by 0.8 and leaving the P/S score unchanged. Of course, a weighting can be applied to either of the rank values or to any of the rank values of other criteria.

With experience, you might find you have a preference for stocks with higher yields or better financial ratios and devise a system of multipliers to have those preferences reflected in your rankings. A complex array of many standards, each carefully weighted to reflect their relative importance, is clearly possible.

Proportional Ranking

Finally, the method used for ranking all these measurements can also be refined. A proportional ranking system can be developed, for example, that measures not only which data item is better, but by how much. Using a racing analogy, it would show you not only who came in first, second, and third, but how long each contestant took to finish. That kind of information could be very useful before you place your next bet on the third place tortoise or the second place hare.

Proportional ranking is actually a very simple concept and one that may be familiar to you from your school days. Each security is "graded" based on the percentage of the best possible grade it achieved in the criteria being measured. Unlike a school test, however, a perfect score doesn't come from having all the right answers. In this case, the best possible answer is simply the best answer among the candidates in your list. If the best (lowest) P/E in your list is an 8, the security with the 8 gets a grade of 100 percent. If the worst (highest) P/E in your list is 28, the stock with the 28 gets a grade of 0 percent. All the other stocks in your list get a grade somewhere in between, depending on where they lie on the 20-point scale that runs from the best score of 8 to the worst score of 28.

Exhibit 10.9 shows a list of hypothetical stocks with the P/E for each, ranked from best (lowest) to worst (highest). Notice that by simply measuring the ranking of these 10 stocks, each candidate is assumed to be exactly the same amount better than the next stock on the list. The distance between 1 and 2 is the same as the distance between 3 and 4. In a list of 10, this distance will always be 10 percent between every consecutive pair of stocks on the list. It's like grading on a curve. No matter what their scores are, the second place stock essentially gets a 90 percent grade, while the ninth place

E X H I B I T   1 0 . 9

Proportional Ranking: P/E (Lowest Is Best)

Best (Lowest) P/E: 8
Worst (Highest) P/E: 28
Span (Highest-Lowest): 20

| | Best data value is: | | Low | High | | |
Rank	% Lower Than Prior Rank	Company Name	P/E	"Grade"	% Lower Than Prior Grade	
1	n/a%	ABC	8	100%	n/a%	best
2	10%	DEF	9	95%	5%	best
3	10%	GHI	10	90%	5%	best
4	10%	JKL	17	55%	35%	so-so
5	10%	MNO	18	50%	5%	so-so
6	10%	PQR	19	45%	5%	so-so
7	10%	ST	20	40%	5%	so-so
8	10%	UV	26	10%	30%	worst
9	10%	WX	27	5%	5%	worst
10	10%	YZ	28	0%	5%	worst

Span = Highest P/E minus the lowest P/E
Grade = (Highest P/E minus this stock's P/E) divided by the Span

stock gets a 10 percent—even if its score is only slightly worse. By "grading" these results instead of simply ranking them, we can get a clearer idea of how close to each other they really are.

To calculate a stock's proportional grade, first find the highest and lowest numerical value among the stocks in your list. Subtract the lower number from the higher number to get the "span"—the total range that covers all the values in your list. In the example shown in Exhibit 10.9, subtracting the P/E of 8 (the lowest value) from the P/E of 28 (the highest value) results in a span of 20 for this theoretical list of stocks. Although P/Es are generally reported only as positive numbers, this calculation works even if one of the values is negative and one is positive, as might be the case for earnings growth rates, for example. Subtracting a negative number is the same as adding the absolute value of that number, so subtracting –10 from 10 equals 20—the span between those two numbers.

Because the best value of a P/E is the lowest number, subtract each stock's P/E from the highest P/E in the list, then divide by the span. The result will be its grade. The grade compares what the span would be if this company had the best value and reflects what percent of the total actual span this represents—essentially what percentage of the best possible value this company's value represents. For company GHI, the stock ranked third on the list in Exhibit 10.9, the calculation would look like this:

Highest P/E minus GHI's P/E: 28 − 10 = 18
18 divided by span: 18 / 20 = .90 or 90%

Repeating the calculation for every stock in the list results in the grades shown in the exhibit. While the order of the stocks remains unchanged, it's now clear that there is a big difference in how they fare in our P/E test. The first place stock, ABC, is 5 percentage points better than the second place stock, DEF, and DEF is 5 points better than third place GHI. GHI's grade of 90 percent, however, is 35 points higher than fourth ranked JKL's grade of 55 percent—a huge gap in their results. Getting a 55 percent on a test in school wouldn't feel much like getting a 90.

Rather than being evenly dispersed at regular intervals as they are according to their rankings alone, the stocks in this example fall into three clear groups: the top three with excellent grades, a pack of four with so-so scores (by the standards of this list), and three with P/E grades clumped at the bottom.

If the highest value of a measure is best, such as yield or revenue growth rate, the grading process is essentially the same, but with a minor alteration of the calculation to account for this difference. In this case the formula is: each stock's criteria value, minus the lowest criteria value in the list, divided by the span. Using company GHI again, but this time assuming you wanted to give the stocks in the list with the highest P/E the best grade, the calculation would look like this:

GHI's P/E minus the lowest P/E: 10 − 8 = 2
2 divided by span: 2 / 20 = .10 or 10%

Now that the formula favors a high P/E, GHI appears at the bottom of the list, in eighth place instead of third (see Exhibit 10.10). Obviously, we wouldn't recommend actually ranking for a high P/E, but this is the version of the formula to use whenever the highest number is the best criteria value.

Like a weighted ranking, proportional ranking changes the order of your candidate list only if results from two or more criteria are being combined, although it will show you the relative merits of

EXHIBIT 10.10

Proportional Ranking: P/E (Highest Is Best)

		Worst (Lowest) P/E:	8		
		Best (Highest) P/E:	28		
		Span (Highest-Lowest):	20		

		Best data value is:	**High**	**High**	
Rank	**% Lower Than Prior Rank**	**Company Name**	**P/E**	**"Grade"**	**% Lower Than Prior Grade**
1	10%	YZ	28	100%	n/a%	best
2	10%	WX	27	95%	5%	best
3	10%	UV	26	90%	5%	best
4	10%	ST	20	60%	30%	so-so
5	10%	PQR	19	55%	5%	so-so
6	10%	MNO	18	50%	5%	so-so
7	10%	JKL	17	45%	5%	so-so
8	**10%**	**GHI**	**10**	10%	35%	worst
9	10%	DEF	9	5%	5%	worst
10	n/a	ABC	8	0%	5%	worst

Span = Highest P/E minus the lowest P/E
Grade = (This stock's P/E minus the lowest P/E) divided by the Span

your choices even if you're looking at a single characteristic of the stocks in a list.

Exhibit 10.11 shows how a proportional ranking system would look using the value criteria from Exhibit 10.2. Using grades instead of ranks moves Chubb and Public Service Enterprise Group into the top 10 from 16th and 12th place, respectively. CMS Energy and Verizon slip from the top 10 down to spots 12 and 13. Eli Lilly's best P/E still doesn't get it into the top 10, but it does bump it all the way from 28th place to 11th.

See the appendix for examples of how to calculate the various rankings as shown in Exhibits 10.2 and 10.8 through 10.11 using a Microsoft Excel spreadsheet. (The appendix also includes an example of the calculation shown in Exhibit 11.7 in the next chapter.)

Just because it's possible, however, doesn't mean that adding complexity to your process is a good idea. Using weighted criteria and proportional grades changed some of the rankings in the examples shown, but the changes were not dramatic. The top choices from one

EXHIBIT 10.11

Value Ranking: Proportional Grades

Best data value is:	P/E	P/S
Best (Lowest):	8.1	0.4
Worst (Highest):	27.9	0.4
Span (Highest-Lowest):	19.8	6.4

Proportional Value Rank	Company Name	P/E Low	P/E High Grade	P/S Low	P/S High Grade	Value "Grade" High	Symbol	Industry	Simple Value Rank
1	AMEREN	9.0	95%	0.85	93%	189%	AEE	MULTI-UTILITIES	1
2	LOCKHEED MARTIN	10.7	87%	0.70	95%	182%	LMT	AEROSPACE/DEFENSE	1
3	CHUBB	8.3	99%	1.56	82%	181%	CB	INSURANCE-PROP/CAS	16
4	EDISON INT'L	10.4	88%	0.89	93%	181%	EIX	ELECTRIC UTILITIES	4
5	PITNEY BOWES	10.5	88%	0.89	93%	180%	PBI	SERVICES-OFFICE/SUPP	6
6	FIRST ENERGY	10.5	88%	0.93	92%	180%	FE	ELECTRIC UTILITIES	9
7	QWEST COMMUNICATIONS	11.5	83%	0.67	96%	179%	Q	INTEG TELECOM SVC	3
8	PROGRESSIVE	11.1	85%	0.80	94%	179%	PGR	INSURANCE-PROP/CAS	4
9	PUBLIC SVC ENTP	9.8	91%	1.25	87%	178%	PEG	MULTI-UTILITIES	12
10	DONNELLEY (RR)	12.6	77%	0.42	100%	177%	RRD	COMMERCIAL PRINTING	7
11	LILLY (ELI)	8.1	100%	1.89	77%	177%	LLY	PHARMACEUTICALS	28
12	CMS ENERGY	12.5	78%	0.58	97%	175%	CMS	MULTI-UTILITIES	8
13	VERIZON COMM	12.4	78%	0.78	94%	173%	VZ	INTEG TELECOM SVC	10

method were generally at or near the top of the other lists as well. That's not to say there isn't a benefit to getting the bestranking you can, but unless you're using a computer and spreadsheet to handle all the calculations, the burden of maintaining advanced strategies might not work for you. After all, a clever method won't prove to be such a smart idea if it's too much trouble to actually use.

See Exhibit 10.12 on pages 164–165 for a complete listing of companies used in the sample rankings, together with their symbols, industries, and the values in March 2010 for the criteria measured.

ENDNOTE

1. All data are as provided by Thomson Baseline, a product of Thomson Reuters.

EXHIBIT 10.12

Company Names, Symbols, Industries, and Criteria Values

Company Name	Symbol	Industry	P/E	P/S	Revenue % Change	EPS % Change	Quick Ratio	OPs CF/ST Debt	Dividend Yield	CF Div Coverage
Abbott Laboratories	ABT	Pharmaceuticals	14.7	2.74	4.2	12	1.26	1.40	3.2	2.88
Altria Group	MO	Tobacco	11.5	1.78	21.7	6	0.25	4.44	6.9	1.36
Amer Electric Power	AEP	Electic Utilities	11.4	1.21	−8.0	−7	0.29	1.33	4.8	3.95
Ameren	AEE	Multi-Utilities	9.0	0.85	−9.5	−4	0.83	8.83	6.0	4.03
AT&T	T	Integ Telecom Svc	11.6	1.23	−0.8	−21	0.51	4.68	6.6	3.30
Automatic Data Proc	ADP	Services-Data Proc	18.2	2.52	−2.5	4	0.13	2.14	3.1	2.29
Bemis	BMS	Paper Packaging	15.9	0.91	−7.0	13	2.92	15.19	3.1	3.62
Block (H & R)	HRB	Special Consm Serv	11.4	1.41	−6.9	−2	0.79	1.15	3.6	3.10
Bristol-Myers Squibb	BMY	Pharmaceuticals	12.8	2.12	0.2	15	1.85	17.60	4.9	1.91
Campbell Soup	CPB	Packaged Foods/Meats	14.4	1.57	−5.0	13	0.44	3.08	3.2	2.69
Caterpillar	CAT	Machinery Const/Farm	27.9	1.16	−36.9	−61	0.97	0.65	2.8	3.52
Centerpoint Energy	CNP	Multi-Utilities	13.3	0.67	−26.9	−18	0.66	1.92	5.5	3.81
CenturyTel	CTL	Integ Telecom Svc	9.9	2.07	91.7	4	0.56	41.81	8.4	2.34
Chevron	CVX	Oil & Gas-Integrated	15.2	0.86	−37.1	−57	1.01	50.45	3.7	4.00
Chubb	CB	Insurance-Prop/Cas	8.3	1.56	−5.5	10	n/a	n/a	2.9	4.27
Clorox	CLX	Household Products	15.1	1.60	1.0	21	0.42	0.74	3.2	2.59
CMS Energy	CMS	Multi-Utilities	12.5	0.58	−8.8	0	0.60	1.16	3.8	6.23
Coca-Cola	KO	Soft Drinks	17.5	3.99	−3.0	−3	0.95	1.20	3.3	2.03
Conagra Foods	CAG	Packaged Foods/Meats	14.8	0.89	−2.9	11	0.67	4.37	3.2	2.79
ConocoPhillips	COP	Oil & Gas-Integrated	14.2	0.50	−37.8	−66	0.58	7.22	3.9	4.96
Consol Edison	ED	Multi-Utilities	14.1	0.94	−4.1	16	0.73	3.37	5.4	2.50
Dominion Resources	D	Multi-Utilities	12.1	1.57	−6.8	3	0.33	1.56	4.6	2.99
Donnelley (RR)	RRD	Commerical Printing	12.6	0.42	−14.9	−45	1.10	4.19	5.1	4.26
DTE Energy	DTE	Multi-Utilities	13.5	0.92	−14.0	16	0.65	1.82	4.7	4.49
Duke Energy	DUK	Electric Utilities	13.4	1.67	−3.6	0	0.80	3.84	5.9	2.74
Dupont	DD	Chems-Diverse	17.4	1.23	−14.5	−24	1.19	3.15	4.6	2.26
Edison Int'l	EIX	Electric Utilities	10.4	0.89	−10.5	−15	0.53	4.44	3.7	6.03
Entergy	ETR	Electric Utilities	11.7	1.38	−17.9	2	0.85	4.36	3.8	4.48
Exelon	EXC	Electric Utilities	10.7	1.68	−8.2	−2	0.96	5.04	4.8	3.83
Federated Investors	FII	Asset Management	12.4	2.28	−3.9	−3	1.04	13.08	3.7	2.64
First Energy	FE	Electric Utilities	10.5	0.93	−4.8	−17	0.43	0.82	5.6	4.72
FPL Group	FPL	Electric Utilities	11.6	1.24	−4.6	6	0.39	1.72	4.2	4.46
Genuine Parts	GPC	Distributors	16.3	0.65	−8.7	−14	1.08	n/a	4.0	1.91
Heinz (H.J.)	HNZ	Packaged Foods/Meats	16.5	1.41	0.6	−5	0.79	17.78	3.6	2.26
Hershey Co (The)	HSY	Packaged Foods/Meats	19.7	1.83	3.2	15	0.73	27.11	3.0	2.32
Home Depot	HD	Retail-Home Improve	19.4	0.83	−7.2	−5	0.31	3.13	2.9	3.05
Hudson City Banc	HCBK	Thrifts&Mortgage Fin	12.8	5.62	34.4	19	n/a	n/a	4.4	2.00
Intel	INTC	Semiconductors	18.2	3.34	−6.5	27	1.52	64.94	3.0	3.30
Johnson & Johnson	JNJ	Pharmaceuticals	13.9	2.86	−2.9	2	1.34	2.62	3.1	2.88
Kimberly-Clark	KMB	Household Products	12.5	1.31	−1.5	16	0.68	5.71	4.4	2.53
Kraft Foods	KFT	Packaged Foods/Meats	14.4	1.26	−5.6	8	0.64	5.26	3.9	2.30
Lilly (Eli)	LLY	Pharmaceuticals	8.1	1.89	7.2	10	1.27	158.23	5.5	2.84
Linear Technology	LLTC	Semiconductors	24.4	6.83	−22.6	−34	2.04	n/a	3.3	1.64
Lockheed Martin	LMT	Aerospace/Defense	10.7	0.70	5.8	−1	0.79	n/a	3.0	3.98
Lorillard	LO	Tobacco	13.3	2.33	24.5	7	1.07	n/a	5.3	1.48
M&T Bank	MTB	Regional Banks	23.0	3.04	7.8	−31	n/a	5.15	3.5	1.82
Marathon Oil	MRO	Oil & Gas-Integrated	19.8	0.41	−30.9	−75	0.75	55.06	3.0	5.52
Marsh & McLennan	MMC	Insurance-Brokers	15.1	1.21	−9.3	14	1.25	1.15	3.3	2.85
Mattel	MAT	Leisure Products	16.7	1.51	−8.2	30	1.76	18.19	3.3	2.44
McDonald's	MCD	Restaurants	16.0	3.11	−3.3	13	0.96	317.73	3.4	2.37
Merck & Co.	MRK	Pharmaceuticals	11.4	4.14	15.0	−5	1.03	2.46	4.1	2.70
Nicor	GAS	Gas Utilities	14.3	0.72	−29.8	15	0.54	1.16	4.4	3.92
Nisource	NI	Multi-Utilietes	14.6	0.70	−30.8	−17	0.26	2.03	5.9	3.48
Northeast Utilities	NU	Electric Utilities	14.0	0.86	−6.2	3	0.26	14.92	3.8	3.67
NYSE Euronext	NYX	Specialized Finance	14.0	1.60	−3.7	−29	0.54	0.76	4.2	2.42
Paychex	PAYX	Services-Data Proc	23.5	5.74	−4.2	−13	0.17	n/a	3.9	1.44
Pfizer	PFE	Pharmaceuticals	8.5	2.76	3.5	−17	1.12	3.03	4.2	3.63
PG&E	PCG	Multi-Utilities	13.3	1.18	−8.4	9	0.57	1.95	4.3	4.65
Philip Morris Int'l	PM	Tobacco	15.1	3.81	−4.1	−2	0.47	13.59	4.6	1.64
Pinnacle W Capital	PNW	Electric-Utilities	16.1	1.14	−3.6	−8	0.52	2.39	5.6	3.19

Company Name	Symbol	Industry	P/E	P/S	Revenue % Change	EPS % Change	Quick Ratio	OPs CF / ST Debt	Divi-dend Yield	CF Div Cov-erage
Pitney Bowes	PBI	Services-Offices/Supp	10.5	0.89	−11.1	−18	1.02	3.65	6.1	2.69
PPG Industries	PPG	Chems-Diverse	21.9	0.88	−21.6	−34	1.03	4.94	3.4	2.69
PPL	PPL	Electric Utilities	14.4	1.41	−6.0	−3	0.45	2.90	5.0	3.03
Progress Energy	PGN	Electric Utilities	12.8	1.09	7.8	1	0.63	4.16	6.4	2.85
Progressive	PGR	Insurance-Prop/Cas	11.1	0.80	12.8	25	n/a	n/a	3.8	2.79
Public Svc Emtp	PEG	Multi-Utilities	9.8	1.25	−7.0	7	0.62	1.76	4.4	3.75
Qwest Communications	Q	Integ Telecom Svc	11.5	0.67	−8.6	−5	0.73	1.51	6.7	5.50
Reynolds American	RAI	Tobacco	11.3	1.81	−4.8	−4	0.69	4.85	6.9	1.42
Sara Lee	SLE	Packaged Foods/Meats	13.9	0.84	−13.4	25	1.02	12.00	3.1	3.55
SCANA	SCG	Multi-Utilities	13.0	1.07	−20.3	−3	0.68	1.87	5.1	2.98
Sempra Energy	SRE	Multi-Utilities	10.5	1.53	−24.7	7	0.32	1.57	3.1	5.08
Southern Company	SO	Electric Utilities	14.0	1.65	−8.1	−2	0.43	1.86	5.4	2.60
Spectra Energy	SE	Oil & Gas-Storage	18.9	3.17	−10.6	−36	0.40	1.81	4.5	2.10
Sysco	SYY	Food Distributors	15.8	0.47	−5.6	−2	1.16	171.99	3.5	2.42
TECO Energy	TE	Multi-Utilities	14.7	1.02	−1.9	26	0.42	4.45	5.0	3.04
Time Warner Cable	TWC	Cable & Satellite	14.4	0.96	3.9	−7	0.58	n/a	3.3	7.58
United Parcel Svc	UPS	Airfrght & Logistics	27.0	1.37	−12.0	−34	1.29	6.20	3.0	2.16
V.F.	VFC	Apparel & Accessory	15.1	1.23	−5.8	−6	1.38	3.92	3.0	2.83
Verizon Comm	VZ	Integ Telecom Svc	12.4	0.78	10.7	−6	0.52	4.38	6.4	4.33
Waste Management	WM	Services-Environmntl	16.7	1.39	−11.9	−10	0.92	3.15	3.8	3.48
Wind Stream	WIN	Integ Telecom Svc	10.7	1.60	−5.9	−3	1.91	47.09	9.1	2.25
Wisconsin Energy	WEC	Multi-Utilities	15.6	1.42	−6.8	6	0.33	0.56	3.2	3.87
Xcel Energy	XEL	Multi-Utilities	14.2	1.00	−13.9	2	0.51	1.91	4.7	3.56

Safeguard Your Capital

Markets can remain irrational longer than you can remain solvent.

—*John Maynard Keynes*

You've done your homework. You've searched and researched. You've screened, you've ranked, and you've finally found an ideal candidate for your portfolio. Its financial statements look great, it has a terrific yield, and it is growing earnings year after year. It's a hidden gem—a steal at its current price. With understandable pride and confidence, you plunk down a hefty chunk of your cash and add it to your portfolio. You sit back and relax, ready to let the dividends start flowing in while other investors come to understand and appreciate its beauty and bid its price steadily higher.

But imagine that, as you drive to work the next morning, you hear the news on the radio—the Securities and Exchange Commission is launching an investigation for accounting fraud into the company you just bought. Apparently, it has been losing money for years and falsifying its documents to cover it up. The assets are gone, and so is the top executive. The hastily appointed new boss announces a halt to the dividend to stave off bankruptcy until the investigation is over. In a related story, a class action lawsuit is filed by thousands of customers who claim to have been seriously harmed by this company's products. Damages could be in the hundreds of millions. And it's going to rain all day.

If only this were harder to imagine!

In addition to the infamous Enron debacle, investors have been shocked by a litany of corporate scandals:

- **WorldCom.** $3.8 billion of "revenue" is allegedly created by fraudulently cooking the books. A criminal investigation of the country's second largest long-distance provider is launched by the Justice Department.
- **Adelphia.** Cable operator files for bankruptcy; admits inflating cash flow and revenue by $500 million and subscribers by 47,000. $3.1 billion loaned to the founding Regis family; criminal investigations follow.
- **Arthur Andersen.** Convicted of a felony for obstruction of justice in the Enron document shredding caper.
- **Global Crossing.** Bankruptcy followed by FBI and SEC investigations of accounting practices. Accounting firm: Arthur Andersen.
- **Tyco.** After resigning, CEO L. Dennis Kozlowski is arrested for tax fraud and tampering with evidence.
- **ImClone.** Insider trading scandal as CEO Samuel Waksal and family sell shares ahead of the public announcement the FDA was refusing application for cancer drug. Waksal resigns and is arrested. Martha Stewart faces sentencing for actions related to receiving a tip about Waksal's sales.
- **Xerox.** Settles with SEC; restates earnings and reverses $1.9 billion of revenue going back to 1997.
- **Merrill Lynch.** Fined $100 million for hyping stocks to investors that its analysts described to one another as excrement.

Sometimes, no matter how hard you try, the stocks you buy are going to flop. There doesn't even have to be any funny business going on for this to happen. Sometimes stocks just go down. *The key is not to go down with them.*

That's not to suggest you can't afford to have any volatility in your portfolio. Stock prices jump up and down all the time, and it's not reasonable to expect otherwise. The risk you have to protect yourself against, though, is suffering losses so large that you'll never be able to recover.

When it comes to the value of your portfolio, gains and losses are not created equal. Exhibits 11.1 and 11.2 show just how precious and fragile gains can be. A 50 percent gain can be wiped out by a

E X H I B I T   1 1 . 1

Wiping Out Gains

A Gain of	Is Wiped Out by
5%	−4.76%
10%	−9.09%
20%	−16.67%
30%	−23.08%
40%	−28.57%
50%	−33.33%
60%	−37.50%
70%	−41.18%
80%	−44.44%
90%	−47.37%
100%	−50.00%

E X H I B I T   1 1 . 2

Getting Back to Even

If the Loss Is	The Gain Must Be
5%	5.26%
10%	11.11%
20%	25.00%
30%	42.86%
40%	66.67%
50%	100.00%
60%	150.00%
70%	233.33%
80%	400.00%
90%	900.00%
100%	**game over**

33 percent loss. And if you're fortunate enough to double your money, losing half of your new pile puts you right back where you started.

On the other hand, a 50 percent loss takes much more away from you than a 50 percent gain gives back. Start with $100, and a 50 percent loss leaves you with $50. A 50 percent gain on the $50 you have left gets you back to only $75. You're still down by $25!

To get your $100 back, you need to double your $50—a 100 percent return. That's just the way the math works. As the losses get bigger, the gains required to get back to where you started from go from unlikely to impossible. Once you've lost 100 percent, you've got to go out and get some new money: $0.00 times any gain still adds up to broke. Exhibit 11.2 shows the challenge investors face as they wonder, "How long will it take me to recover?"

The decade of the 2000s demonstrated that 50 to 100 percent losses are not out of the question; on the flip side, however, from a practical standpoint, 50 to 100 percent gains just aren't all that common. You certainly wouldn't want to have to come up with them on a regular basis to keep your portfolio alive. At some point along the way, there's a point of no return, a loss of capital so large that there is no real possibility of ever achieving financial goals with what's left in the portfolio during a normal lifetime. If you're young enough and can inject new cash into your account, you can start over. If you're in or near retirement, starting over probably just isn't an option.

A much better approach, one that doesn't rely on hitting the occasional lottery, is to limit your losses to levels that can be sustained. It might be tough to find investments that will double your money every year. But add a 3 or 4 percent dividend yield to some reasonable price appreciation, and hitting the long-term historical stock return of around 10 percent shouldn't require too much luck. Even small losses aren't fun, but if you can find a way to keep them from turning into big losses, your chances of bouncing back and just moving on ahead are a whole lot better.

Diversifying your holdings among a variety of dividend-paying stocks, spreading your money across different industries, and adding tactical and noncorrelating assets to the mix will help control the overall volatility of your portfolio. None of this, however, will help you prevent unacceptable losses at the individual security level. For that job, we recommend using a stop loss system.

THE STOP LOSS SYSTEM

The way we're using the term here, a *stop loss system* is any method of setting a predetermined selling price under the current price that, if hit, will cause a security to be sold. It forces the investor to decide in advance the maximum price decline that will be tolerated before a security is removed from the portfolio.

One of the fundamental benefits of a stop loss is that it helps take the emotion out of the decision-making process. It's easy to grasp the importance of limiting losses, but it can be hard to let go of a stock once you've bought it. It's especially hard to sell a stock at a loss. You've invested your time as well as your money in deciding to buy a piece of this company. You proved to yourself it was a good opportunity and backed up your judgment with cash. No one likes to admit they were wrong. It's easy to tell yourself that as long as you still own the stock, maybe you'll turn out to be right after all. It could come roaring back and vindicate you.

Or it could just keep on falling until it turns into one of those big losses you know you absolutely have to avoid. An old Wall Street adage advises the smart investor to "cut your losses, and let your winners run." Still, most people seem to be more comfortable selling their winners ("to lock in my profits") and holding onto their losers ("just until they come back"). Imagine a sports team trying to reach the championship by cutting its starters every year and playing the benchwarmers.

It's important to understand and accept that using a stop loss process will cause you to sell things you don't want to sell yet. You also need to prepare yourself for the reality that sometimes the stock you didn't want to sell will go up right after you sell it. It's okay. That's the trade-off for protecting yourself from the bottomless pit of unlimited losses.

How far below the current price should you set your stop for a given security? To a certain extent, of course, that depends on the security. A quick look at its price range should give you a fair idea of what's reasonable. You should also consider your appetite for risk when setting your loss limits. If the price of a security you're considering routinely moves outside of your comfort range, don't buy it. Find a candidate whose typical price swings are more acceptable to you. You can perform all kinds of complex trend analyses to figure out the exact percentage to use in setting your stops, but in most cases 10 percent does pretty well as a rule of thumb. Let's face it, if you thought a stock was about to drop 10 percent right after you bought it, you'd probably hold off buying it in the first place. Unless we're tracking a very volatile stock, we generally would not set a stop more than 16 percent below the purchase price.

EXHIBIT 11.3

Stop Order

Shares Owned	Stop Order	Expected Proceeds
200	$9.00	$1,800.00
Stock Price Hits:	$8.95	Stop Hit
	Market order to sell 200 shares	

Shares Sold	Sale Price	Actual Proceeds
100	$8.75	$875.00
50	$8.50	$425.00
50	$8.00	$400.00
200	$8.50	$1,700.00

You can place a *stop order* with your broker for securities traded on a stock exchange. The primary advantage is that this automates the process a bit for you. You don't have to continually watch the price yourself so you can jump in and sell if your stop is hit. One problem is that a stop order placed with your broker becomes a "market order" once your stop is hit. That means your shares will be sold at whatever price is then being offered in the market, even if it's fallen right through your target to a price substantially below your stop. (See Exhibit 11.3.)

Example: Say you own 200 shares of a stock you bought at $10 per share, and you set a stop order at a price of $9 per share. Your stock opens the day at $9.05 and then drops to $8.95. Since your stop has been hit, your stop order is activated as a market order to sell 200 shares. The next bid that hits the market for your stock is for 100 shares at $8.75. Your first 100 shares are sold. The next bid is for just 50 shares at a price of $8.50. You sell 50 more shares. Your last 50 shares sell for just $8, the next bid to hit the market. You've successfully gotten out of your position, but at an average price of just $8.50. Your proceeds (before commissions) are $1,700—$100 less than you were hoping for when you set your stop order.

A *stop limit order* can be used to set the minimum price you'll accept if your stop is hit, but you run the risk that your shares won't be sold at all if no one cares to pay your price. Let's assume that

EXHIBIT 11.4

Stop Limit Order

Shares Owned	Stop Limit	Expected Proceeds
200	$9.00	$1,800.00
Stock Price Hits:	$8.95	Stop Hit
Limit order to sell 200 shares @ $9 +		

Shares Sold	Bid	Value
0	$8.75	$0.00
0	$8.50	$0.00
0	$8.00	$0.00
100	$9.00	$900.00
0	$8.00	$0.00
Sold: 100	**$9.00**	**$900.00**
Held: 100	**$8.00**	**$800.00**

instead of placing a stop order, as in the previous example, you set a stop limit order on those same 200 shares—again at $9. Once again, when the stock trades at $8.95, your order is activated, but this time it's activated as a limit order for $9 or better. This means your shares will be sold only if you can get a price of at least $9 for them. In our example, the first three bids that hit the market are below your limit price, so none of your shares are sold. (See Exhibit 11.4.) If a fourth bid arises for 100 shares at $9, your first 100 shares can be sold. If all the rest of the day's trading takes place below $9, you won't sell any more of your shares that day. You will have sold some of your shares but will end up holding the rest at the current lower price.

With either of these types of stop orders, your target price doesn't change by itself. If you want to keep your stop price no more than 10 percent away from the latest price, you'll have to change your order periodically, especially if the price is rising.

If you own mutual funds, you'll have to keep track of any stops you set on your own. Brokerage firms generally don't execute stops on fund shares, and the fund companies themselves are not interested in having you "stop out" of their shares if they start falling. Exceptions are exchange-traded funds and closed-end funds, both of which trade on stock exchanges instead of directly with fund families. Like stocks, these kinds of funds can be protected with brokerage stop orders.

We prefer tracking stops independently rather than placing brokerage stop orders. Using your own stop tracking system allows you to:

- Track any security you happen to own, including mutual funds
- Control your trading activities when your stops have been hit
- Set goals for the securities you buy, so you can be as objective about the rise of your holdings as you are about their decline
- Set "goal stops" to let your winners run even after your performance expectations have been met, yet still capture gains once the price begins to fade
- Use "trailing" stops that track the upward movement of the securities you own

TRAILING STOPS

A *trailing stop* follows the price of the security higher as it rises but holds firm should its price start to fall. To calculate your trailing stop, start by multiplying the current price by your stop percentage. Subtract that number from the current price to get your stop price for the day. For example, if your stock's price is $10 and you've set a stop percentage of 10 percent, your stop price for that day would be $9. (See Exhibit 11.5.)

EXHIBIT 11.5

Calculating a Stop Price

Step 1: Find the distance in dollars to your stop.

Stock Price		Stop Percent		$ to Stop Price
$10.00	×	10.00%	=	$1.00

Step 2: Subtract from the price to find your stop price.

Stock Price		$ to Stop Price		Stop Price
$10.00	−	$1.00	=	$9.00

EXHIBIT 11.6

Trailing Stop

Day	Price	$ to Stop Price	New Stop Price	Trailing Stop Price
		Stop % = 10%		
Monday	$10.00	$1.00	$9.00	$9.00
Tuesday	$11.00	$1.10	$9.90	$9.90
Wednesday	$10.50	$1.05	$9.45	$9.90
Thursday	$12.00	$1.20	$10.80	$10.80
Friday	$11.00	$1.10	$9.90	$10.80

To create the trailing stop, repeat the stop price calculation every day with the stock's new price, then compare the new stop price to the old one, and keep whichever is higher. If the price in our example moved to $11 the next day, the new stop price would be $9.90: $11 × 10% = $1.10, and $11 − $1.10 = $9.90. Since the new stop price of $9.90 is higher than the old stop price of $9, the new $9.90 becomes the trailing stop. Every day, that day's new stop price is compared to the trailing stop price from the day before, and the higher number becomes the new trailing stop. Exhibit 11.6 provides an example of how this might look over the course of a few days.

Notice that Wednesday's stop price of $9.45 is lower than Tuesday's trailing stop price of $9.90, so the trailing stop stays at the higher number: $9.90. Thursday's price jump in the stock to $12 pulls the trailing stop up to $10.80. Even though Friday's price of $11 is the same as Tuesday's, the trailing stop stays at $10.80 rather than sliding back down to $9.90 again.

If the stock had dropped right to $9 on Tuesday instead of rising to $11, it would have been sold, just as with a typical stop. By allowing the stop to trail higher, however, Friday's stop has already risen to $10.80. Instead of holding onto the stock from Thursday's high of $12 all the way back down to $9 before selling, the stock would be sold as soon as it hit $10.80, potentially capturing an $0.80 gain from the purchase price.

Many brokerage firms now offer the ability to set trailing stops for exchange-traded securities held in their accounts, so you don't have to do the daily math yourself. Trailing stops are generally available as market or limit stops, so make sure you understand how to enter your instructions correctly if you are entering the stops through your broker's trading system.

GOALS AND GOAL STOPS

We recommend using stops because we recognize the possibility that a stock's price may unexpectedly fall. Goals and goal stops exist because there's also the possibility of a pleasant surprise. Your stock's price may climb much higher than expected. The kind of goal we recommend using, therefore, is not an automatic sell trigger. Rather, it's a limit on how high to watch a holding rise before you tighten up its stop percentage to try to capture as much of the gain as possible.

Example: Imagine we expect a 10 percent gain on a stock, with an acceptable downside of 10 percent as well. If we watched our stock rise 10 percent exactly as predicted but continued to hold it as it fell right back down to where we bought it, we would feel a little foolish. Our prediction about the stock's possible gain would have been accurate, but our purchase wouldn't have resulted in a profit. Of course, we could simply sell the stock as soon as its price hits our goal target. But what about letting our winners run and keeping the first string on the field as long as possible? Maybe this particular stock will prove to be a superstar and climb 20, 30, 40 percent or more before losing steam. Again, we risk being right but leaving most of the benefit on the table—this time by walking away too soon.

Combining a goal with a goal stop helps solve this problem. Instead of selling a winner as it's still rising, we simply raise the trailing stop. As long as the stock continues to rise, we continue to hold it. But with the tighter goal stop in place, we'll get a sell signal on a much smaller percentage decline than we would by sticking with the initial stop percentage. Exhibit 11.7 shows the goal stop in action.

The process initially works exactly as before. However, once the goal is hit (on Thursday, in this example), the stop percentage changes from 10 percent to 3 percent. Now, instead of waiting for a drop of more than a dollar, a decline of just 33 cents will trigger a sale. The new trailing goal stop of 3 percent continues to track the price higher, as always, until the new tighter stop is finally hit

E X H I B I T   1 1 . 7

Trailing Stop with Goal and Goal Stop

| | | | | | New | Trailing | $ Above |
| | | | Goal | Stop % | Stop | Stop | Trailing |
	Date	Price	Price	to Use	Price	Price	Stop
			Initial Stop % = 10.00%				
			Goal % = 10.00%				
			Goal Stop % = 3.00%				
	Monday	$10.00	$11.00	10.00%	$9.00	$9.00	$1.00
	Tuesday	$10.75	$11.00	10.00%	$9.68	$9.68	$1.08
	Wednesday	$10.50	$11.00	10.00%	$9.45	$9.68	$0.82
GOAL!	Thursday	**$11.00**	**$11.00**	3.00%	$10.67	$10.67	$0.33
	Friday	$11.50	$11.00	3.00%	$11.16	$11.16	$0.35
	Monday	$12.50	$11.00	3.00%	$12.13	$12.13	$0.38
	Tuesday	$13.00	$11.00	3.00%	$12.61	$12.61	$0.39
SELL	Wednesday	**$12.50**	$11.00	3.00%	$12.13	$12.61	**($0.11)**

(in this case on Wednesday, when our theoretical stock closes at $12.50, 11 cents below the trailing stop for that day of $12.61).

Using only an initial stop of 10 percent instead of a goal stop that tightens to 3 percent once the goal is hit, the investor in our hypothetical example would still be holding the stock at the end of the period, waiting for a price of $11.70 to sell. That's still better than selling as soon as the price first hits $11 but puts a lot more of the gain at risk after the expected profit target has already been hit.

The appropriate percentage decline to use for your goal stops should vary depending on the normal performance of the stocks you're buying and on your personal feelings about "giving back" gains. We have found that using about a third of the initial stop (rounded) works pretty well. If you're using a 10 percent initial stop (as in our examples), a 3 percent goal stop should work; for a 12 percent initial stop, you can use a 4 percent goal stop, and so on.

As a practical matter, using the closing price of a stock in your calculations will be sufficient to provide the desired effect in most cases. You could track prices all day long to see if you've hit your goals and stops, but, except in rare cases, the time and effort required would probably not improve your outcome enough to be worthwhile. Executing trades on the basis of the prior day's close works for mutual funds as well, since intraday prices are not available (except for ETFs and closed-end funds).

We haven't seen brokerage firms offer trailing stop orders that automatically convert to a tighter stop at a predetermined price like the goal/goal stop method we've described here, so if you enter a trailing stop order, you'll probably have to keep track of whether or not your goal price has been hit and change the trigger on the order yourself.

With the business section of your newspaper, a calculator, and a pad of paper to track your results, you can easily keep a list of 30 stocks up to date in just a few minutes a day. If you're handy with a computer and a spreadsheet or database, you can track your list in as little time as it takes you to enter (or download) your daily prices.

Exhibit 11.8 gives another view of how the complete stop loss process, with an initial stop, goal, and goal stop, might look. (See the appendix for an example of how to calculate a trailing goal stop as shown in Exhibit 11.7 using a Microsoft Excel spreadsheet.)

EXHIBIT 11.8

The Stop Loss Process

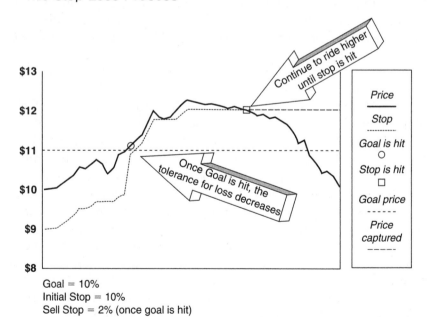

Goal = 10%
Initial Stop = 10%
Sell Stop = 2% (once goal is hit)

For illustration purposes only. Actual prices, goals, stops, and results will vary.

RESETTING STOPS

The passage of time will gradually cause your targets to lose some of the relevance they had when you first set them. For example, it's unlikely you'd be satisfied holding a stock that hasn't moved even a little toward your initial 10 percent goal after several years. The goals and stops you set should be revisited on a periodic and systematic basis. The dates should be chosen in advance, and you should follow the same analysis process you used when you first added the security to your portfolio. You should review your portfolio holdings at least quarterly, and this would be the perfect occasion to revisit and reset your goals and stops as well. Be as dispassionate as possible in your review.

If you wouldn't buy a stock you already own (if you didn't already own it), give serious consideration to selling it—or at least setting a very tight stop under it. We strongly advise against rethinking a stop just because it's been hit. One of the powerful advantages of the stop process is that it helps to keep emotion from overruling your careful analysis, and even a pretty cool head can get a little flustered when a favorite "old friend" has to go.

After bidding a fond (or not so fond) farewell to one of your holdings, it's generally wise to allow some time to pass before buying it back. If you're taking a loss in a taxable account, a 30-day wait moves you past the "wash sale" issues discussed earlier. Whether you're selling at a gain or loss, however, a month is a decent minimum cooling off period before repurchasing a stock in either taxable or nontaxable accounts.

TAX CONSIDERATIONS

Don't stop loss systems like these create unnecessary tax liabilities? What about tax efficiency? The effect of taxes on your ability to accumulate wealth is certainly important. In fact, tax benefits are one of the advantages of investing in dividend-paying stocks. Still, we believe it's a mistake to focus so intently on avoiding taxes that the very foundation of your wealth, your invested capital, is put at risk.

There *is* something worse than paying tax on a gain. *It's watching a gain melt away into a loss.* How many people who once had huge gains in high-flying Internet and technology stocks wouldn't gladly turn back the clock to the heady days of late 1999, sell their now worthless shares, and gleefully pay the tax on their fortune?

How many investors in one-time blue chip financial or automotive stocks wish a trailing stop had capped their losses at something close to 10 percent during the market meltdown of 2007–2009? If stocks only went up, it would be foolish to create an unnecessary tax liability by selling them and thereby shrinking your portfolio. But stocks also go down. If you're going to put the preservation of your capital first, you have to be prepared to sell.

Example: Remember, you have to pay tax only on your gain, not on your proceeds. Let's take a closer look at exactly how big a bite that really puts on your progress. Imagine you've got a stock in your portfolio that's done really well for you. You've held it for just over a year, and you've made 25 percent on your initial investment of $20,000. Using tax rates in effect in 2009, if you sell today for $25,000, assuming you pay the highest federal rate on long-term capital gains, the 15 percent tax on your $5,000 gain amounts to $750. (See Exhibit 11.9.) State tax consequences vary by state and are therefore not considered in this example. Now, $750 is nothing to sneeze at, but it represents only 3 percent of the current value of your investment! That means if you decide to hold your shares, and they fall in value by just 3 percent, you'll be right where you would have been if you had sold, paid the tax, and pocketed the $4,250 difference. Well, not exactly the same place—you'd still have the potential tax liability on your unsold shares and their unrealized 21 percent gain!

The tax rates on short-term gains (on securities held for less than a year) would be the same as on your ordinary income, so that would make the tax cost of selling higher. Still, even at an assumed top federal tax rate of 35 percent, the tax amounts to 7 percent of the stock's total value. You still net $3,250 after taxes. (See Exhibit 11.10.)

EXHIBIT 11.9

Weighing Your Risks: Taxes versus Capital Loss (at 15 Percent Tax Rate)

Value	Cost	Long-Term Gain	% of Gain	Tax Rate	Tax	% of Value
$25,000	$20,000	$5,000	25%	15%	$750	3%

EXHIBIT 11.10

Weighing Your Risks: Taxes versus Capital Loss
(at 35 Percent Tax Rate)

Value	Cost	Short-Term Gain	% of Gain	Tax Rate	Tax	% of Value
$25,000	$20,000	$5,000	25%	35%	$1,750	7%

EXHIBIT 11.11

Weighing Your Risks: Taxes versus Capital Loss
(Showing High and Low Tax Rates)

Value	Yield	Quarterly Dividend	High Tax	Low Tax	Difference	% of Value
$25,000	3%	$187.50	$65.63	$28.13	$37.50	0.15%

Minor bad news about a stock has been known to wipe out more than 7 percent of its value in a single day.

Missing the qualifying period for a particular dividend payment will cost you the special tax treatment for that payment. For a stock with a 3 percent yield, however, the difference between paying the high tax rate of 35 percent or the low tax rate of 15 percent on one dividend payment is just 0.15 percent of the stock's value. (See Exhibit 11.11.)

Future tax rates may differ from those used in this example, but the concept remains the same. Holding onto a security just to avoid paying tax on your gains opens you up to the risk of losing the gains themselves.

By all means, pay attention to the tax implications of your decisions. Where it makes sense to do so, take losses to offset your realized portfolio gains. You might have unused losses from prior tax years that can help offset your taxable gains. But don't avoid using a stop loss system out of fear of the possible tax consequences, or you might end up giving away a whole lot of capital just to save a little bit of tax.

CHAPTER 12

DRIPs, Folios, Mutual Funds, and ETFs

Tall oaks from little acorns grow.

—David Everett

Everybody has to start somewhere. What if you're just starting out and don't have a lot to invest, or you've been saving for years but still haven't accumulated the $50,000 to $100,000 in your brokerage account that is recommended for a diversified portfolio of individual stocks?

You agree that the benefits of dividend investing are compelling, and the process makes sense to you. But how do you take advantage of this information to grow your wealth without already having a pretty decent chunk of wealth in your pocket to get you started? Is there some way to harness the power of dividends while you're still in the early stages of building your fortune?

Fortunately, there are several. Each is tailor-made for smaller accounts, but the approach that fits you best will depend on your tastes and preferences—as well as on the size of your account.

DRIPs

Most public companies that pay cash dividends offer a *dividend reinvestment plan* (DRIP). These plans allow current shareholders to reinvest their dividends directly with the company to buy additional shares. Many companies also offer *direct share purchase plans,* which allow investors who are not yet shareholders to buy stock directly from the company so they can begin to take advantage of the DRIP. The features and services offered by DRIPs vary by company. Before investing in a DRIP, you should read its disclosure information to learn how that particular plan works. The plan description will tell you how to enroll, the number of shares you need to open an account, the minimum and maximum optional investments you can make, and how to sell shares. You'll also find a description of any fees or charges that apply.

These programs began in the 1960s and have been gaining popularity with investors ever since. That popularity is one of the reasons companies are encouraged to pay cash dividends and maintain the level of the payments. DRIPs are also popular with the companies that offer them. By issuing new shares of stock, a company can raise capital from investors joining the plan. Since the company can also pay the plan's participants their dividends in the form of newly issued stock rather than in cash, the plan also helps to conserve the firm's liquid assets. Offering investors a convenient, economical way to invest in its shares can help a company build goodwill and create a class of loyal shareholders.

For investors who want to do their own security selection, DRIPs offer some compelling advantages. One of the top attractions of DRIPs is their affordability. Many DRIPs allow an initial investment of as little as the cost of a single share. You can add to your plan with small deposits and buy a fraction of a share without a problem. Some companies even offer a discount on the shares you purchase with reinvested dividends. Buying shares directly through the DRIP can eliminate brokerage commissions. While some brokerage firms will also allow shareholders to reinvest their dividends at no cost, they will charge commissions for the purchase of the initial shares and any shares bought in excess of the dividend being reinvested.

DRIPs are a great way to introduce the discipline of a systematic savings plan to your budget. People who become financially successful do so because they save. Some plans make it easy to save by allowing you to set up automatic deductions from your checking or savings account. Even without adding new cash to your plan, reinvesting your dividends each quarter will still lock you in to the two big benefits of systematic saving: the *magic of compounding* and *dollar cost averaging*.

The magic of compounding has always been one of the classic advantages of dividend investing, as illustrated by the dramatically different outcomes Robert and Michael experienced in our story at the beginning of this book. DRIPs show in simple terms how the power of compounding takes hold.

Example: Let's say you own 1,000 shares of a $10 stock with a 5 percent yield in a DRIP (see Exhibit 12.1). For simplicity's sake, we'll assume the stock price never goes up or down. Over the course of the first year, you receive $500 in dividends, which buys you 50 new shares. In the second year, you're now entitled to dividends on 1,050 shares. That adds up to $525. This buys you 52.50 new shares. Each year, as the number of shares you own grows, so does the amount of your dividend income, creating a cycle of accelerated wealth accumulation. Within 15 years, your initial investment will have doubled *entirely from reinvested dividends*—and without the benefit of the stock price rising by a single penny.

EXHIBIT 12.1

The Effects of Compounding

| | | Starting Value: | $10,000.00 | | | |
| | | Annual Dividend Yield: | 5.00% | | | |
Year	Shares	Price	Dividend	New Shares	Total Shares	Value
1	1000.00	$10.00	$500.00	50.00	1050.00	$10,500.00
2	1050.00	$10.00	$525.00	52.50	1102.50	$11,025.00
3	1102.50	$10.00	$551.25	55.13	1157.63	$11,576.25
4	1157.63	$10.00	$578.81	57.88	1215.51	$12,155.06
5	1215.51	$10.00	$607.75	60.78	1276.28	$12,762.82
6	1276.28	$10.00	$638.14	63.81	1340.10	$13,400.96
7	1340.10	$10.00	$670.05	67.00	1407.10	$14,071.00
8	1407.10	$10.00	$703.55	70.36	1477.46	$14,774.55
9	1477.46	$10.00	$738.73	73.87	1551.33	$15,513.28
10	1551.33	$10.00	$775.66	77.57	1628.89	$16,288.95
11	1628.89	$10.00	$814.45	81.44	1710.34	$17,103.39
12	1710.34	$10.00	$855.17	85.52	1795.86	$17,958.56
13	1795.86	$10.00	$897.93	89.79	1885.65	$18,856.49
14	1885.65	$10.00	$942.82	94.28	1979.93	$19,799.32
15	1979.93	$10.00	$989.97	99.00	2078.93	$20,789.28

EXHIBIT 12.2

Dollar Cost Averaging

Amount Invested	Share Price	Shares Bought	Total Shares	Account Value
$1,000	$40	25.00	25.00	$1,000
$1,000	$50	20.00	45.00	$2,250
$1,000	$30	33.33	78.33	$2,350
$1,000	$40	25.00	103.33	$4,133

Total Cost: $4,000
Average Price: $40
Gain: $133

In real life, of course, stock prices don't stay perfectly still for 15 years. That's a good thing when you're systematically saving in a DRIP, because it's the volatility of a stock's price that drives the engine of dollar cost averaging.

Dollar cost averaging is what happens when you add to an investment at frequent regular intervals, such as monthly or quarterly, while the price of the investment rises and falls. The fluctuation in the price causes you to buy more shares at low prices and fewer shares at high prices, reducing the average cost of your overall investment. Exhibit 12.2 shows a simple example.

Example: At a price of $40, your $1,000 investment buys 25 shares. As the price rises to $50, your next $1,000 investment buys only 20 shares. By investing the same dollar amount, you automatically buy fewer shares at the higher price. The bargain price of $30 allows you to pick up 33.33 shares for your investment. Finally, the price returns to its original $40 per share—but look at what's happened. If you had just bought $4,000 worth of stock all at once at $40 per share, you would own 100 shares. Because you were dollar cost averaging, however, you actually were able to buy 103.33 shares for your investment of $4,000. Even though the average price you paid was $40, and the price started and ended at $40, you have a gain of $133! In a DRIP, volatility isn't such a bad thing after all.

As compelling as the benefits of reinvesting all of your dividends can be, if you need to take income from your portfolio, a DRIP can still work for you. Most plans allow you to split your dividend income, reinvesting a portion and receiving the balance in cash.

Not all the news about DRIPs is good news, however. They do have a few drawbacks.

Although many companies issue new stock to cover the shares your dividends buy, others use your dividends to buy stock on the open market, incurring a transaction charge or commission. Some plans charge annual plan fees or service charges, which are usually deducted automatically from your account. As is always the case with stocks that aren't held in a pension plan or IRA, you'll have to pay tax on your dividend income. If you're reinvesting all the income, you'll have to come up with the cash to pay the tax from somewhere else. Any discounts you receive on your share purchases are treated as an additional dividend and would also be taxable to you.

Most plans now offer Internet access to your account statements and the ability to make additional investments, sell shares, and withdraw certificates online. Still, if you assemble a portfolio of 30 stocks, the administration of 30 separate DRIPs can pose a challenge.

If you participate in a DRIP over a long period of time, determining the tax consequences of selling your shares can be a real challenge unless you keep detailed records as you go along. To know whether you have a gain or loss on your shares, you have to know their *cost basis*.

The cost basis is the cost your shares have for tax purposes. Your basis includes the price you've paid for each of your shares, including the shares you bought with the dividends you reinvested. Even though you didn't take money out of your pocket to buy your "reinvestment" shares, for tax purposes they are treated the same as if the DRIP had sent you a check and you used the money to buy those shares. To know your basis in these shares, you not only have to know the amount of the dividend you were paid but the price at which that dividend bought each new share added to your account.

Several software programs are available to help you maintain your records. Both Intuit's Quicken (www.quicken.intuit.com) and Drip Wizard (www.dripwizard.com) have features designed to make it easier for you to handle the challenge of keeping track of all your DRIP investment information.

Even if you can keep your information under control, actually managing a portfolio held in a collection of DRIPs could still pose some problems. Suppose you decide it's time to sell one of your stocks and buy a new candidate that ranks high on one of your lists. Maybe you've hit an initial stop or a goal stop. You not only have to get the money out of the old DRIP, but you have to set up an account in the new company's DRIP as well. These plans are intended for the "buy it and forget it" investor. While there's usually some flexibility *within* the plan, they're not particularly well suited to the active management of an ever-changing roster of holdings.

Assuming the benefits of DRIP investing outweigh the drawbacks in your situation, how do you go about picking a good DRIP? You don't!

It's important to understand how a DRIP will work, but the most important factor in the success of a DRIP isn't the plan—*it's the merits of the stock that's in it*. No wonderful collection of features and benefits in the plan can make up for a lousy stock. Dollar cost averaging is a powerful force, and the magic of compounding can work miracles, but neither can bring a dying company back to life.

Imagine using a DRIP to systematically invest in a company over decades, reinvesting the dividends to buy more shares, only to see your investment waste away as your company turns to dust. If you trust your research to find the companies you want to buy, and you monitor the stocks you already own, the DRIPs you end up holding them in should work out just fine.

The idea of making small, systematic investments has broad appeal, and a number of companies have stepped forward with Internet-based solutions to facilitate the process in one way or another. DRIP Central (www.dripcentral.com) provides a source of reference information and online links for further research.

ShareBuilder (www.sharebuilder.com), BUYandHOLD (www.buyandhold.com), and My Stock Fund (www.mystock fund.com) are offered by brokerage firms with special programs designed to facilitate systematic investments at reduced costs. While their specific offerings vary, these firms typically offer some discount brokerage services and lower-cost window trading pricing, either as part of a subscription service or on a price per trade basis. *Window trading* involves collecting customer orders and then placing them in bulk form at predetermined times or "windows."

Keep in mind that Web sites, software solutions, and broker-age firms come and go. This sampling of resources available in 2010 might or might not exist when you're ready to invest in a DRIP, or other better solutions may have taken their place. Still, it's likely services and vendors of some kind will be available to help DRIP investors for as long as companies continue to offer DRIPs.

THE FOLIO CONCEPT

One of the more flexible and interesting online brokerage options comes from FOLIOfn (www.folioinvesting.com). *Folios* are baskets of up to 100 stocks that you can either build yourself or select from a collection of "prepackaged" sets. (The High Dividend Folio, for example, consists of "established companies paying above average dividends.")

There is no minimum account size, and you can buy fractional shares of the stocks in your Folio. The available pricing plans and terms change over time, so check the Web site for details of current costs and options. At the time this is being written, there is an "Unlimited Plan" offering unlimited window trading for a monthly or annual subscription fee, and a "Basic Plan" with per-trade com-missions but no subscription fees.

One big advantage of the Folio approach is the convenience of being able to build and maintain your portfolio in one account. Executing your own stop loss program is not a problem in this envi-ronment, as both stop and stop limit orders are available. You have the flexibility to use your research to build a well rounded, custom built, dividend-based portfolio of 30 or more securities with as few or as many shares of each as you can afford. Since there's no mini-mum account size and fractional shares aren't a problem, you don't have to limit your selection process—even if you have limited funds.

Keep in mind, though, that if you *do* have limited funds, the cost of your Folio could make a serious dent in your account. Compared to typical discount brokerage commissions, the price of a window trade is likely to look pretty cheap. Even so, the trading costs of establishing a portfolio of 30 stocks on a per-trade basis will still set you back a few dollars, and you'll also have to pay again every time you buy or sell a stock as you actively manage your portfolio. A monthly or annual subscription fee might not seem terribly expensive, but if you're investing only a little bit of money, it could whack your portfolio for a pretty big percentage of its value. Still, if you plan to make regular additions to your account and can seed it with $10,000 or so, the Folio concept may be a good way to start growing your very own dividend portfolio.

MUTUAL FUNDS

Mutual funds aren't so much a type of investment as they are a method of investing. Investors essentially pool their assets and hire investment professionals to manage their money for them. Just about anything you can invest in directly can be invested in through a mutual fund. Stocks, bonds (both foreign and domestic), real estate, gold and other commodities, and even cash equivalents are all available from mutual fund companies. You can't invest directly in a market index, but you can invest in a mutual fund designed to mimic the performance of that index. Funds can be used in an individual retirement account (IRA), and many 401(k) pension plans offer them among the investment choices.

One of the primary purposes of all types of mutual funds is to relieve you of the burden of managing the portfolio yourself. Whether it's evaluating companies or matching the performance of an index, the fund company chooses and trades the stocks for you. Of course, that also removes the opportunity for you to pick which stocks you want to own. When you hand off the responsibility for making the choices, you also give away the flexibility to adapt the portfolio to your needs and preferences. Maybe you'd like a higher dividend yield than the stocks in your fund offer, or maybe your fund's biggest holdings are on your "veto list." You can try to work around these issues by choosing one fund over another, but even with the vast selection of funds available, you're probably going to have to make some compromises.

For some investors, the benefits of professional management will more than compensate for the drawbacks. They understand the advantages of being an investor but find it impractical, impossible, or just not in their nature to take on the task of doing it all themselves. If they don't have sufficient assets to meet the account minimums typically required by investment advisors for private account management, mutual funds can be a great solution for them.

There are three main types of mutual funds:

- Open-end funds
- Closed-end funds
- Exchange-traded funds, or ETFs

If you build your portfolio with funds, feel free to mix and match open-end, closed-end, and exchange-traded funds in whatever combination fits your needs and circumstances.

Open-End Mutual Funds

Open-end funds are probably the most familiar kind of mutual fund and are very popular with investors. Open-end funds continually offer their shares to the public as new money comes in, and the price of each share is calculated based on the value of all the holdings in the fund—the *net asset value* or NAV. The NAV is set once per day, usually based on the prices of the fund's holdings at the close of the regular trading session. While investors can add or withdraw money from the fund at any time during the day, the price they get is based on the fund's closing NAV, not a price that varies throughout the trading day. Orders that arrive before the close get that day's closing price, while orders coming in after the close would be priced at the next business day's NAV.

If the market closes at 4 p.m., an order coming in on Monday at 3 p.m. would be priced at Monday's NAV, but one coming in at 5 p.m. would get Tuesday's NAV. No one knows exactly what price he or she will get until after the fact. (At least that's how it's supposed to work. The mutual fund industry endured a scandal in 2003 about certain investors being allowed to buy or sell fund shares after the market closed and the daily prices were already known.)

Minimum investment amounts for open-end funds start as low as $250, although many funds require an initial purchase of $5,000 or more to open an account. Additional investments can typically be made in much smaller amounts, and most open-end funds offer systematic savings programs as well.

Open-end funds are probably what most people think of when they hear "mutual fund," and for the balance of this chapter we will refer to them simply as mutual funds.

Dividend Investing with Mutual Funds

The basic steps to creating a portfolio using mutual funds are the same as those for creating a stock portfolio:

- Define a universe of funds to follow
- Rate your candidates by specific standards
- Select candidates to fill in the portfolio
- Monitor your holdings to control your risk

Some of the details will change, of course, to accommodate the unique characteristics of funds, but the importance of following a process remains the same.

Narrowing Your Universe

With thousands of mutual funds to choose from, how can you hope to find the ones that will meet your needs? As with stocks, you'll need a good source of information. Morningstar is well known for its fund information and rating reports, and Value Line offers a competing set of services. With the advent of mutual fund "supermarkets" at some brokerage firms, companies like Charles Schwab & Co., Inc., also offer research and information about the extensive collection of funds on their list.

Zeroing in on funds that focus on dividend-paying stocks hasn't always been easy. Many funds tend to include such stocks in their portfolios but often don't concentrate on them as part of the fund's stated objective. Funds with *value, growth and income,* and *blue chip* in their names don't necessarily hunt for dividends but end up owning stocks that pay dividends anyway. Utility and financial services funds tend to produce good dividend income because they specialize in industries in which high dividend payments are fairly common. Looking for *dividend* in the fund name is a good place to start, but unfortunately many good candidates would slip through that screen undetected. The Thornburg Investment Income Builder Fund springs to mind.

Based on what's been happening lately, though, the problem of finding funds with a dividend focus may be fading away. The tax treatment of dividends has started a rush in the mutual fund industry to offer funds designed to capitalize on this opportunity and to clearly advertise those dividend-focused funds already in the market.

If this trend continues, we wouldn't be surprised to find dividend funds appearing as a separate category of stock funds, just as municipal bonds are considered a separate category of bonds. It would certainly make building your universe of candidates a lot simpler.

Rating Your Candidates

Examining financial statements won't give you the information you need to evaluate your fund candidates. Even if you had the time and energy to examine the data of every stock in a mutual fund, there would be no assurance that the list of holdings wouldn't change the next day as the fund manager did his or her job. Some funds will give you the average of some of the key financial measures of the stocks in the portfolio, but since the fund could have hundreds of stocks with a wide range of profiles, that information can give you only the broadest idea of the nature of the stocks owned.

The screens and standards used to evaluate an individual stock just don't transfer well to the process of picking the right mutual fund for your portfolio. The criteria for rating mutual funds may be more subjective than P/E ratios and debt levels are, but they can form the basis for some solid decision making nonetheless. Six key factors to examine when reviewing your fund candidates are

- Investment objective
- Tenure
- Performance
- Service
- Tax considerations
- Cost

The first thing you want to understand about a fund is its *investment objective*. This sounds obvious, but you need to make sure you know exactly what the fund is trying to do and how it plans to do it. You can't always rely on the name or description; sometimes you have to dig deeper.

In the late 1990s, a number of "utility funds" loaded up on high-flying technology and telecommunications stocks. Why own stodgy old electric companies when you could own fiber-optic cable companies? After all, telephones are utilities, aren't they? Investors who understood what was going on in their funds might have felt the risks were worth the rewards. Investors who expected the funds to be conservative stalwarts in a bear market were probably shocked by their losses as the technology and telecom bubble burst.

Read the prospectus and check the fund's holdings on a regular basis. The process the fund tells you it will follow should result in its owning the kinds of stocks you would expect to find there. You know the part this fund is supposed to play in your overall portfolio. Look for a good match between what the fund does and what you need it to do.

One of the most important things you're buying when you select a mutual fund is the expertise of the portfolio management team. But what if the people responsible for the good results that attracted you to a fund no longer work there? Be sure to find out the *tenure* of the people responsible for investing your money. Portfolio managers sometimes move from one fund family to another. A portfolio management team may be new to a fund but have a track record established elsewhere. Check the fund's prospectus or annual report for information about the prior experience of any new additions.

Past *performance* may not be indicative of future results, but it's usually the first thing investors look at when trying to pick a fund. Who can blame them? All the disclaimers in investment ads usually appear right under the past performance numbers. Unfortunately, a simple reading of performance can lead you astray in your research. A high return number may tell you more about the performance of a particular kind of investment than it does about the skill of the manager.

If gold soars as bonds plummet, the typical gold fund will look great and the typical bond fund will look terrible. Unless you can accurately predict how gold and bonds will perform next year, comparing the performance of those two funds will be pointless. On the other hand, comparing how several gold funds did versus one another and how different bond funds held up over the same period could give you some insight into which funds of either type you'd rather own.

You may not have to contact a fund company often, but when you do, the quality of the *service* it provides can be critical. Try calling the company and see how long you have to wait on hold before you actually get to talk to someone. Do you have to sit through one list of prerecorded menu items after another, hitting 1 and the # sign, then 3 and the * sign, and then having to hang up and call again because you hit the wrong button? How long does it actually take for materials you request to arrive? A fund company with a culture of helpfulness and competence is more likely to come through when you need help than one where every contact is a hassle.

These might seem like trivial issues, but sometimes your service request is important. If you need cash wired to a bank account in an emergency, you want to be confident it will get to your bank on time—and into the right account.

Mutual funds have become increasingly sensitive to investors' concerns about *tax considerations*. Tax efficiency became a buzz-word during the latter stages of the raging bull market of the 1990s as investors frequently got hit with tax liabilities on "other people's" gains. Mutual funds don't pay tax on their investment activities but pass all their income and gains through to their shareholders instead. The concept is fairly straightforward, but it can seem very unfair to those adversely affected.

Example: Consider two investors: Mr. Tried buys shares of a mutual fund in August 1981; Mr. True invests in the same fund in August 2002. In 1981 the fund buys shares in a host of companies at very low prices. Over the years, Mr. Tried watches as his fund's price rises with the value of the stocks it owns.

In early 2002 the fund sells some of the stocks it holds. Because these stocks are much higher than they were in 1981 when they were first purchased, the fund realizes a gain on their sale. By August 2002, when Mr. True invests, the fund is at its highest price of the year. Unfortunately, between August and the end of the year, the price of the fund falls with the market.

At the end of the year, the fund is required to distribute the gain it realized earlier that year when it sold some of its holdings. It makes a distribution payment, passing the gain through to *all of its present investors*, including Mr. Tried and Mr. True. Mr. Tried feels fine about the gain distribution. After all, he rode the stocks that were sold all the way up, and he's still way ahead on the price of his fund shares. Mr. True is appalled. The fund's price has done nothing but fall since he bought it in August, and now he has to pay tax on gains that were realized by the fund before he was even a shareholder!

This is only a theoretical example. But in the real-world market meltdown of Internet and technology stocks during the Y2K bear market, investors who bought into some high-flying funds near their peaks had tax liabilities on huge realized gain distributions as the plummeting funds sold off their holdings to meet redemptions. Not only did their initial investment in the fund dwindle, but they also had to pay tax on their "gains."

To evaluate the risk of this kind of thing happening to you, look for the size of a prospective fund's unrealized gains, sometimes referred to as "embedded gains" or "contingent gains," before you invest. Of course, mutual funds can pile up losses on the stocks they've sold during bear markets, which can help them offset future gains.

Finally, evaluate the *cost* of a prospective fund choice to see if it's fair and in line with the cost of owning other similar funds. Costs are clearly spelled out in a fund's prospectus, including operating expenses, sales charges, management fees, and marketing costs. All other things being equal, lower costs are better than higher costs. But "all other things" are almost never equal. Superior service, management experience, solid performance, and an excellent match to your portfolio objectives are worth something. As a consumer, you often have to pay more for better quality. More value can justify a higher price. Keep a close eye on your costs, but don't put your hard-earned dollars at risk by pinching pennies in your portfolio.

Selecting Candidates to Fill Your Portfolio

Although you won't be choosing the individual stocks in your fund, keep your overall portfolio design in mind as you select the funds to include. Try to keep around 70 percent of your money in funds that focus on dividend-paying stocks. You might not be able to break this up further into value, growth, quality, yield, and overall slices, but if your account size permits, try to include funds with different approaches to investing in dividend-paying stocks.

Split the balance of your portfolio between funds that suit your tactical objectives and those that will serve as noncorrelators.

Monitoring Your Portfolio and Controlling Your Risk

Review your fund positions at least quarterly to see if there have been any material changes in the fundamental reasons you added them to your portfolio.

- Has the objective changed, either overtly through a change in the fund's prospectus, or through a drift in the kinds of securities you find among its holdings?
- Is the portfolio management team still intact? If managers or analysts have moved on, what can you learn about their replacements?
- Is the performance of your fund falling behind that of other similar funds? It's not unusual for funds to spend some time leading and some time lagging their peers, but

a disappointing trend that persists for more than a year might indicate it's time for a change. Don't worry about how your funds fare relative to others that are outside your universe. You're trying to hold the best fund of its kind, not chase the hottest fund of the day.

- Has the service you've been receiving from the fund company deteriorated, or are you still comfortable with the way you're being treated?
- Are there signs that a large gain distribution may be on the way?
- Have new fees, charges, or other costs been introduced? If so, have there been corresponding improvements to the fund that are likely to flow through to the shareholders?

As you review your holdings, compare them again to the other funds in your candidate list for each tier of your portfolio. Frequent changes to your fund holdings can be inefficient and costly, but don't become so attached to a fund that you won't replace it—even when a clearly superior alternative appears.

Although a mutual fund may be less volatile than an individual stock, fund prices will follow the prices of the securities they hold. Whether you're investing in stocks or funds, you've still got to confront the emotional challenges of investor risk. The professional management and diversification that mutual funds offer won't be enough to protect your account from a major drop in the market. The trailing stop loss process described earlier can be used to help protect the capital you've invested from unacceptable losses. If you're committed to using stops to control your losses in mutual funds, you're probably going to have to set and monitor them yourself.

Closed-End Funds

Closed-end funds raise money from investors when shares are first issued and then invest that pool in a collection of securities. The fund is "closed" to new investment, but the fund's shares trade on an exchange like a stock. While these funds also have a net asset value, their shares can trade at a discount or premium to the value of the securities they own, depending on the demand for the fund's shares in the market. If a fund becomes unpopular with investors,

EXHIBIT 12.3

Closed-End Fund Pricing

Popular Fund		Unpopular Fund	
Holdings	**Price**	**Holdings**	**Price**
Company A	$10	Company A	$10
Company B	$10	Company B	$10
Company C	$10	Company C	$10
Fund NAV	$30	Fund NAV	$30
Fund Price	$33	Fund Price	$27
Premium	$3	Discount	($3)

it may sell at a discount, while strong demand for its shares can cause it to sell at a premium.

Exhibit 12.3 gives an example of two funds with identical holdings selling at a premium or discount. The popularity of a closed-end fund can be affected by the prospects of its holdings or investors' opinion of the fund's managers. Investors can buy or sell a closed-end fund's shares throughout the trading day at the prevailing market price.

Closed-end funds have been a popular vehicle for income investors, and many are invested in bonds. After the tax treatment of dividends improved with the passage of the Jobs and Growth Tax Relief Reconciliation Act (JGTRRA) in 2003, five dividend-focused closed-end funds were launched on the same day, January 28, 2004:

- Eaton Vance Tax-Advantaged Global Dividend Fund (symbol: ETG)
- Nuveen Tax-Advantaged Total Return Strategy Fund (symbol: JTA)
- Pioneer Tax-Advantaged Balanced Trust (symbol: PBF)
- Dreman/Claymore Dividend & Income Fund (symbol: DCS)
- Cohen & Steers REIT & Utility Income Fund (symbol: JNC)

The cost of buying a closed-end fund can be as low as the cost of one share plus commission. Even owning one share creates an instant portfolio of stocks selected and managed to meet a particular objective.

Exchange-Traded Funds (ETFs)

Exchange-traded funds (ETFs) are a relatively new addition to the fund universe, and they share some of the features of both open-end and closed-end funds. Like closed-end funds, ETFs trade on a stock exchange and may be purchased or sold throughout the trading day at a known price. Unlike closed-end funds, however, they rarely trade at much of a premium or discount to the underlying value of their holdings. This is because, as in an open-end fund, shares can be issued or redeemed to match demand. The sponsoring fund company allows certain institutional investors to deliver a "basket" of shares that exactly matches the fund's holdings in exchange for new shares of the fund, essentially "creating" new shares.

These investors are also allowed to give their fund shares back to the fund company in exchange for the underlying basket of securities. If the fund's share price drifts too far above or below the value of its holdings, the institutional investors will buy and sell either the baskets of stocks or the fund's shares to capture the price difference, until their buying and selling brings both sets of prices back into line.

The first ETF in the United States was launched in 1993. The Standard & Poor's 500 Depositary Receipts (SPDRs or "spiders"), ticker symbol SPY, was designed to track the performance of the S&P 500 Index. ETFs built to track other popular benchmarks, such as the NASDAQ 100 (symbol QQQQ) and Dow Jones Industrial Average (symbol DIA), soon followed. On November 7, 2003, Barclays Global Investors introduced an ETF based on 50 of the highest-dividend-yielding stocks in the Dow Jones U.S. Total Market Index (excluding REITs): the iShares Dow Jones Select Dividend Index Fund (symbol DVY). By the end of 2009, there were well over 800 ETFs, offered by at least 17 sponsors. Exhibit 12.4 lists these sponsors, the product name under which they offer their ETFs, and their Web addresses as of March 2010.

Inventories of available ETF choices seem to become obsolete almost as soon as they appear, with announcements of new offerings appearing almost daily in early 2010. Among these were at least 37 ETFs that focus on dividend-paying stocks, both in the U.S. and abroad, across many indices and company sizes. Twenty-three of those were offered by WisdomTree, a sponsor that has clearly embraced the dividend story. There are even more ETFs that focus on dividend-rich sectors, such as utilities, financials, health care, energy, and industrials.

ETF Sponsors

Product	Sponsor	Web Site
Claymore	Claymore Securities, Inc.	www.claymore.com/etf
Direxion Shares	Direxion	www.direxionshares.com/etfs
Emerging Global Shares	Emerging Global Shares	www.egshares.com
Fidelity	Fidelity Investments	www.fidelity.com
First Trust	First Trust Portfolios LP	www.ftportfolios.com/Retail/etf/home.aspx
Grail Advisors	Grail Advisors LLC	www.grailadvisors.com
iShares	Black Rock	www.iShares.com
Market Vectors	Van Eck Global	www.vaneck.com
Pimco ETFs	PIMCO	www.pimcoetfs.com
Powershares	Invesco PowerShares Capital Management LLC	www.invescopowershares.com
ProShares	ProFunds Group	www.proshares.com
Revenue Shares	Pacer Financial, Inc.	www.revenuesharesetfs.com
Rydex Shares	Rydex SGI	www.rydex-sgi.com
Schwab ETFs	Charles Schwab Investment Management Inc.	www.schwabetfs.com
SPDR	State Street Global Advisors	www.spdrs.com
Vanguard	Vanguard Group	vanguard.com/jumppage/etfs/index.html
Wisdom Tree	Wisdom Tree Funds	www.wisdomtree.com

ETFs have become a viable choice for starting a dividend portfolio for investors with limited funds, and, as discussed in Chapter 10, "Building Your Portfolio," they can be used to fill in the tactical and noncorrelator tiers of dividend portfolios of all sizes. Whether you want to pursue tactical sector opportunities or diversify with commodities, currencies, bonds (including TIPs), REITs, specialty choices, or some leveraged hedging strategy, there's probably an ETF that offers the exposure you're looking for.

In addition to the wide range of choices available, other advantages of ETFs include their typically low expenses and the fact that they trade throughout the day, so you don't have to wait until 4 p.m. to know the price of your trades. There's no minimum investment amount except, of course, the price of a single share. Because of the way ETF shares are created and redeemed, surprise tax distributions, like the one the open-end fund in the earlier example delivered to Mr. True, have been virtually unheard of.

Like stocks, ETFs are subject to trading commissions (although the occasional promotion by a sponsor and/or brokerage firm has been known to waive these costs). The early wave of ETFs tended to track passive market indices, although some actively managed ETFs have started to appear. The diversification offered by mutual funds, including ETFs, can reduce volatility but can also reduce the opportunity for superior stock selection. For better or worse, an ETF—especially a passively managed index ETF—can lock you into an allocation to a group of stocks you might prefer to avoid. Several dividend-focused ETFs remained true to their indices and rode their exposure to financial stocks right down the road to ruin during the banking crisis of 2008.

You may have to become familiar with some tax forms and reporting issues you haven't seen before if you invest in certain ETFs. Some are organized as master limited partnerships or grantor trusts and deliver a Schedule K–1 or grantor trust letter for their investors to use in preparing their tax returns. This has been especially common among commodity and currency related ETFs. Tax laws frequently change, and ETF sponsors may someday find a way to eliminate the need for these forms, but in the meantime investors should be aware of any special tax considerations that come with the ETFs they buy.

In many respects, evaluating ETFs is similar to evaluating an open-end mutual fund. Does the investment objective match what you want in your portfolio? The top holdings of the fund are often available on the sponsor's Web site. If the ETF is supposed to be tracking an index, how closely does its performance mirror that index? Is the fund capitalization weighted, equal weighted, or weighted by some fundamental method, such as dividend, revenue, or earnings? If the ETF is actively managed, do the managers have experience using that management method (perhaps in an open-end mutual fund offering)? Are the ETF's expenses in line with those of similar funds? If two ETFs are tracking the same passive index with about the same accuracy, why pay more for one than the other? Does the sponsor have a helpful Web site, with robust, easy-to-use reference information about its products—including information about tax considerations and how to use any required special forms to complete your tax return?

A concern typically relevant only to some ETFs and closed-end funds is the amount of trading volume in the fund. Many ETFs trade millions of shares each day, so trading effectively at a fair price is not a problem. Still, for some new, small, or unusual ETFs, we have seen days go by without a single share trading hands. The spread between the bid and ask prices can be unacceptably wide, making it harder to get in or out of a position without sacrificing some return. This tends to be a fairly temporary condition, because if the fund doesn't grow enough in popularity among investors for volume to pick up, the sponsor will often shut it down.

Finally, investments commonly marketed alongside ETFs are exchange-traded notes, or ETNs. Unlike ETFs, which typically hold the underlying assets of an index or strategy (stocks, bonds, bars of gold bullion, etc.), ETNs are unsecured notes offered by the sponsor. Their value is also based on the performance of an index, commodity, or benchmark, but it is backed only by the promise to pay an amount based on that value, not by those assets themselves. Because of their design, ETNs have been able to match index performance with almost no tracking error and can be created to produce exposure to virtually any performance measurement. Obviously, however, as unsecured debt of the issuer, the creditworthiness of the sponsor is a critical element in the evaluation of an ETN. In September 2008, as Lehman Brothers tumbled into bankruptcy, its ETNs were delisted and collapsed into bankruptcy with the company.

CHAPTER 13

Staying on Course

I went to a bookstore and asked the saleswoman, "Where's the self-help section?" She said if she told me, it would defeat the purpose.

—*George Carlin*

To some people, "do it yourself" is a rude answer to a perfectly civil request. For others, it's a way of life. "Some assembly required" may quicken your pulse with excitement or fill your heart with dread. Maybe you find yourself somewhere in between; you like to dabble a bit with some things but are happy to give up the drudgery of other things. When it comes to digging in by yourself or wisely delegating to others, there's no right answer. There's only what's right for you.

When it comes to your investments, we hope you'll find that the information we've shared in this book gives you exactly the help you're looking for, no matter how you plan to use it. If you decide to build your portfolio entirely on your own, this book can serve as a valuable how-to guide, with all the background information you need to lay a solid foundation for your project and the tools you'll need to get the job done.

LAYING THE FOUNDATION: THE BASIS FOR DIVIDEND INVESTING

- You've seen how one investor's experience can differ dramatically from another's, both in accumulating wealth and producing income at retirement, depending on the way dividends are used in a portfolio over the course of an investment lifetime.

- You've reviewed some of the basic information you need to know about dividends, including what they are, how they're paid, and what kinds of companies are most likely to pay them.

- You've explored how the powerful demographic forces unleashed more than 50 years ago are likely to alter the nature of investing tomorrow, and how changes in the tax law could affect investor preferences today. You've reviewed some of the important elements of the tax treatment of dividends and how to use those changes to your advantage in your portfolio.

- You've assessed the traditional investment alternatives used by income investors and have uncovered their limitations. You've seen the insidious long-term effects inflation can have on your purchasing power and how dividends can provide a rising stream of income to help sustain your lifestyle in retirement.

- You've looked at the performance illusion and seen how volatility can rob growth investors of their hard-earned gains. You've seen how dividends can cushion volatility and help protect against market risk. You've learned about the possible consequences of investing too aggressively, and about the perils of investor risk—the risk you face just by being human.

- You have seen examples based on real investor experiences of how conventional wisdom has repeatedly failed investors in the pursuit of their important life goals.

USING THE TOOLBOX: HOW TO GET IT DONE

- You have a guide to financial statements and key measures that you can use to evaluate companies and the value of their stocks. You have a variety of sources for the information you need to do your analysis, whether you prefer to see your data in print or have it delivered electronically.

- You have screens and standards you can use to create a manageable list of stocks to follow. You've seen how to use an investment policy statement to match your choices to your needs and goals.

- You have a template for a model dividend portfolio. You have a list of standards you can use in implementing its design, including measures for value, growth, quality, yield, and overall promise. You've seen examples of what to look for in tactical candidates and have looked at the kinds of noncorrelating investments that can add stability and balance to your portfolio.

- You have a method for ranking your candidates and selecting the stocks you'll use to actually build your portfolio. You've learned how to limit your exposure to any one industry and what to do when your rankings end in a tie or produce duplicates. You have sampled some advanced ranking strategies, including weighting your criteria and using a proportional ranking system.

- You have a system for protecting your portfolio from the unforeseeable by using a combination of trailing stops, goals, and goal stops.

- You have information about DRIPs, Folios, mutual funds, and ETFs in the event these approaches are the most appropriate in your situation.

Even with all the right tools, however, building your portfolio on your own might not be the best strategy for you. Personally executing each step of the plan is a huge undertaking. The endless cycle of research can become tedious. The daily demands of living your life may be far more important than handling all the details of your investments. Common sense may call you to use your time and your talents elsewhere.

Investing takes time, and someone must take the time to do the work or the process will suffer. It's better to bring in some help than to struggle along with questionable results—or, worse yet, give up altogether. Abandoned, half-finished projects are a monument to wasted time and effort.

Perhaps you're more suited to drawing up the blueprint and hiring professionals to do the heavy lifting. You still must supervise their actions and progress. Supervision requires skill and dedication to assure a successful outcome. It's the coach who gets carried off the field on the shoulders of the victorious players. The coach wins the game from the sidelines. Let the players run around on the field; that's what they do best. The top professionals in every field have one thing in common: they're very good at what they do. That's why people hire them. The best use of your skills may be to draw up the game plan, select the right players, and keep the team focused on winning.

If this kind of approach feels right to you, the principles and procedures described in this book can serve as your blueprint for success. Hold on to the parts of the process you want to control, and find the right people to handle the rest. You have everything you need to effectively communicate every step of the process, so you can transfer as much or as little of the work as you wish. The time you spend managing your money can be reserved for the things you enjoy doing and making sure everything else is still being done right.

Some of the most intelligent, talented, successful, creative, hardworking, and interesting people we know delegate virtually all of their investment management process. They are our clients. Among them are executives and entrepreneurs, physicians and attorneys, accountants and artists, scientists and engineers, developers and consultants, philanthropists and community leaders. Many are retired. They lead rich and rewarding lives, and they have chosen to have us manage their money for them. They have decided to rely on us just as others rely on them for their judgment and expertise in their chosen fields.

After reading this book, you may realize that your interests would be best served by delegating the management of your portfolio to an investment professional. In that case, this book can be a guide to the investment experience you're looking for. As you interview prospective advisors, you can use what you've learned to measure the likelihood that he or she will be able to deliver exactly what you want. If the dividend-based approach makes sense to you, you have all the information you need to cut through the jargon and focus on finding a good fit between the advisor's skills and preferences and your goals and concerns.

Over the years, we've seen many investments do very well while many investors have failed. Some failed because they were too cautious, squirreling away all their money in the bank as taxes and inflation ate them alive. Some failed from being too aggressive, betting their future on greed and a dream. Some failed because they ran hot and cold, jumping in and out of investments with the mood of the market, buying too early and selling too late. *And others failed because they never got started.*

Whatever you decide to do, we hope this book helps you decide to *do something.* If investing for dividends is not for you, cross it off your list and go learn about another way to invest. But if dividend-based investing does make sense to you, now is the time to take the first step.

All About Dividend Investing provides you with a disciplined strategy and the tools you need to implement it. It incorporates the fundamental principles of investing for value, unlocking the power of dividend cash flows, and managing risk. Still, the success of this book can be measured only by your success as an investor. We want you to win as an investor because we understand why winning is so important. It's not about the money; it's about the things money can bring you: security, peace of mind, a brighter future for your children, and dignity in retirement.

Spreadsheet Versions of Selected Exhibits

Several of the processes and calculations discussed in Chapters 10 and 11 of this book can be facilitated through the use of a spreadsheet. This appendix includes examples of the formulas that can be used in Microsoft Excel to generate the results shown in selected exhibits from those chapters. Simple ranking, weighted ranking, proportional ranking, and trailing goal stop calculations are shown. Columns that have no bearing on the method being demonstrated have been omitted from the appendix version of the exhibit.

Each exhibit has two parts. The top part shows the formulas used in the calculations. The bottom part shows the result of those calculations when applied to the sample data in the exhibits. Column letters, row numbers, and spreadsheet grid lines are shown in both parts to make it easier to identify the cell locations referenced in the formulas. Data entries (as opposed to formulas) are identified with "ENTER" above the description at the top of the relevant columns.

Some basic understanding of Excel formulas is assumed. All formulas in the examples begin with the "=" mathematical operator, and absolute (fixed) cell references include the "$" before the column (letter) and/or row (number) of a cell. The formulas shown are simple versions that use only cell references.

Although not shown in any of the exhibits in this section, there are other Excel features and functions available that can make these spreadsheets easier to use and maintain. Named arrays (cell ranges) can be created and substituted for the absolute cell reference ranges used in the formulas.

Example: Use a named range like *valuerank* instead of *$G$8:$G$90* in ranking formulas.

Lookup tables can be created for the complete list of candidates (similar to the list shown in Exhibit 10.12) that contain all the relevant data so that data values have to be entered only once for all rankings, instead of everywhere data entries are required.

Example: Use a formula like *=vlookup*(B8, datalist, 3, *FALSE*) instead of typing *AEROSPACE/DEFENSE.*

Refer to Microsoft Excel help for information about changing cell references in formulas to names and for instructions on how to create and use a lookup table with the "vlookup" function.

EXHIBIT A 10.2

Value Ranking

	A	B	C	D	E	F	G	H	I	J
3		Best data value is:								
4	Value	ENTER NAMES	ENTER	Low	ENTER	Low	Low Value	ENTER	ENTER	ENTER
5	Rank	Company Name	P/E	Rank	P/S	Rank	Score	Symbol	Industry	Yield
6	=RANK(G6,$G$6:$G$88,1)	AMEREN	9.0	=RANK(C6,$C$6:$C$88,1)	0.85	=RANK(E6,$E$6:$E$88,1)	=+D6+F6	AEE	MULTI-UTILITIES	6.0
7	=RANK(G7,$G$6:$G$88,1)	LOCKHEED MARTIN	10.7	=RANK(C7,$C$6:$C$88,1)	0.70	=RANK(E7,$E$6:$E$88,1)	=+D7+F7	LMT	AEROSPACE/DEFENSE	3.0
8	=RANK(G8,$G$6:$G$88,1)	QWEST COMMUNICATIONS	11.5	=RANK(C8,$C$6:$C$88,1)	0.67	=RANK(E8,$E$6:$E$88,1)	=+D8+F8	Q	INTEG TELECOM SVC	6.7
9	=RANK(G9,$G$6:$C$88,1)	PROGRESSIVE	11.1	=RANK(C9,$C$6:$C$88,1)	0.80	=RANK(E9,$E$6:$E$88,1)	=+D9+F9	PGR	INSURANCE-PROP/CAS	3.8
10	=RANK(G10,$G$6:$G$88,1)	EDISON INT'L	10.4	=RANK(C10,$C$6:$C$88,1)	0.89	=RANK(E10,$E$6:$E$88,1)	=+D10+F10	EIX	ELECTRIC UTILITIES	3.7
11	=RANK(G11,$G$6:$G$88,1)	PITNEY BOWES	10.5	=RANK(C11,$C$6:$C$88,1)	0.89	=RANK(E11,$E$6:$E$88,1)	=+D11+F11	PBI	SERVICES-OFFICE/SUPP	6.1
12	=RANK(G12,$G$6:$G$88,1)	DONNELLEY (RR)	12.6	=RANK(C12,$C$6:$C$88,1)	0.42	=RANK(E12,$E$6:$E$88,1)	=+D12+F12	RRD	COMMERCIAL PRINTING	5.1
13	=RANK(G13,$G$6:$G$88,1)	CMS ENERGY	12.5	=RANK(C13,$C$6:$C$88,1)	0.58	=RANK(E13,$E$6:$E$88,1)	=+D13+F13	CMS	MULTI-UTILITIES	3.8
14	=RANK(G14,$G$6:$G$88,1)	FIRST ENERGY	10.5	=RANK(C14,$C$6:$C$88,1)	0.93	=RANK(E14,$E$6:$E$88,1)	=+D14+F14	FE	ELECTRIC UTILITIES	5.6
15	=RANK(G15,$G$6:$G$88,1)	VERIZON COMM	12.4	=RANK(C15,$C$6:$C$88,1)	0.78	=RANK(E15,$E$6:$E$88,1)	=+D15+F15	VZ	INTEG TELECOM SVC	6.4
16	EXTEND ALL COLUMNS TO CONTAIN THE FULL LIST OF CANDIDATES. THIS EXAMPLE WOULD EXTEND TO ROW 88 TO INCLUDE ALL 83 CANDIDATES.									

	A	B	C	D	E	F	G	H	I	J
3		Best data value is:								
4	Value	ENTER NAMES	ENTER	Low	ENTER	Low	Low Value	ENTER	ENTER	ENTER
5	Rank	Company Name	P/E	Rank	P/S	Rank	Score	Symbol	Industry	Yield
6	1	AMEREN	9.0	4	0.85	16	20	AEE	MULTI-UTILITIES	6.0
7	1	LOCKHEED MARTIN	10.7	11	0.70	9	20	LMT	AEROSPACE/DEFENSE	3.0
8	3	QWEST COMMUNICATIONS	11.5	19	0.67	7	26	Q	INTEG TELECOM SVC	6.7
9	4	PROGRESSIVE	11.1	14	0.80	13	27	PGR	INSURANCE-PROP/CAS	3.8
10	4	EDISON INT'L	10.4	7	0.89	20	27	EIX	ELECTRIC UTILITIES	3.7
11	6	PITNEY BOWES	10.5	8	0.89	20	28	PBI	SERVICES-OFFICE/SUPP	6.1
12	7	DONNELLEY (RR)	12.6	29	0.42	2	31	RRD	COMMERCIAL PRINTING	5.1
13	8	CMS ENERGY	12.5	27	0.58	5	32	CMS	MULTI-UTILITIES	3.8
14	9	FIRST ENERGY	10.5	8	0.93	25	33	FE	ELECTRIC UTILITIES	5.6
15	10	VERIZON COMM	12.4	25	0.78	12	37	VZ	INTEG TELECOM SVC	6.4
16	EXTEND ALL COLUMNS TO CONTAIN THE FULL LIST OF CANDIDATES. THIS EXAMPLE WOULD EXTEND TO ROW 88 TO INCLUDE ALL 83 CANDIDATES.									

EXHIBIT A 10.8

Value Ranking: Weighted Scores

	A	B	C	D	E	F	G	H	I
1									
2									
3		Best data value is:	Low		Low		Low		
4									
5	Weighted								
6	Value	ENTER NAMES	ENTER	ENTER Weight: 1.2	ENTER	ENTER Weight: 1.2	Value	ENTER	ENTER
7	Rank	Company Name	P/E	Rank	P/S	Rank	Score	Symbol	Industry
8	=RANK(G8,$G$8:$G$90,1)	LOCKHEED MARTIN	10.7	=RANK(C8,$C$8:$C$90,1)*$D$6	0.70	=RANK(E8,$E$8:$E$90,1)*$F$6	=+D8+F8	LMT	AEROSPACE/DEFENSE
9	=RANK(G9,$G$8:$G$90,1)	AMEREN	9.0	=RANK(C9,$C$8:$C$90,1)*$D$6	0.85	=RANK(E9,$E$8:$E$90,1)*$F$6	=+D9+F9	AEE	MULTI-UTILITIES
10	=RANK(G10,$G$8:$G$90,1)	QWEST COMMUNICATIONS	11.5	=RANK(C10,$C$8:$C$90,1)*$D$6	0.67	=RANK(E10,$E$8:$E$90,1)*$F$6	=+D10+F10	Q	INTEG TELECOM SVC
11	=RANK(G11,$G$8:$G$90,1)	PROGRESSIVE	11.1	=RANK(C11,$C$8:$C$90,1)*$D$6	0.80	=RANK(E11,$E$8:$E$90,1)*$F$6	=+D11+F11	PGR	INSURANCE-PROP/CAS
12	=RANK(G12,$G$8:$G$90,1)	EDISON INT'L	10.4	=RANK(C12,$C$8:$C$90,1)*$D$6	0.89	=RANK(E12,$E$8:$E$90,1)*$F$6	=+D12+F12	EIX	ELECTRIC UTILITIES
13	=RANK(G13,$G$8:$G$90,1)	DONNELLEY (RR)	12.6	=RANK(C13,$C$8:$C$90,1)*$D$6	0.42	=RANK(E13,$E$8:$E$90,1)*$F$6	=+D13+F13	RRD	COMMERCIAL PRINTING
14	=RANK(G14,$G$8:$G$90,1)	PITNEY BOWES	10.5	=RANK(C14,$C$8:$C$90,1)*$D$6	0.89	=RANK(E14,$E$8:$E$90,1)*$F$6	=+D14+F14	PBI	SERVICES-OFFICE/SUPP
15	=RANK(G15,$G$8:$G$90,1)	CMS ENERGY	12.5	=RANK(C15,$C$8:$C$90,1)*$D$6	0.58	=RANK(E15,$E$8:$E$90,1)*$F$6	=+D15+F15	CMS	MULTI-UTILITIES
16	=RANK(G16,$G$8:$G$90,1)	FIRST ENERGY	10.5	=RANK(C16,$C$8:$C$90,1)*$D$6	0.93	=RANK(E16,$E$8:$E$90,1)*$F$6	=+D16+F16	FE	ELECTRIC UTILITIES
17	=RANK(G17,$G$8:$G$90,1)	VERIZON COMM	12.4	=RANK(C17,$C$8:$C$90,1)*$D$6	0.78	=RANK(E17,$E$8:$E$90,1)*$F$6	=+D17+F17	VZ	INTEG TELECOM SVC
18	EXTEND ALL COLUMNS TO CONTAIN THE FULL LIST OF CANDIDATES. THIS EXAMPLE WOULD EXTEND TO ROW 90 TO INCLUDE ALL 83 CANDIDATES.								

	A	B	C	D	E	F	G	H	I
1									
2									
3		Best data value is:	Low		Low		Low		
4									
5	Weighted								
6	Value	ENTER NAMES	ENTER	ENTER Weight: 1	ENTER	ENTER Weight: 1.2	Value	ENTER	ENTER
7	Rank	Company Name	P/E	Rank	P/S	Rank	Score	Symbol	Industry
8	1	LOCKHEED MARTIN	10.7	11	0.70	10.8	21.8	LMT	AEROSPACE/DEFENSE
9	2	AMEREN	9.0	4	0.85	19.2	25.2	AEE	MULTI-UTILITIES
10	3	QWEST COMMUNICATIONS	11.5	19	0.67	8.4	27.4	Q	INTEG TELECOM SVC
11	4	PROGRESSIVE	11.1	14	0.80	15.6	24.6	PGR	INSURANCE-PROP/CAS
12	5	EDISON INT'L	10.4	7	0.89	24	31	EIX	ELECTRIC UTILITIES
13	6	DONNELLEY (RR)	12.6	29	0.42	2.4	31.4	RRD	COMMERCIAL PRINTING
14	7	PITNEY BOWES	10.5	8	0.89	24	32	PBI	SERVICES-OFFICE/SUPP
15	8	CMS ENERGY	12.5	27	0.58	6	33	CMS	MULTI-UTILITIES
16	9	FIRST ENERGY	10.5	8	0.93	30	38	FE	ELECTRIC UTILITIES
17	10	VERIZON COMM	12.4	25	0.78	14.4	39.4	VZ	INTEG TELECOM SVC
18	EXTEND ALL COLUMNS TO CONTAIN THE FULL LIST OF CANDIDATES. THIS EXAMPLE WOULD EXTEND TO ROW 90 TO INCLUDE ALL 83 CANDIDATES.								

EXHIBIT A 10.9

Proportional Ranking: P/E (Lowest Is Best)

	A	B	C	D
1				
2				
3		Best (Lowest) P/E:	=MIN(C10:C19)	
4		Worst (Highest) P/E:	=MAX(C10:C19)	
5		Span (Highest-Lowest):	=C4-C3	
6				
7		*Best data value is:*	*Low*	*High*
8		**ENTER NAMES**	**ENTER**	
9	**Rank**	**Company Name**	**P/E**	*"Grade"*
10	=RANK(D10,$D$10:$D$19)	ABC	8	=($C$4-C10)/$C$5
11	=RANK(D11,$D$10:$D$19)	DEF	9	=($C$4-C11)/$C$5
12	=RANK(D12,$D$10:$D$19)	GHI	10	=($C$4-C12)/$C$5
13	=RANK(D13,$D$10:$D$19)	JKL	17	=($C$4-C13)/$C$5
14	=RANK(D14,$D$10:$D$19)	MNO	18	=($C$4-C14)/$C$5
15	=RANK(D15,$D$10:$D$19)	PQR	19	=($C$4-C15)/$C$5
16	=RANK(D16,$D$10:$D$19)	ST	20	=($C$4-C16)/$C$5
17	=RANK(D17,$D$10:$D$19)	UV	26	=($C$4-C17)/$C$5
18	=RANK(D18,$D$10:$D$19)	WX	27	=($C$4-C18)/$C$5
19	=RANK(D19,$D$10:$D$19)	YZ	28	=($C$4-C19)/$C$5
20				
21	Span = Highest P/E minus the lowest P/E			
22	Grade = (Highest P/E minus this stock's P/E) divided by the Span			

	A	B	C	D
1				
2				
3		Best (Lowest) P/E:	8	
4		Worst (Highest) P/E:	28	
5		Span (Highest-Lowest):	20	
6				
7		*Best data value is:*	*Low*	*High*
8		**ENTER NAMES**	**ENTER**	
9	**Rank**	**Company Name**	**P/E**	*"Grade"*
10	1	ABC	8	100%
11	2	DEF	9	95%
12	3	GHI	10	90%
13	4	JKL	17	55%
14	5	MNO	18	50%
15	6	PQR	19	45%
16	7	ST	20	40%
17	8	UV	26	10%
18	9	WX	27	5%
19	10	YZ	28	0%
20				
21	Span = Highest P/E minus the lowest P/E			
22	Grade = (Highest P/E minus this stock's P/E) divided by the span			

EXHIBIT A 10.10

Proportional Ranking: P/E (Highest Is Best)

	A	B	C	D
1				
2				
3		Worst (Lowest) P/E:	=MIN(C10:C19)	
4		Best (Highest) P/E:	=MAX(C10:C19)	
5		Span (Highest-Lowest):	=C4-C3	
6				
7		*Best data value is:*	*High*	*High*
8		ENTER NAMES	ENTER	
9	**Rank**	**Company Name**	**P/E**	*"Grade"*
10	=RANK(D10,$D$10:$D$19)	YZ	28	=(C10-$C$3)/$C$5
11	=RANK(D11,$D$10:$D$19)	WX	27	=(C11-$C$3)/$C$5
12	=RANK(D12,$D$10:$D$19)	UV	26	=(C12-$C$3)/$C$5
13	=RANK(D13,$D$10:$D$19)	ST	20	=(C13-$C$3)/$C$5
14	=RANK(D14,$D$10:$D$19)	PQR	19	=(C14-$C$3)/$C$5
15	=RANK(D15,$D$10:$D$19)	MNO	18	=(C15-$C$3)/$C$5
16	=RANK(D16,$D$10:$D$19)	JKL	17	=(C16-$C$3)/$C$5
17	=RANK(D17,$D$10:$D$19)	GHI	10	=(C17-$C$3)/$C$5
18	=RANK(D18,$D$10:$D$19)	DEF	9	=(C18-$C$3)/$C$5
19	=RANK(D19,$D$10:$D$19)	ABC	8	=(C19-$C$3)/$C$5
20				
21	Span = Highest P/E minus the lowest P/E			
22	Grade = (This stock's P/E minus the lowest P/E) divided by the Span			

	A	B	C	D
1				
2				
3		Worst (Lowest) P/E:	8	
4		Best (Highest) P/E:	28	
5		Span (Highest-Lowest):	20	
6				
7		*Best data value is:*	*High*	*High*
8		ENTER NAMES	ENTER	
9	**Rank**	**Company Name**	**P/E**	*"Grade"*
10	1	YZ	28	100%
11	2	WX	27	95%
12	3	UV	26	90%
13	4	ST	20	60%
14	5	PQR	19	55%
15	6	MNO	18	50%
16	7	JKL	17	45%
17	8	GHI	10	10%
18	9	DEF	9	5%
19	10	ABC	8	0%
20				
21	Span = Highest P/E minus the lowest P/E			
22	Grade = (This stock's P/E minus the lowest P/E) divided by the span			

EXHIBIT A 10.11

Value Ranking: Proportional Grades

A	B	C	D	E	F	G	H	I
		P/E		P/S		High		
	Best (Lowest):	=MIN(C12:C94)		=MIN(E12:E94)				
	Worst (Highest):	=MAX(C12:C94)		=MAX(E12:E94)				
	Span (Highest-Lowest):	=C5-C4		=E5-E4				
	Best data value is:	Low	High	Low	High	High		
Proportional						Value		
Value	ENTER	ENTER		ENTER		"Grade"	ENTER	ENTER
Rank	Company Name	P/E	Grade	P/S	Grade	Grade	Symbol	Industry
=RANK(G12,$G$12:$G$94,0)	AMEREN	9.0	=($C$5-C12)/$C$6	0.85	=($E$5-E12)/$E$6	=D12+F12	AEE	MULTI-UTILITIES
=RANK(G13,$G$12:$G$94,0)	LOCKHEED MARTIN	10.7	=($C$5-C13)/$C$6	0.70	=($E$5-E13)/$E$6	=D13+F13	LMT	AEROSPACE/DEFENSE
=RANK(G14,$G$12:$G$94,0)	CHUBB	8.3	=($C$5-C14)/$C$6	1.56	=($E$5-E14)/$E$6	=D14+F14	CB	INSURANCE-PROP/CAS
=RANK(G15,$G$12:$G$94,0)	EDISON INT'L	10.4	=($C$5-C15)/$C$6	0.89	=($E$5-E15)/$E$6	=D15+F15	EIX	ELECTRIC UTILITIES
=RANK(G16,$G$12:$G$94,0)	PITNEY BOWES	10.5	=($C$5-C16)/$C$6	0.89	=($E$5-E16)/$E$6	=D16+F16	PBI	SERVICES-OFFICE/SUPP
=RANK(G17,$G$12:$G$94,0)	FIRSTENERGY	10.5	=($C$5-C17)/$C$6	0.93	=($E$5-E17)/$E$6	=D17+F17	FE	ELECTRIC UTILITIES
=RANK(G18,$G$12:$G$94,0)	QWEST COMMUNICATIONS	11.5	=($C$5-C18)/$C$6	0.67	=($E$5-E18)/$E$6	=D18+F18	Q	INTEG TELECOM SVC
=RANK(G19,$G$12:$G$94,0)	PROGRESSIVE	11.1	=($C$5-C19)/$C$6	0.80	=($E$5-E19)/$E$6	=D19+F19	PGR	INSURANCE-PROP/CAS
=RANK(G20,$G$12:$G$94,0)	PUBLIC SVC ENTP	9.8	=($C$5-C20)/$C$6	1.25	=($E$5-E20)/$E$6	=D20+F20	PEG	MULTI-UTILITIES
=RANK(G21,$G$12:$G$94,0)	DONNELLEY (RR)	12.6	=($C$5-C21)/$C$6	0.42	=($E$5-E21)/$E$6	=D21+F21	RRD	COMMERCIAL PRINTING

EXTEND ALL COLUMNS TO CONTAIN THE FULL LIST OF CANDIDATES. THIS EXAMPLE WOULD EXTEND TO ROW 94 TO INCLUDE ALL 83 CANDIDATES.

A	B	C	D	E	F	G	H	I
		P/E		P/S		High		
	Best (Lowest):	8.1		0.4				
	Worst (Highest):	27.9		6.8				
	Span (Highest-Lowest):	19.8		6.4				
	Best data value is:	Low	High	Low	High	High		
Proportional						Value		
Value	ENTER	ENTER		ENTER		"Grade"	ENTER	ENTER
Rank	Company Name	P/E	Grade	P/S	Grade	Grade	Symbol	Industry
1	AMEREN	9.0	95%	0.85	93%	189%	AEE	MULTI-UTILITIES
2	LOCKHEED MARTIN	10.7	87%	0.70	95%	182%	LMT	AEROSPACE/DEFENSE
3	CHUBB	8.3	99%	1.56	82%	181%	CB	INSURANCE-PROP/CAS
4	EDISON INT'L	10.4	88%	0.89	93%	181%	EIX	ELECTRIC UTILITIES
5	PITNEY BOWES	10.5	88%	0.89	92%	180%	PBI	SERVICES-OFFICE/SUPP
6	FIRSTENERGY	10.5	88%	0.93	92%	180%	FE	ELECTRIC UTILITIES
7	QWEST COMMUNICATIONS	11.5	83%	0.67	96%	179%	Q	INTEG TELECOM SVC
8	PROGRESSIVE	11.1	85%	0.80	94%	179%	PGR	INSURANCE-PROP/CAS
9	PUBLIC SVC ENTP	9.8	91%	1.25	87%	178%	PEG	MULTI-UTILITIES
10	DONNELLEY (RR)	12.6	77%	0.42	100%	177%	RRD	COMMERCIAL PRINTING

EXTEND ALL COLUMNS TO CONTAIN THE FULL LIST OF CANDIDATES. THIS EXAMPLE WOULD EXTEND TO ROW 94 TO INCLUDE ALL 83 CANDIDATES.

EXHIBIT A 11.7

Trailing Stop with Goal and Goal Stop

	A	B	C	D	E	F	G	H
1			*Enter Targets Here*					
2		Initial Stop % =	10%					
3		Goal % =	10%					
4		Goal Stop % =	3%					
5								
6			*Enter Values Daily*					
7		Date	Price	Goal Price	Stop % to Use	New Stop Price	Trailing Stop Price	$ to Trailing Stop Price
8	Enter the values here ->	1/4/2010	$ 10.00	=C8+(C8*$C$3)	=IF(C8<D8,$C$2,$C$4)	=C8-(C8*E8)	=F8	=C8-G8
9	from the purchase date	1/5/2010	$ 10.75	=D8	=IF(C9<D9,$C$2,$C$4)	=C9-(C9*E9)	=IF(F9>G8,F9,G8)	=C9-G9
10	or date of reset	1/6/2010	$ 10.50	=D9	=IF(C10-D10,$C$2,$C$4)	=C10-(C10*E10)	=IF(F10>G9,F10,G9)	=C10-G10
11		1/7/2010	$ 11.00	=D10	=IF(C11<D11,$C$2,$C$4)	=C11-(C11*E11)	=IF(F11>G10,F11,G10)	=C11-G11
12		1/8/2010	$ 11.50	=D11	=IF(C12<D12,$C$2,$C$4)	=C12-(C12*E12)	=IF(F12>G11,F12,G11)	=C12-G12
13		1/11/2010	$ 12.50	=D12	=IF(C13<D13,$C$2,$C$4)	=C13-(C13*E13)	=IF(F13>G12,F13,G12)	=C13-G13
14		1/12/2010	$ 13.00	=D13	=IF(C14<D14,$C$2,$C$4)	=C14-(C14*E14)	=IF(F14>G13,F14,G13)	=C14-G14
15		1/13/2010	$ 12.50	=D14	=IF(C15<D15,$C$2,$C$4)	=C15-(C15*E15)	=IF(F15>G14,F15,G14)	=C15-G15
16								

	A	B	C	D	E	F	G	H
1			*Enter Targets Here*					
2		Initial Stop % =	10%					
3		Goal % =	10%					
4		Goal Stop % =	3%					
5								
6			*Enter Values Daily*					
7		Date	Price	Goal Price	Stop % to Use	New Stop Price	Trailing Stop Price	$ to Trailing Stop Price
8	Enter the values here ->	1/4/2010	$ 10.00	11.00	10.00%	$ 9.00	$ 9.00	$ 1.00
9	from the purchase date	1/5/2010	$ 10.75	11.00	10.00%	$ 9.68	$ 9.68	$ 1.08
10	or date of reset	1/6/2010	$ 10.50	11.00	10.00%	$ 9.45	$ 9.68	$ 0.82
11		1/7/2010	$ 11.00	11.00	3.00%	$ 10.67	$ 10.67	$ 0.33
12		1/8/2010	$ 11.50	11.00	3.00%	$ 11.16	$ 11.16	$ 0.35
13		1/11/2010	$ 12.50	11.00	3.00%	$ 12.13	$ 12.13	$ 0.38
14		1/12/2010	$ 13.00	11.00	3.00%	$ 12.61	$ 12.61	$ 0.39
15		1/13/2010	$ 12.50	11.00	3.00%	$ 12.13	$ 12.61	$ (0.11)
16								

GLOSSARY

Advisor One who gives investment advice in return for compensation.

Aggressive Growth High-risk/reward investments, funds, or securities classes.

Analysis Process of evaluating individual financial instruments (often stock) to determine whether they are appropriate purchases.

Analysts Those on Wall Street who study and recommend securities.

Annual Interest Income The annual dollar income for a bond or savings account, calculated by multiplying the bond's coupon rate by its face value.

Annualized Return The total return on an investment or portfolio over a period other than one year, restated as an equivalent return for a one-year period.

Appreciation That part of the total return on an investment due to the increase in its price.

Asset Allocation The decision as to how a customer should be invested among major asset classes in order to increase expected risk-adjusted return. Asset allocation may be two-way (stocks and bonds), three-way (stocks, bonds, and cash), or many-way (e.g., value mutual funds, growth mutual funds, small mutual funds, cash, foreign mutual funds, foreign bonds, real estate, and venture capital).

Asset Mix Combination of investable asset classes within a portfolio.

Average Daily Trading The number of shares of stock traded in the preceding calendar month, multiplied by the current price and divided by 20 trading days.

Average Return The measure of the price of an asset, along with its income or yield, on average over a specific period. The arithmetic mean is the simple average of the returns in a series. The arithmetic mean is the appropriate measure of typical performance for a single period.

Balance Sheet A financial statement that indicates, at a given point in time, what the firm owns and how these assets are financed.

Basis Point One-hundredth of a percentage point, or 0.01 percent. Basis points are often used to express changes or differences in yields, returns, or interest rates. Thus, if a portfolio has a total return of 10 percent versus 7 percent for the S&P 500, the portfolio is said to have outperformed the S&P 500 by 300 basis points.

Bear Market A prolonged period of falling stock prices. There is no consensus on what constitutes a bear market or bear leg. We consider a bear market or bear market leg as a drop of at least 20 percent from high to low.

Beginning Value The market value of a portfolio at the inception of the period being measured by the customer statement.

Benchmark A standard by which investment performance or trading execution can be judged. The most widely used performance benchmark is the total return of the S&P 500.

Beta The linear relationship between the return on the security and the return on the market. By definition, the market, usually measured by the S&P 500 Index, has beta of 1.00. Any stock or portfolio with a higher beta is generally more volatile than the market, while any with a lower beta is generally less volatile than the market.

Bond Long-term, short-term, and high-yield. Debt instruments are loans that pay lenders a regular return. Short-term bonds are for five years or less. High-yield bonds pay lenders a higher rate of return because of perceived risk.

Bond Rating Method of evaluating the possibility of default by a bond issuer. Standard & Poor's, Moody's Investors Service, and Fitch's Investors Service analyze the financial strength of each bond's issuer, whether a corporation or a government body. Their ratings range from AAA (highly unlikely to default) to D (in default). Bonds rated B or below are not investment grade—in other words, institutions that invest other people's money may not, under most state laws, buy them.

Book Value The current value of an asset on a company's balance sheet according to its accounting conventions. The shareholders' equity on a company's balance sheet is the book value for that entire company. Many times when investors refer to book value, they actually mean book value per share, which is the shareholders' equity (or book value) divided by the number of shares outstanding. Theoretically the book value is what a company could be sold for (liquidation value). This book value number is sometimes used by active managers as a guide as to whether or not the shares are undervalued.

Bull Market A prolonged period of rising stock prices. We consider a bull market or bull market leg to be a period of generally rising stock prices that has not been interrupted by a bear market decline of 20 percent or more.

Business Cycle Short-term swings in economic activity encompassing expansionary and recessionary periods that generally occur over two to four year periods.

Business Day A day when the New York Stock Exchange is open for trading.

Business Life Cycle The movement of a firm through stages of development: start-up, growth, expansion, maturity, decline, and extinction.

Cap Small cap, large cap. The stock market worth of an individual equity. Large-cap stocks can be found on the New York Stock Exchange. Small-cap stocks are often listed on the NASDAQ.

Capital Appreciation or Depreciation An increase or decrease in the value of a mutual fund or stock due to a change in the market price of the fund. For example, a stock that rises from $50 to $55 has a capital appreciation of 10 percent. Dividends are not included in appreciation. If the price of the stock fell to $45, it would have a depreciation of 10 percent.

Capital Preservation Investing in a conservative manner so as not to put capital at risk.

Cash Investment in any instrument (often short-term) that typically does not fluctuate in value and is easily liquidated.

CFP® or CERTIFIED FINANCIAL PLANNER™ Individuals who have met the CFP board's rigorous certification standards and are authorized to use the certification marks. Certified Financial Planner Board of Standards, Inc., owns the certification marks CFP®, CERTIFIED FINANCIAL PLANNER™, and CFP (with flame logo)®, which it awards to individuals who successfully complete initial and ongoing certification requirements.

Closed-End Mutual Fund A mutual fund that issues a fixed number of shares. These shares then trade on a stock exchange at a premium or discount to the value of the underlying investments owned by the fund.

Commission A transaction fee commonly levied by brokers.

Compound Annual Return Geometric mean. The geometric mean is more appropriate when one is comparing the growth rate for an investment that is continually compounding.

Compounding The reinvestment of dividends and/or interest and capital gains. This means that over time dividends, interest, and capital gains grow exponentially. For example, $100 earning compound interest at 10 percent per year accumulates to $110 at the end of the first year and $121 at the end of the second year, etc., based on this formula: compound sum = principal (1 + interest rate) (number of periods).

Conservative A characteristic relating to a mutual fund, a stock, or an investment style. There is no precise definition of the term. Generally, the term is used when the mutual fund manager's emphasis is on the below market betas.

Contrarian An investment approach characterized by buying securities that are out of favor.

Correction A reversal in the price of a stock, or the stock market as a whole, within a larger trend. While corrections are most often thought of as declines within an overall market rise, a correction can also be a temporary rise in the midst of a longer-term decline.

Correlation A statistical measure of the degree to which the movement of two variables is related.

Coupon The periodic interest payment on a bond. When expressed as an annual percentage, it is called the *coupon rate*. When multiplied by the face value of the bond, the coupon rate gives the annual interest income.

CPI Consumer price index, maintained by the Bureau of Labor Statistics, a measure of the changes in the cost of a specified group of consumer products relative to a base period. Because it represents the rate of inflation, the CPI can be used as a general benchmark for gauging the maintenance of purchasing power.

Current Return on Equity (ROE) A ratio that measures profitability as the return on common stockholders' equity. It is calculated by dividing the reported earnings per share for the latest 12-month period by the book value per share.

Current Yield A bond's annual interest payment as a percentage of its current market price. The current yield is calculated by dividing the annual coupon interest for a bond by the current market price. The coupon rate and the current yield on a bond are equal when the bond is selling at par. Thus, a $1,000 bond with a coupon of 10 percent that is currently selling at $1,000 will have a current yield of 10 percent. However, if the bond's price drops to $800, the current yield becomes 12.5 percent.

Demographics The study of population characteristics over time. Demographic analysis studies the population on the basis of age and the statistical effects of population on economic conditions.

Depression That portion of the business cycle in which production and prices are at their lowest point, unemployment is highest, and general economic activity is low.

Dissimilar Price Movement The process whereby different asset classes and markets move in different directions.

Diversification A way to reduce risk by using multiple investments. In broad terms, a first-time investor might diversify his or her investments among mutual funds, real estate, international investments, and money market instruments. A mutual fund might diversify by investing in many companies in many different industry groups.

Dividend A dividend is defined in Code Section 316 as a distribution by a corporation to its shareholders out of its current or accumulated earnings and profits. The distribution, therefore, must be made by a corporation, not some other kind of entity. It must be received by shareholders in their capacity as shareholders, not by lenders, employees, or customers. And the corporation must have earnings and profits. A distribution to shareholders by a corporation without earnings and profits is a return of capital, not a dividend. Confusion over what is a dividend derives from mislabeling interest as dividends.

Dividend Coverage Ratio This ratio measures how secure the dividend payment is relative to the company's operating income. Formula: divide operating income per share by dividends per share. Ratio should be more than 100 percent.

Dividend Reinvestment Plan (DRIP) Company sponsored plans that allow investors to automatically reinvest dividends in additional shares of company stock, often at low cost or on other favorable terms.

Dollar Cost Averaging A system of buying stock or mutual funds at regular intervals with a fixed-dollar amount. Under this system an investor buys according to a fixed-dollar amount rather than by the number of shares. This reflects an attempt to buy more shares at a lower average price.

Dow Jones Industrial Average (DJIA) A price-weighted average of 30 leading blue chip industrial stocks, calculated by adding the prices of the 30 stocks and adjusting by a divisor, which reflects any stock dividends or splits. The Dow Jones Industrial Average is the most widely quoted index of the stock market, but it is not widely used as a benchmark for evaluating performance. The S&P 500 Index, which is more representative of the market, is the benchmark most widely used by performance measurement services.

Economic Tax Recovery Act The Economic Tax Recovery and Tax Act of 1981 reduced business taxes and lowered the maximum marginal tax rate to 50 percent while lowering the capital gains tax to 20 percent.

EPS (Earnings per Share) Growth The annualized rate of growth in reported earnings per share of stock.

Equities Stocks of various corporations often traded on national securities exchanges.

Exchange-Traded Funds (ETFs) A relatively new addition to the fund universe, ETFs trade on a stock exchange and may be purchased or sold throughout the trading day at a known price.

Execution Price The negotiated price at which a security is purchased or sold.

Expenses Costs of maintaining an invested portfolio.

Fed The Federal Reserve serves as the central banking authority for the United States. The Fed enacts monetary policy and plays a major role in regulating commercial banking operations and controlling the money supply.

Financial Advisor or Planner One who helps investors with a wide variety of financial and investing issues including retirement, estate planning, etc.

The Financial Industry Regulatory Authority (FINRA) The largest independent regulator for all securities firms doing business in the United States. It was created in July 2007 through the consolidation of NASD and the member regulation, enforcement, and arbitration functions of the New York Stock Exchange.

Financial Metric Formula used to express a company's financial results at a per share level. Example: dividend per share metric (divide total dividend paid by shares outstanding).

Fiscal Policy Government spending and taxing practices designed to promote or inhibit economic activity.

Folio A basket of stocks that an investor can either build or select from a collection of prepackaged sets.

Forecasts Predictions of analysts usually associated with stock picking and active money management.

Foreign Corporations The House and Senate had different views as to whether the favorable dividend rates should apply to dividends received from foreign corporations as well as domestic corporations. The result, as with most compromises, is complexity—some foreign corporate dividends meet the definition of qualified dividend income; others do not. In general, for dividends from a foreign corporation to qualify for favorable treatment, the foreign corporation must be incorporated in a U.S. possession, traded on a U.S. exchange, or incorporated in a country covered by a comprehensive tax treaty with the United States.

401(k) Plan (Section of the Internal Revenue Code) In simplest terms, a before-tax employee savings plan. A defined contribution plan that permits employees to have a portion of their salaries deducted from their paychecks and contributed to an account. Federal (and sometimes state) taxes on the employee contributions and investment earnings are deferred until the participant receives a distribution from the plan (typically at retirement). Employers may also make contributions to a participant's account.

Front-End Load A fee charged when an investor buys a mutual fund.

Fund Rating Evaluation of the performance of invested money pools, often mutual funds, by such entities as Chicago-based Morningstar.

Fund Shares Shares in a mutual fund.

Fundamentals The financial statistics that traditional analysts and many valuation models use. Fundamental data include stock, earnings, dividends, assets and liabilities, inventories, debt, etc. Fundamental data are in contrast to items used in technical analysis, such as price momentum, volume trends, and short-sales statistics.

Global Diversification Investment of funds around the world in regions and markets with dissimilar price movements.

Gross Profit Sales less the direct cost of producing a product. Formula: sales – cost of goods sold.

Gross Profit Margin This ratio expresses the company's ability to generate earnings from a product after the cost of goods is deducted from sales. The ratio indicates the percentage that selling prices can fall, or costs can increase, to eliminate gross profit. Formula: gross profit/sales.

Guaranteed Interest Rate In a fixed annuity or certificate of deposit, the minimum interest rate that is guaranteed by the insurance company or bank to be credited each year to the cash value.

Income That part of the total return on an investment delivered to an investor in the form of cash.

Income Statement A financial statement that shows the profitability of a firm over a given period.

Index Fund A passively managed portfolio designed and computer-controlled to track the performance of a certain index, such as the S&P 500. In general, such mutual funds have performance within a few basis points of the target index. The most popular index mutual funds are those that track the S&P 500, but special index funds, such as those based on the Russell 1000 or the Wilshire 5000, are also available.

Indexing Disciplined investing in a specific group (asset class) of securities so as to benefit from its aggregate performance.

Individual Investor Buyer or seller of securities for personal portfolio.

Investment Objective The money goals one wishes to reach.

Inflation Inflation is the pervasive and sustained rise in the aggregate level of prices measured by an index of the cost of various goods sold. Inflation results when actual economic pressures and anticipation of future developments cause the demand for goods and services to exceed the supply available at existing prices.

Institutional Investor Corporation or fund with market presence.

Interest The rate a borrower pays a lender.

Interest Rate Guarantee Guarantee that the renewal rate will never fall below a particular level.

Intrinsic Value The theoretical valuation or price for a stock. The valuation is determined by using a valuation theory or model. The resulting value is compared with the current market price. If the intrinsic value is greater than the market price, the stock is considered undervalued.

Invest Place, in a disciplined fashion, money in financial instruments so as to gain a return.

Investment Advisor See *Advisor.*

Investment Discipline A specific money strategy one espouses.

Investment Philosophy Strategy justifying short- or long-term buying and selling of securities.

Investment Policy An investment policy statement that forces the investor to confront risk tolerance, return objectives, time horizon, liquidity needs, the amount of funds available for investment, and the investment methodology to be followed.

Investment Policy Statement Embodiment of the essence of the financial planning approach to investing. It includes (1) assessing where you are now, (2) detailing where you want to go, and (3) developing a strategy to get there.

Investment Wisdom Process of understanding valid academic research concerning asset allocation.

Investor Discomfort Realization that risk is not appropriate and reward is not predictable in a given portfolio.

Investor Risk The risk that an investor will make a poor decision because of emotional or subjective responses to market conditions.

iShares Trade name for exchange-traded funds offered by BlackRock, Inc

Jobs and Growth Tax Relief Reconciliation Act of 2003 Taxing capital gains and dividend income on the same rate structure (5 percent and 15 percent).

The long-term capital gain rates dropped

- From 20 percent down to 15 percent
- From 10 percent down to 5 percent, with 0 percent in 2008

Dividends tax rates dropped on qualifying dividends

- From 38.6 percent down to 15 percent
- From 15 percent down to 5 percent

These new rates were scheduled to expire after 2008 unless new tax laws were passed. Under this act, mutual fund companies have passed through earnings to fund holders in the form of dividends or capital gains. These two forms of distributions were distinguished because of the different tax treatment of the two. Interest on money market and bond funds was reported as dividends because there was no strong reason to distinguish between interest and dividends. Now dividends will be taxed the same as capital gains. Mutual fund holders will need to distinguish interest-paying funds from dividend-paying and capital-gain-paying funds. Dividends and capital gains may also be treated differently on state income tax returns.

Junk Bonds High risk, low-grade bonds, rated BBB or lower. They often perform like common stock yet have high coupon rates.

Limit Order An order to buy or sell a security, but only if the trade can be executed at a specified price.

Liquidity Ability to generate cash on demand when necessary.

Load Fund A mutual fund that is sold for a sales charge (load) by a brokerage firm or other sales representative. Such funds may be stock, bond, or commodity funds, with conservative or aggressive objectives.

Management Fee Charge against investor assets for managing the portfolio of an open- or closed-end mutual fund as well as for such services as shareholder relations or administration. The fee, as disclosed in the prospectus, is a fixed percentage of the fund's asset value.

Margin A loan often offered to investors by broker dealers for the purpose of allowing the investors to purchase additional securities. In a down market, margin loans can be called and portfolios liquidated when the value of the loan threatens to exceed the value of the portfolio.

Market In investing terms, a place where securities are traded. Formerly meant a physical location but now may refer to an electronic one as well.

Market Bottom The date that the bear leg of a market cycle reaches its low, not identified until some time after the fact. Market bottoms can also be defined as the month or quarter end closest to the actual bottom date.

Market Capitalization The current value of a company, determined by multiplying the latest available number of outstanding common shares by the current market price of a share.

Market Order An order to buy or sell a security at the prevailing market price.

Market Timing The attempt to base investment decisions on the expected direction of the market. If stocks are expected to decline, the timer may elect to hold a portion of the portfolio in cash equivalents or bonds. Timers may base their decisions on fundamentals (e.g., selling stocks when the market's price/book ratio reaches a certain level), on technical considerations (such as declining momentum or excessive investor optimism), or a combination of both.

Market Value The market or liquidation value of a given security or of an entire pool of assets.

Maturities For bonds, the date at which a borrower must redeem the capital portion of the loan.

Model Portfolio A theoretical construct of an investment or series of investments.

Money Market Fund Fund of short-term fixed instruments and cash equivalents. These instruments make up the portfolio, and their objective is to maximize principal protection. Even though these accounts have short-term (one-day) liquidity, they typically pay more like 90- to 180-day CDs versus passbook or one-week CDs.

Municipal Bonds Fixed-income securities issued by government agencies.

Mutual Fund A pool of managed money, regulated by the Securities and Exchange Commission, in which investors can purchase shares. Funds are not managed individually as they might be by a private money manager.

Mutual Fund Families A number of funds with different investment objectives within a family of funds. For example, a mutual fund family may include a money market fund, a government bond fund, a corporate bond fund, a blue chip stock fund, and a more speculative stock fund. If an investor buys a fund in the family, she or he is allowed to exchange that fund for another in the same family. This is usually done with no additional sales charge.

NASDAQ NASDAQ is the largest electronic stock market in the United States. The name NASDAQ began as an acronym for the National Association of Securities Dealers Automated Quotations.

NASDAQ Composite Index A market-value weighted index of all common stocks listed on the NASDAQ.

National Association of Securities Dealers, Inc. (NASD) Former name of the Financial Industry Regulatory Authority (FINRA). The NASD was the principal association of over-the-counter (OTC) brokers and dealers that established legal and ethical standards of conduct for its members. NASD was established in 1939 to regulate the OTC market in much the same manner as organized exchanges monitor actions of their members.

Net Asset Value (NAV) The market value of each share of a mutual fund. This figure is derived by taking a fund's total assets (securities, cash, and receivables), deducting liabilities, and then dividing that total by the number of shares outstanding.

No-Load Fund Mutual fund offered by an open-end investment company that imposes no sales charge (load) on its shareholders. Investors buy shares in no-load funds directly from the fund companies rather than through a broker, as is done in load funds. Because no broker is used, no advice is given on when to buy or sell.

Nominal Return The actual current dollar growth in an asset's value over a given period. See also *Total Return* and *Real Return*.

Operating Expense Cost associated with running a fund or portfolio.

Optimization A process whereby a portfolio, invested using valid academic theory in various asset classes, is analyzed to ensure that risk/reward parameters have not drifted from stated goals.

Outperform Exceed expectations or historical performance for any given market.

Over-the-Counter (OTC) A market made between securities dealers who act as either principal or broker for their clients. This is the principal market for U.S. government and municipal bonds.

Payout Ratio The percentage of earnings that a company is paying out to shareholders as dividends. Formula: dividends per share/earnings per share.

Percentage Points Used to describe the difference between two readings that are percentages. For example, if a portfolio's performance was 18.2 percent versus the S&P 500's 14.65, it outperformed the S&P by 3.6 percentage points.

Portfolio A collection of investment assets organized to meet a particular financial goal.

Portfolio Turnover The replacement of one security in a portfolio with another. Portfolio turnover is often described as the percentage of a portfolio replaced in one year. A portfolio with 100 percent turnover has replaced all of its original holdings in the course of the year.

Preferred Stock The distribution from preferred stock is coming from a corporation with earnings and profits to someone holding something labeled preferred stock. The distribution would appear to qualify as a dividend eligible for the reduced tax rates. However, much of what has been marketed as preferred stock is not preferred stock. It is debt masquerading as preferred stock. It has been developed and marketed to corporations to enable corporations to deduct the distributions as interest expense on the corporate tax return. If the corporation is entitled to an interest expense deduction, it is not preferred stock, and the distributions with respect to that instrument are not dividends.

Price/Earnings (P/E) Ratio The current price divided by reported earnings per share of stock for the latest 12-month period. For example, a stock with earnings per share of $5 during the trailing year and currently selling at $50 per share has a price/earnings ratio of 10.

Price/Sales (P/S) Ratio This ratio indicates a company's share price relative to its ability to generate sales. Formula: current stock price/sales per share.

Principal The original dollar amount invested.

Prospectus The document required by the Securities and Exchange Commission that accompanies the sale of a mutual fund or annuity, outlining risks associated with certain types of funds or securities, fees, and management. At the core of the prospectus is a description of the fund's investment objectives and the portfolio manager's philosophy.

Put Right of the investor to sell a security at a preset price within a specified time.

Quartile A ranking of comparative portfolio performance. The top 25 percent of mutual fund managers are in the first quartile, those ranking from 26 to 50 percent are in the second quartile, from 51 to 75 percent in the third quartile, and the lowest 25 percent in the fourth quartile.

Quick Ratio A conservative measure of the ability to repay short-term debt. Since inventory is less liquid than other current assets, it is deducted from current assets to determine what portion of current liabilities could be retired very quickly by liquidating quick assets. Formula: current assets – inventory/current liabilities.

Rate of Return The profits earned by a security, measured as a percentage of earned interest and/or dividends and/or appreciation.

Real Estate Investment Trusts (REITs) Bundled, securitized real estate assets often traded on the New York Stock Exchange. As they relate to dividends, REITs are corporations that make distributions to holders. However, they are required to distribute to their holders most of the REIT earnings for the year. If some portion of REIT earnings is retained in the REIT, it is taxed at the REIT level, and distributions with respect to those earnings would qualify for the reduced dividend tax rates. Also, if a REIT happened to be a shareholder in a corporation and passed dividends it received from the corporation through to its holders, that distribution would also qualify for favorable dividend treatment. *These are exceptions to the general rule that most REIT distributions are not true dividends and would not qualify for the favorable tax rates.*

Real Return The inflation-adjusted return on an asset. Inflation-adjusted returns are calculated by subtracting the rate of inflation from an asset's apparent, or nominal, return. For example, if common stocks earn a total return of 10.3 percent over a period of time, but inflation during that period is 3.1 percent, the real return is the difference, or 7.2 percent.

Rebalancing A process whereby funds are shifted within asset classes and between asset classes to ensure the maintenance of the efficient frontier. See *Optimization*.

Reinvested Dividends Dividends paid by a particular stock or mutual fund that are reinvested in that same mutual fund or in shares of the stock. Some mutual funds offer automatic dividend reinvestment programs. In the complex equation theoretically used to determine the performance of the S&P 500, each company's dividend is reinvested in the stock of that company.

Relative Return The return of a stock or a mutual fund portfolio compared with some index, usually the S&P 500.

Return on Investment (ROI) The amount of money generated over time by placement of funds in specific financial instruments.

Risk The uncertainty of future rates of return, which includes the possibility of loss. This variability or uncertainty causes "rational" investors to expect higher returns on investments where the actual timing or amount of payoffs is not guaranteed.

Risk, Systematic Potential for predictable, quantifiable loss of funds through the application of valid academic research to the process of disciplined asset class investing.

Risk, Unsystematic Associated with investment in an undiversified portfolio of individual instruments through active management.

Risk-Free Rate of Return The return on an asset that is considered virtually riskless. U.S. government Treasury bills are typically used as the risk-free asset because of their short time horizon and the low probability of default.

Risk Tolerance Risk is the variability of returns from an investment, and tolerance is leeway for variation from a standard—in other words, your capacity to tolerate unfavorable conditions during the time period you hold your investments.

Rule of 72 Divide the number 72 by the compound interest rate you have chosen. The result is the number of years it takes your money to double.

Securities Tradable financial instruments.

Securities and Exchange Commission (SEC) The keystone law in the regulation of securities markets. It governs exchanges, over-the-counter markets, broker-dealers, the conduct of secondary markets, extension of credit in securities transactions, the conduct of corporate insiders, and principally the prohibition of fraud and manipulation in securities transactions. It also outlines the powers of the Securities and Exchange Commission to interpret, supervise, and enforce the securities laws of the United States.

Securities Investor Protection Corporation (SIPC) A government-sponsored organization created in 1970 to insure investor accounts at brokerage firms in the event of the brokerage firm's insolvency and liquidation. The maximum insurance of $500,000, including a maximum of $100,000 in cash assets per account, covers customer losses due to brokerage house insolvency, not customer losses caused by security price fluctuations. SIPC coverage is conceptually similar to Federal Deposit Insurance Corporation coverage of customer accounts at commercial banks.

Security Selection Process of picking securities, especially stocks for investment purposes.

Shares Specific portions of a tradable equity; a share of stock. It generally refers to common or preferred stocks.

S&P Common Stock Rankings Rankings that measure historical growth and stability of earnings and dividends. The system includes eight rankings: A+, A, and A− (above average); B+ (average); B, B−, and C (below average); and NR (insufficient historical data or not amenable to ranking process). As a matter of policy, S&P does not rank the stocks of foreign companies, investment companies, and certain finance-oriented companies.

S&P 500 Index The performance benchmark most widely used by sponsors, managers, and performance measurement services. This index includes 400 industrial stocks, 20 transportation stocks, 40 financial stocks, and 40 public utilities. Performance is measured on a capitalization-weighted basis. The index is maintained by Standard & Poor's Corporation, a subsidiary of The McGraw-Hill Companies, Inc.

Stagflation An economic period when inflation and recession occur simultaneously.

Standard Deviation How far from the mean historic performance has been, either higher or lower. Volatility can be statistically measured using standard deviation. The mean is simply the middle point between the two historic extremes of the performance of the investment you are examining. The standard deviation measurement helps explain what the distribution of returns likely will be. The greater the range of returns, the greater the risk. Generally, the current price of a security reflects the expected total return of its investment and its perceived risk. The lower the risk, the lower the return expected.

Stock The equity or ownership interest in a corporation, represented by certificates for transferable shares. Divided into preferred stock (which has preferenced rights to earnings and assets ahead of common stock) and common stock (which represents the residual interest in earnings and assets of the company after all other claims have been satisfied).

Stock Dividend A dividend paid by issuing more stock, which results in retained earnings being capitalized.

Stop Limit Order A limit order to trade a security once a specified price target has been reached. This order will be executed only if the limit price is available in the market after the target price has been hit.

Stop Order A market order to trade a security once a specified price target has been reached. This order will be executed at the prevailing market price once the target price has been hit, irrespective of the market price.

Strategic Asset Allocation Determination of an appropriate asset mix for an investor based on long-term capital market conditions, expected returns, and risks.

Systemic Withdrawal Plan A program in which shareholders receive payments from their mutual fund investments at regular intervals. Typically, these payments are drawn first from the fund's dividends and capital gains distribution, if any, and then from principal as needed.

Tactical Allocation Investment strategy allocating assets according to investor expectations of directions of regional markets and asset classes.

Tax-Efficient Fund A mutual fund that deliberately attempts to limit the taxable distributions made to investors.

Technical Analysis Any investment approach that judges the attractiveness of particular stocks or the market as a whole based on market data, such as price patterns, volume, momentum, or investor sentiment, as opposed to fundamental financial data, such as earnings or dividends.

Time Horizon The amount of time someone can wait to generate or take profits from an investment.

Time-Weighted Rate of Return The rate at which $1 invested at the beginning of a period would grow if no additional capital were invested and no cash withdrawals were made. It provides an indication of value added by the investment manager and allows comparisons to the performance of other investment managers and market indexes.

Total Return A standard measure of performance or return including both capital appreciation (or depreciation) and dividends or other income received. For example, a stock is priced at $60 at the start of a year and pays an annual dividend of $4. If the stock moves up to $70 in price, the appreciation component is 16.7 percent, the yield component is 6.7 percent, and the total return is 23.4 percent. That oversimplification does not take into account any earnings on the reinvested dividends.

Trading Costs Fees or commissions paid to move money from one financial instrument to another.

Transaction Costs Any fees or commissions generated and paid in the management of a portfolio. Another term for execution costs. Total transaction costs (or the cost of buying and selling stocks) have three components: (1) the actual dollars paid to the broker/advisor in commissions; (2) the market impact (i.e., the impact a manager's trade has on the market price for the stock—this varies with the size of the trade and the skill of the trader); and (3) the opportunity cost of the return (positive or negative) given up by not executing the trade instantaneously.

Treasury Bills A U.S. financial security issued by Federal Reserve banks for the Treasury as a means of borrowing money for short periods. The bills are sold at a discount from their maturity value, pay no coupons, and have maturities of up to one year. Because they are a direct obligation of the federal government, they are free of default risk. Most Treasury bills are purchased by commercial banks and held as part of their secondary reserves. Treasury bills regulate the liquidity base of the banking system in order to control the money supply. For example, if the authorities wish to expand the money supply, they can buy Treasury bills, which increases the reserves of the banking system and induces a multiple expansion of bank deposits.

Treasury Inflation-Indexed Securities (TIPs) The principal on these Treasury bonds is adjusted with changes in inflation as measured by the Consumer Price Index (CPI). As inflation rises, so does the principal amount of the bond. The interest payments are based on the adjusted principal amount. The adjusted principal amount is paid at maturity. In the event of deflation, the final payment will not be less than the original par value.

Underperform Fail to meet expectations; applies to securities or markets.

Value Added Value of returns over and above that of the stock market.

Value Stocks Stocks with high book-to-market valuations (i.e., companies doing poorly in the market that may have the potential to do better).

Volatility The extent to which market values and investment returns are uncertain or fluctuate. Another word for *risk*, volatility is gauged by using such measures as beta, mean absolute deviation, and standard deviation.

Wash Sale The sale of a security at a loss within 30 days before or after the purchase of a substantially identical security to the one sold. Losses from wash sales may not be deducted for tax purposes.

Weighting A term usually associated with proportions of assets invested in a particular region or securities index to generate a specific risk/reward profile. It may also refer to the relative importance attached to a particular characteristic in a ranking system when evaluating investment alternatives.

Yield (Current Yield) For stocks, the percentage return paid in dividends on a common or preferred stock, calculated by dividing the indicated annual dividend by the market price of the stock. For example, if a stock sells for $40 and pays a dividend of $2 per share, it has a yield of 5 percent (or $2 divided by $40). For bonds, the coupon rate of interest divided by the market price is called current yield. For example, a bond selling for $1,000 with a 10 percent coupon offers a 10 percent current yield. If the same bond were selling for $500, it would offer a 20 percent yield to an investor who bought it for $500. (As a bond's price falls, its yield rises, and vice versa.)

Yield Curve A chart or graph showing the price of securities (usually fixed income) through time. A flat or inverted yield curve of fixed-income instruments is thought by many to be an indicator of recession. This is because those who borrow at the far end of the curve usually pay more for their money than those who borrow for only a little while. When the yield curve is flat or inverted, there is little demand for long-term money, and this can be interpreted as a signal that there is little demand in the economy for the products that long-term borrowing would generate.

Yield to Maturity The discount rate that equates the present value of the bond's cash flows (semiannual coupon payments, the redemption value) with the market price. The yield to maturity will actually be earned if (1) the investor holds the bond to maturity, and (2) the investor is able to reinvest all coupon payments at a rate equal to the yield to maturity. When a bond is selling at par, the yield to maturity and the coupon rate are equal.

INDEX

Page numbers followed by *n.* indicate endnotes.

Accounting frauds, 168
Accounts payable, 86
Accumulated depreciation, 86
Additional paid-in capital, 86–87
Adelphia, 168
After-tax yields (income
    investments), 43
Alcatel-Lucent, 128–129
Annual report, 104–105
Arthur Andersen, 168
Asbestos liability, 120
Asset coverage, 95–96
Assets, 84–86
AT&T, 22
Average rate of return (DJIA), 10

Baby boomers, 25
Balance sheet:
    assets, 84–86
    equity, 86–87
    liabilities, 86
    sample statement, 85
    uses, 89
Bank of New York, 15–16
Banking, 15
Barclays Global Investors, 199
Barron's, 103–104
Barron's Annual Reports Service, 104
Barron's Fund Info Service, 104
Barron's Market Lab section, 104
Baseball card, 65
Basic financial metrics, 90–94
Bear market, 9–11
Bear market cycles, 9–10
Behavioral finance, 66
BellSouth Corporation, 22
Berkshire Hathaway, 154

Blueprint, 123–124
Bonds:
    corporate, 43
    defined, 54
    fixed returns, 39
    further information, 40
    government, 43
    higher yields, 39
    inflation, 55–56
    junk, 43
    municipal, 43
    noncorrelator tier, 138
    overview, 40
    weakness of, as investment, 54–56
Brokerage stop orders, 174
Building your portfolio, 141–165
    absence of reliable information, 153
    additional standards, 156
    advanced strategies, 155–163
    cash equivalents, 152
    cautionary note, 143
    choices you don't like, 153
    commodity exposure, 152
    company names, symbols, criteria
        values, 144, 164–165
    duplicate choices, 154
    growth ranking, 146, 147
    high vs. low, 142–143
    how many stocks to buy?, 141–142
    industry sectors, 152–153
    noncorrelator candidates, 152
    order of precedence, 154
    overall ranking, 148, 151
    patience, 153
    proportional ranking, 158–163
    quality ranking, 148, 149
    required characteristics, 143

Building your portfolio (*Cont.*)
  same dollar amount, 154
  tactical picks, 152
  tiebreaker rule, 148
  trading costs, 142
  value ranking, 144–146
  weighting of standards,
    156–158
  yield ranking, 148, 150
Bull market, 9
Bull overperformance cycle, 9, 12
Bush, George W., 30
Business and dividend life cycles,
    20–23
Business life cycle, 20–22
BUYandHOLD, 188
Buy-and-hold approaches, 71, 72
Buy high, sell low, 74, 76
Buy low and sell high, 37, 71, 139

California power crisis, 135
Capital preservation. *See* Safeguard
    your capital
Cash/cash equivalents, 48–51
Cash flow per share, 91, 94
Cash investments, 49
Cash tier, 125–126
Certificate of deposit (CD), 43, 48, 49,
    51–53
Certified Financial Planner Board of
    Standards, Inc., 124
Charles Schwab, 192
Chat rooms, 108
Citicorp, 16
Classic dividend story, 4–7
Classic investor mistakes:
  doing things right, 77–78
  greed, 77
  make hay while the sun shines,
    73–75
  sitting on the sidelines, 75–76
  thinking you're really smart, 76
Closed-end fund pricing, 198
Closed-end funds, 197–198

Cohen & Steers REIT & Utility Income
    Fund, 198
Commodities, 138
Common stock, 23
Company Web sites, 105
Company's dividend history, 18
Complete Book of the Olympics, The
    (Wallechinsky), 134
Compounded rate of growth, 8
Compounding, 6, 184–185
Contingent gains, 195
Corporate bonds, 43
Corporate scandals, 168
Cost basis, 187
Cost of goods sold, 87
Coupon, 54
Creating a stock portfolio. *See* Building
    your portfolio
Current assets, 84
Current liabilities, 86
Cut your losses, and let your winners
    run, 171
Cutting dividends, 17

Debt ratios, 91, 95–96
Decline phase, 22
Delegating the investment
    management process, 206
Demographic effect, 25–26
Direct share purchase plans, 183–184
Distribution date, 18
Distribution rate (monthly income
    need), 115
Diversification, 72, 127, 141, 142
Dividend(s):
  benefits, 7–8. *See also* Dividend
    advantage
  cushioning effect, 63
  defined, 15
  example, 62–64
  holding period requirement,
    34–35
  mutual fund, 35
  not guaranteed, 119

qualifying/nonqualifying, 33–34
reducing, 17
stock, 15, 24
tax treatment, 31, 33–34
Dividend advantage:
compounded rate of growth, 8
dollar cost averaging, 8
price volatility, 8
steady stream of income, 7–8
stock prices increase over time, 8
Dividend coverage ratio, 91, 97–98,
132–133
Dividend cut, 17
Dividend effect, 63
Dividend investing, 46–47
new advantages of. See New
advantages of dividend investing
Dividend payers tier, 126–134
growth, 131–132
overall best, 134
quality, 133–134
value, 127–131
yield, 132–133
Dividend payout ratio, 91, 98, 99.
See also Payout ratio
Dividend policy, 16–18
Dividend portfolio design, 124–139
cash tier, 125–126
dividend payers tier. See Dividend
payers tier
noncorrelator tier, 137–139
objectives, 124
tactical choices tier, 134–137
Dividend ratios, 91, 97–99
Dividend reinvestment plans. See DRIPs
Dividend safety, 119
Dividend stocks:
high-yielding, 41–42, 43
low-yielding, 40–41, 43
medium-yielding, 41, 43
Dividend yield, 11–12, 47, 94, 117–119
by industry, 118
Dividends per share, 91, 92
DJIA dividend yield (1920–2003), 17

DJIA dividends reinvested summary:
1966–1981, 13
1982–1999, 13
2000–2009, 14
DJIA index correction and rally cycles
(1900–2009), 36
DJIA return from price appreciation, 9
DJU (Dow Jones Utilities Index),
135–136
Dollar cost averaging, 6, 8, 62, 186
Dollar lost averaging, 46, 47–48, 114
Dot com bubble, 30
Dow Jones Utilities Index (DJU),
135–136
Dreman/Claymore Dividend &
Income Fund, 198
DRIP Central, 188
Drip Wizard, 187
DRIPs (dividend reinvestment plans),
183–189
affordability, 184
compounding, 184–185
dollar cost averaging, 186
drawbacks, 187–188
Internet Web sites, 188
recordkeeping, 187
taking out cash, 186–187
taxes, 187

Early growth phase, 20
Earnings growth rate ratio, 91, 99
Earnings per share, 88, 91, 92
Eaton Vance Tax-Advantaged Global
Dividend Fund, 198
Economic Tax Recovery Act, 75
EDGAR, 108
Electric utilities, 101
Embedded gains, 195
Energy Policy Act of 1992, 135
Enron, 135
Equity section (balance sheet), 86–87
ETF sponsors, 200
ETFs, (exchange-traded funds), 138, 152,
199–202
ETNs (exchange-traded notes), 138, 202

Evaluating dividend-paying
  companies, 18–20
Everett, David, 183
Ex-dividend, 18
Examples. *See* Vignettes
Excel spreadsheets. *See* Spreadsheet
  versions of some exhibits
Exchange-traded funds (ETFs), 138,
  152, 199–202
Exchange-traded notes (ETNs), 138, 202
Expansion phase, 21

Failures, 207
Fear, 72, 74
Federal income tax brackets, 31–32
Financial planner, 122*n.*
Financial ratios. *See* Ratio analysis
Financial statement analysis, 83–89
  balance sheet, 84–87, 89
  income statement, 87–89
  statement of retained earnings, 88–89
Financial strength, 133
First preferred stocks, 23
Fixed assets, 85–86
Fixed income investing, 46
Fixed-income investments, 43
Folio, 189–190
Franklin, Benjamin, 25
FreeEDGAR, 108

Galbraith, John Kenneth, 69
General Motors, 20
Global Crossing, 168
Goals and goal stops, 176–178
Government bonds, 43, 55
Great Depression, 69
Greed, 73, 74
Gross profit, 87
Growth investor, 57–67
Growth ratios, 91, 99

High dividend folio, 189
High-yielding stocks, 41–42, 43
Holding period requirement, 34–35

Hypothetical fact situations.
  See Vignettes
ImClone, 168
Income from operations, 96
Income statement, 87–88, 89
Income tax brackets, 31–32
Income tax rates, 31
Industries (dividend yield), 118
Industry sectors, 152–153
Inflation:
  bonds, 55–56
  cash investments, 49
  effect of, 45
  historical rates, 50
  interest rates, 50
  retirement plan, 50
  TIPs (Treasury inflation-protected
    securities), 138, 152
Information sources, 102–110
  cost, format, content, 102–103
  Internet sources, 105–109
  library, 109–110
  printed materials, 103–105
  software and data sources, 109
Interest rates, 50, 138
Internet sources (as information
  source), 105–109
Investment policy statement (IPS),
  113–117
Investment professional, 206. *See also*
  Professional assistance
Investments (balance sheet), 85
Investor mistakes. *See* Classic investor
  mistakes
Investor risk, 66–67
IPS (investment policy statement),
  113–117
Irises (van Gogh), 65
iShares Dow Jones Select Dividend
  Index Fund, 199

Jenner, Bruce, 134
JGTTRA, 6, 26, 27, 30–33, 198
JGTTRA sunset provisions, 32–33

Jobs and Growth Tax Relief
    Reconciliation Act (JGTTRA),
    6, 26, 27, 30–33, 198
Johnson, Rafer, 134
Junk bonds, 43, 55
Jury-rigging dividend payouts, 29

Keynes, John Maynard, 167
Kozlowski, L. Dennis, 168

Late-stage growth phase, 21
Laying the foundation, 123–140
    blueprint, 123–124
    caution, 124
    questions to ask, 123–124
    tier design. *See* Dividend
        portfolio design
Lehman Brothers, 202
Lemonade drink business (example), 88
Leverage, 77, 78, 95
Liabilities, 86
Library, 109–110
Limiting your losses. *See* Safeguard
    your capital
Liquidity ratios, 91, 94
Litigation risk, 120
Long-term debt, 86
Lookup tables, 210
Lovland, Helge, 134
Low-yielding stocks, 40–41, 43
Lucent, 128–129

Marathon Oil, 106–107
Margin, 77
Market performance cycles (DJIA
    index), 10
Markowitz, Harry, 69–70
Master limited partnership (MLP), 33,
    41, 43, 121–122
Mature industries, 47
Maturity phase, 21
Medium-yielding stocks, 41, 43
Merrill Lynch, 168
Microsoft Excel spreadsheets. *See*
    Spreadsheets

MLP (master limited partnership),
    33, 41, 43, 121–122
Modern portfolio theory (MPT), 70
Money market instruments, 43, 49
Morningstar, 105, 192
MPT (modern portfolio theory), 70
Multiple, 130
Municipal bonds, 43
Mutual fund, 190–202
    closed-end funds, 197–198
    commodities, 138, 152
    controlling risk, 197
    costs, 196
    ETFs, 199–202
    ETNs, 202
    investment objective, 193
    narrowing your focus, 192
    open-ended funds, 191
    quality of service, 194
    quarterly reviews, 196–197
    rating the funds, 192–196
    selecting the funds, 196
    steps in process, 191
    stop loss system, 173
    tax considerations, 195–196
    unrealized gains, 195
Mutual fund dividends, 35
Mutual fund supermarkets, 192
My Stock Fund, 188

NASDAQ Composite Index, 59, 60
Net asset value (NAV), 191
Net income, 88
New advantages of dividend
    investing, 25–38
    demographic effect, 25–26
    holding period requirement, 34–35
    JGTTRA, 30–33
    qualifying dividends, 33–34
    relief rallies, 36–37
    swimming with the tide, 28–29
    tax effect, 26–28
    tech stock factor, 29–30
Newton's third law of motion, 3

Nonqualifying dividends, 33–34
Noncorrelator tier, 137–139
Noncumulative preferred stock, 23
Nuveen Tax-Advantage Total Return
    Strategy Fund, 198

One-year earnings growth ratio, 99
One-year revenue growth ratio, 99
Open-end mutual funds, 191
Operating cash flow to short-term
    debt ratio (ops cf/st debt), 134
Operating income, 88, 96
ops cf/st debt, 134
O'Shaughnessy, James P., 131
Out of favor stocks, 153
Overall best selections, 134
Overperformance cycle, 9–12

Panic, 114
Patience, 153
Payout ratio, 16, 28, 91, 98, 99, 133.
P/E (price-to-earnings) ratio, 91, 97,
    129–130
Penny stocks, 120–121
Perfect income portfolio, 39, 43
Performance illusion, 58–62
Periodic rebalancing, 139
Phases in company's development,
    20–22
Pioneer Tax-Advantaged Balanced
    Trust, 198
Predictability, 35, 44
Preferred A stock, 23
Preferred B stock, 23
Preferred stock, 23, 121
Price-to-earnings (P/E) ratio, 91, 97,
    129–130
Price-to-sale (P/S) ratio, 91, 97, 131
Price volatility, 8, 61, 170
Printed materials (as information
    source), 103–105
Professional assistance, 122n. 124
Proportional ranking, 158–163
Protecting your capital. See Safeguard
    your capital

P/S (price-to-sale) ratio, 91, 97, 131
Public library, 109–110
Qualified financial planner, 122n.
Qualified foreign corporation, 33
Qualifying dividends, 33–34, 35
Quick ratio, 91, 94
Quicken, 187

Rallies off market bottoms, 37
Ratio analysis, 90–100
    debt coverage ratio, 95–96
    dividend ratios, 97–99
    growth ratios, 99
    overview, 91
    quick ratio, 94
    valuation ratios, 96–97
Real estate investment trust (REIT), 33,
    41, 43, 121, 136
Record date, 18
Reducing dividends, 17
REIT (real estate investment trust), 33,
    41, 43, 121, 136
Relative performance to a
    benchmark, 72
Relief rallies, 36–37
Resetting stops, 179
Retained earnings, 87, 89, 98
    statement of, 88–89
Retirement income, sources of:
    dividend investing, 46–47
    fixed income investing, 46
    systematic withdrawal plans, 45–46
Reuters Web site, 108
Revenue growth rate ratio, 91, 99
Rogers, Will, 57
Rules of thumb, 90, 101

Safeguard your capital, 167–181
    effect of losses, 168–170
    goals and goal stops, 176–178
    stop loss system, 170–181
    trailing stops, 174–176
Safety of principal, 48, 49
Sales, 87

Sales per share, 91, 92
Screens:
    defined, 112
    dividend safety, 119
    dividend yield, 117–119
    security types, 120–122
    veto list, 119–120
Second preferred stock, 23
Secondary share offerings, 86–87
Security types, 120–122
Selection process. See Building
    your portfolio
Selling and administrative
    expenses, 87
Shareholders equity, 86
Short-term debt coverage ratio, 91,
    95–96
Short-term rallies, 37
Sitting on the sidelines, 75–76
Small companies, 121, 137
Software and data sources, 109
S&P 500 century dividend payers, 16
S&P 500 Dividend Aristocrats Index,
    18–20
S&P 500 Index, 16
SPDRs (Standard & Poor's Depositary
    Receipts), 199
Spreadsheets, 209–216
    proportional ranking: P/E (highest
        is best), 214
    proportional ranking: P/E (lowest is
        best), 213
    trailing stop with goal and goal
        stop, 216
    value ranking, 211
    value ranking
        proportional grades, 215
        weighted scores, 212
Stagflation, 11, 27
Standard & Poor's 500 Depository
    Receipts (SPDRs), 199
Standard & Poor's Stock Reports, 105
Standards, 112
Start-up phase, 20

Statement of retained earnings, 88–89
Steady stream of income, 7–8
Stewart, Martha, 168
Stock dividend, 15, 24
Stock selection. See Building your
    portfolio
Stocks, 23, 40
    dividend. See Dividend stocks
    noncumulative preferred, 23
    out of favor, 153
    penny, 120–121
    preferred, 23, 121
Stop limit order, 172, 173
Stop loss system, 170–181
    advantages, 179
    brokerage stop orders, 174
    goals and goal stops, 176–178
    mutual funds, 173
    overview (figure), 178
    repurchasing a stock, 179
    resetting stops, 179
    tax considerations, 179–181
    trailing stops, 174–176
Stop order, 172
Supervision, 206
Systematic liquidation plan, 46
Systematic withdrawal plans,
    45–46

Tactical choices tier, 134–137
Tax cut, 27, 30, 31
Tax effect, 26–28
Taxes:
    capital gains, 30
    dividends, 31, 33–34
    DRIPs, 187
    income investments, 43
    investor behavior, 26–27
    JGTRRA, 30–33
    mutual funds, 195–196
    stock dividend, 24
    stop loss system, 179–181
Taxes due, 86
Tech stock factor, 29–30

Thomson Baseline, 109, 163n.
Thornburg Investment Income Builder
    Fund, 192
Thorpe, Jim, 134
Time horizon, 114
TIPs (Treasury inflation-protected
    securities), 138, 152
Tobacco companies, 120
Total assets, 86
Total liabilities, 86
Total return, 58
Trading costs, 142
Traditional income alternatives, 43
Trailing stop with goal and
    goal stop, 177
Trailing stops, 174–176
Treasury bills, 49
Treasury inflation-protected securities
    (TIPs), 138, 152
TreasuryDirect Web site, 138
Trench example, 62
Trend analysis, 100, 101
Tyco, 168

Underperformance cycle, 10–12
U.S. demographics by age, 26
U.S. population census by age group, 26
Utilities, 135–136

Valuation ratios, 91, 96–97
Value Line, 192
Value Line Investment Survey, 105,
    106–107

Veto list, 119–120
Vietnam War, 12
Vignettes:
    classic dividend story, 4–7
    doing things right, 77–78
    dollar lost averaging, 47–48
    greed, 74–75, 77
    relying on prior experience in other
        fields, 76
    safe but sorry (investing in CDs),
        51–53
    sitting on the sidelines, 75–76
vlookup, 210
Volatility, 8, 61, 170

Waksal, Samuel, 168
Wallechinsky, David, 134
Wash sale, 179
Weighting of standards,
    156–158
What Works on Wall Street
    (O'Shaughnessy), 131
Window trading, 188
WisdomTree, 199
WorldCom, 168

Xerox, 168

Yahoo! Finance section, 108
Yield, 91, 94
Yield categories, 40–42
Y2K, 29
Y2K bear market, 60, 63, 76, 195